HEADS, HATS AND TALL TALES

TRAVELS IN INDIA, NEPAL AND EGYPT

by

ALUN BUFFRY

HEADS, HATS AND TALL TALES
TRAVELS INDIA, NEPAL AND EGYPT
by Alun Buffry

Published by ABeFree Publishing 2025
ISBN 9781919212906
http://www.buffry.org.uk/abefreepublishing.html

Copyright©AlunBuffry2022

The right of Alun Buffry to be identified as author of this work has been asserted by him in accordance with section 77 and 78 of the Copyright, designs and Patents Act 1988.

All rights reserved. No part of this publication may be reproduced, stored in a retrieval system, or transmitted in any form or by any means, electronic, mechanical, photocopying, recording, or otherwise, without the prior permission of the publishers.

Any person who commits any unauthorised act in relation to this publication may be liable to criminal prosecution and civil claims for damages.

This book comprises of work extracted from and previously published under the titles "All About My Hat The Hippy Trail 1972", "Back To The East" and "Myhat in Egypt Through the Eyes of a God" by the same author.

In Memory Of

Lesley James

Susan Beswick

The Baktoo Family
Sultan, Ali, Ahmed,
Farook, Madeleine
and Jimmy

Habib

1972: INTRODUCTION	1
First Meeting	3
Turkey	8
Istanbul and The Pudding Shop	11
Afyonkaraishar	15
Pamukkale	19
Ephesus / Efes	21
Antalya	24
Iskenderun, Antakya, Antioch	27
Aleppo, Deir El Zur, Syria	33
Al Qu'im, Iraq	41
Baghdad	47
Tehran, Iran	54
The Opium Farm, Iran	58
Mashhad, Iran	65
Afghanistan, Herat and Kandahar	66
Miriam	79
Kabul	85
Chicken Street and Sigis	93
Boiled Eggs	95
The Khyber Pass and Hellmut	102
Peshawar, Pakistan	105
Lahore, Pakistan	109
Amritsar and The Golden Temple, India	117
The Journey to Delhi with Miriam	123
Delhi	125
Agra and The Taj Mahal	129
Fatepur Sikri	131
Haridwar and Rishikesh	132
A Dip in the Ganges	140
The Journey Home	144
Hospital in Delhi	144
Diane	146
Back Towards Kabul	152
Kabul and Hospital Again	157
Tripping in Kabul	163
Leaving Diane	172
Kabul to Tehran and Hospital Again	173
Back to the UK	178
Guru Maharaji	182
BACK TO THE EAST	186
Introduction	187

1981 Kashmir with Lizzie	188
Srinagar and Dal Lake	191
The Baktoo Family	197
Kashmir Lakes (poem)	208
Pahalgam	212
River Alive (poem)	215
Aru	217
Waiting for Habib (poem)	219
Houseboat	223
1985 India, Nepal and Kashmir with Lesley	230
Dalhi	231
Lal Qika The Red Fort	234
Agra	239
Agra Red Fort	243
Agramaxi (poem)	240
The Taj Mahal	250
Fatepur Sikri	258
Kharjuraho	266
Varanasi (Benares) and Sarnath	276
Trying to Fly and Wondering Why (poem)	282
Back to Delhi and Visiting The Zoo	283
Jodhpur	285
Jaiselmer	286
Camel Rides	289
Rajasthan Desert Song (poem)	291
Jaiselmer (poem)	294
Eyes (poem)	297
Delhi yet again	299
Praying for the Bus (poem)	305
Kathmandu	308
Waking in Nepal (poem)	309
Katmandonein (poem)	315
Patan	319
Looking for New Year (poem)	321
Pokhara	323
As the Mind Flies ... (poem)	329
Annapurna For Sale (poem)	331
Hotel Eden, Kathmandu	334
Bus Back to Delhi	338
Ram Ram Buses (poem)	343
Jammu	345
Srinagar	347

Valley of the Shepherds, Palagam	355
Pony Trek	356
Sonamarg	361
Gulmarg	363
Saying Goodbyes	367
Back to the UK	369
Afterthoughts	370
MYHAT IN EGYPT THROUGH THE EYES OF A GOD	378
Out of My box	380
1989 Cairo and the Pyramids at Giza	382
Father of Fear: The Sphinx	395
Saqqara	396
The National Museum, Tahir Square	397
1989 Luxor	399
Luxor Temple	404
Karnak Temple	406
The Valley of the Kings	419
1990 Ayman	424
The Temple of Hatshepsut	432
Alqunah and Uncle Mustafa	437
2010 Back to the Nile	444
OO-ARE-SET	461
Saleem and Cinderella	468
Professor Bertie	472
Abamira	479
Sex Among The Ancients	490
Ameny	498
Lovely Ana	511
The Returning	526
Through The Eyes of a God	531
Pyramids	539
Kareem and Mustafa	543
Panic: Death on the Nile	547
Run Away	553
Al and Myhat	560
Al and The Undead	562

BY THE SAME AUTHOR

FROM DOT TO CLEOPATRA: PUBLISHED BY FRONTIER PUBLISHING :ISBN 9781872914098

DAMAGE AND HUMANITY IN CUSTODY WITH WILLIAM D. HUTCHINSON: ISBN 9781533026244

OUT OF JOINT-TWENTY YEARS OF CAMPAIGNING FOR CANNABIS: ISBN 9781508420211

TIME FOR CANNABIS: THE PRISON YEARS 1991 TO 2011. ISBN 97809923210761

MYHAT IN EGYPT: THROUGH THE EYES OF A GOD ISBN 9780993210778

THE EFFIE ENIGMA: THE MOTHERLESS MOTHERS ISBN 9780993210792

AND THERE I WAS: ISBN 9781916310742

MY LIFE OF JOY: ISBN 9781916310735

IF ONLY SUOMI: ISBN 9781916310773

BACK TO THE EAST: ISBN 9781916310797

THE AUTOBIOGRAPHY OF A HEAD:
ISBN 9781838440107

MY PIECE OF PEACE: ISBN 9782838440121

Al with some locals in village of Al Qu'im, Iraq, 1972

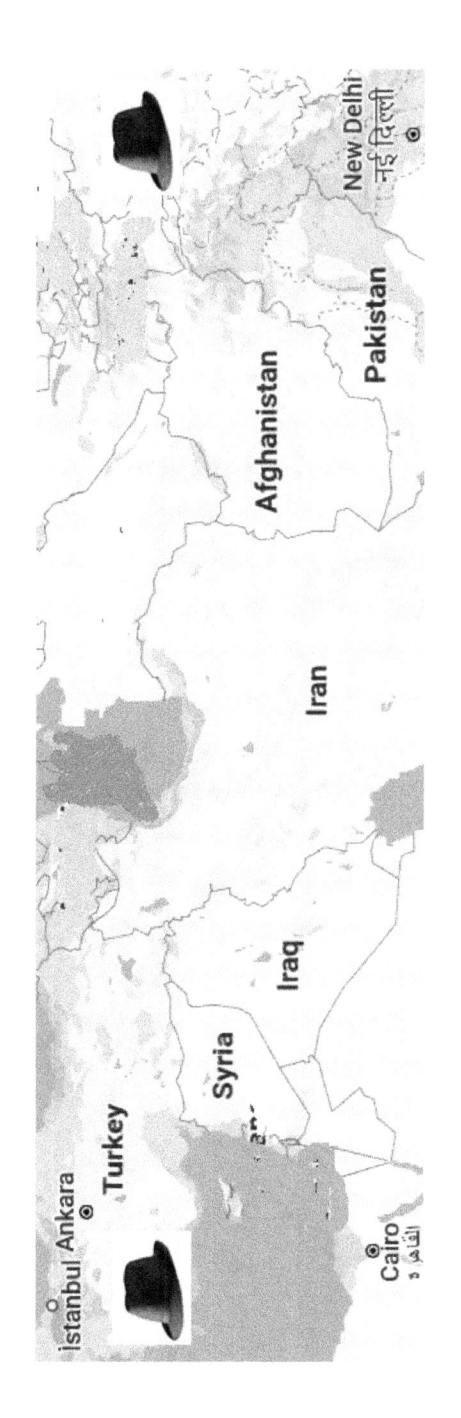

INTRODUCTION

Let me introduce myself.

I am called Myhat. I was also known as Kapelomou.

I am quite an old hat. I was made decades ago. I had been passed many times to different heads, yet had seldom found one that I felt really comfortable on.

About forty years ago, everything changed. I found myself upon a head that I had a close affinity with and I found myself seeing, hearing, smelling much through this young man, Al and even picking up on his emotions and thoughts.

I was lost then for several years, stored in a cupboard until, once again, I found myself on Al's head and now I can tell my tales.

Al and I spent some nine months together on our first trip, visiting many big cities and several small villages, in eight countries, all different, all new to myself and my new head. an adventure of a lifetime.

I sat on Al's head and witnessed all sorts of strange places and events while we travelled to India and then to the UK.

When Al arrived back in the UK, he was quite ill, having suffered from a problem called Infectious Hepatitis and also dysentery. Al went to his parent's house in Wales and then to hospital. But after he was in that hospital, I was never on his head so often.

I didn't know what was happening. Why was Al leaving me? How long was I to be here? What would become of me now? Would I get a new head? Would I get more adventures? Would I be treasured or neglected?

Heads, Hats and Tall Tales

Then one day, Al took me out of my box and put me back on his head.

That is how I came to find myself back on Al's head. I have been on and off Al's head for about forty years and now I can tell my tales. We have done a lot of travelling over those forty years.

I had always been able to understand any language spoken and understood by whatever head I was placed on, but never been able to utter anything myself – until now! I have discovered that I can help Al remember the places we had experienced together and somehow I managed to place the idea of writing my tale for me. Anyway, that idea came upon Al and here he is, writing this for me!

As well as understanding the thoughts, memories and feelings of my head, I felt as he felt, I have been able to see through the eyes, hear through the ears and even taste through the mouth and tongue of my head – Al – and over the days developed a strange connection so that so long as Al was nearby, I could watch what was going on around him – even when not on his head!

I watched, I listened and I remembered – and that is how I come to write this story through a head called Al.

Al had travelled from a country called Britain, a place I had never been to and knew little about.

Al, through me, Kapelomou or Myhat, is writing this account in 2014, forty-two years after the events of 1972.

For my younger readers, I'll say that as Al looks back he remembers there were no mobile or cellular phones out there for the public to be able to buy: no Ipads or Ipods, no digital cameras, no microwave ovens, no 'Sat Nav'. Life was slower, sometimes maybe easier, without the 21st century rush.

In some places there were no telephones at all. And mail was often very slow. Communication was often very difficult outside of the immediate area, especially in the villages and towns of the Middle East.

And Al himself was thinner and fitter if less experienced with the world. I know he doubts whether he could make the same journey now, as he did back in 1971.

Al will tell you, I know, that he feels that apart from the differences in technology and in himself, little has changed. Some things are better, some things are worse.

In his opinion most countries in the world are being run by members of elite families, or Secret Societies or Military men. And almost all of them live lives of luxury at the expense of the people they are supposed to both rule and look after. In even the richest countries there are poor and homeless people sleeping on the streets.

So, on with my account of my first incredible journey into the unknown. It is all about Myhat.

FIRST MEETING

My first meeting with Al took place outside a barber's shop in the Greek town of Thessaloniki.

It was 1972.

Heads, Hats and Tall Tales

At that time, I understood the Greek language, hence my name Kapelomou that means My hat, and I understood just a little English, but that was to change.

It seemed like months since I'd been left on the hook. I had been on the head of a local man who had come to the shop and left me there, never to come back.

During my time in the barber's shop, for long periods my vision and hearing had been impaired, but sometimes a young lad would come to the shop and place me on his head – then I could see and hear more clearly, and pick up on his thoughts and ideas to some extent. Later, of course, I realised that the lad's view of the world was very limited. Listening to the barber's shop chat, I learned about football and sport, politics and war, the rich and the poor – but I honestly considered the world to be quite small, and that everything that happened in it was within walking distance. I thought the rich were one side of the shop and the poor on the other and the shop itself was the great division. Much was still a mystery to me.

Most of the time at the barber's shop I was ignored, just left hanging there, waiting for my head to come back, occasionally being picked up and tried on by customers, always after a haircut!

Konstantinos, the barber, occasionally gave me a rough dust off. He used to sometimes put me on his head and stand in his doorway when there was no hair to cut. I cannot say I felt appreciated.

One thing that Konstantinos often said was the have great influence on my life: he used to say "Watch, listen and remember!"

My life was to change in a big way. I watched, I listened and I remembered.

One day, sun-shining, dusty and quiet, with no hair to cut and no chins to shave, Konstantinos was standing in his shop doorway watching the street. I was on his head. He did that a lot on fine dusty days: street watching was almost a local custom and what was seen was often the topic of barber's chair chat. I could see through the open door and some way up the street.

A group of young people was walking towards the outside of the shop, chatting and laughing. Four males and one female. As they approached I saw that two of the males had long hair; I wondered if they would come into the shop to get it cut.

Three of the young men wore hats. Well I cannot say they were as well made as myself, but there they were. Whilst I had been left hanging there for months, those hats were out seeing the world.

Konstantinos shouted something across the road – he was calling over one of the young men. He said to one: "I see you have no hat!" The young man said that he did not have one – and suddenly I found myself taken off my head, briefly dusted, and presented to him by Konstantinos.

The young man, whom I soon learned was called "Al", put me on his head. I saw the world through his eyes, a world I sensed was very different to my life so far, a world of mystery, strangeness and adventure. A world that Al was exploring with plenty of new experiences, new people and new ideas.

Brilliant! I had a new head.

I instantly understood the new language, English, spoken by my new head. I began to see with different eyes and understand the world in a way new to me.

The others were Keith, John and Mike and the female was called Marion. It doesn't take long to learn those things when all you can do is watch and listen. The fact that the humans did not know that I could watch and listen had the potential of being very useful to me as well as educational.

From the conversations I heard, I was to learn that they had all been students in a country called England, a city called Norwich and most had studied Chemistry. They had finished with schools and had set out to travel and explore, in a small van. At night they huddled together and by day they drove. We were, I gleamed, heading for Turkey, eastwards.

John, Mike and Al had been at a University together for three years, but before that had come from different places. John, Al knew, was from Slough and Mike from London; Al himself was from South Wales. Marion had studied Biology at the same University and Keith, the oldest of them, from Birmingham, was Marion's boyfriend. Of them all, Al regarded Keith as the only experienced traveller. He seemed much more confident than the others, although Al did not know much about him and had only known him for about a year. Al felt safe with all of them, feeling that they were honest and non-violent people like himself

So, I found myself saying goodbye to what had been my home for several months, wondering what the future had in stall for us all. Wondering how long I would be staying with my new head, called Al. Wondering if he too would forget me, leave me on another hook, in some dark place maybe or would I get to travel far?

It wasn't long before we all piled into the van – they had bought some of the local sweet 'Halva' and were saying how good it was, crumbling all over, getting in my brim. I did not care, I felt free.

We were heading for Istanbul, a large city in a country called Turkey.

That evening we pulled up along the sea front near the town of Alexandroupoli. Keith read from his book that this town was an important port and the capital of the Evros region in the Thrace region of Greece.

We did not go into the city itself though, as it was getting late, so stopped and built a camp fire then everyone went to sleep.

The next morning, when Al woke up, Keith and Marion were already awake and making tea, which they all drank with milk added, unlike the Greek people I had seen. They were also cooking eggs for breakfast.

As Al was pouring himself some of this tea, along came a weathered and aged looking man with a donkey, smiling broadly, he pointed at the fire and the tea.

"I think he wants some tea," said Al, and he got up and poured another cup, adding some milk and sugar, and passed the mug to the old man.

"The old man first said thank you, then sipped the hot tea – only to spit it out shouting "Baba, baba!" Clearly, he did not like it. Then he opened his bag and pulled out a bottle of Ouzo.

I knew about "ouzo", an aniseed-flavoured alcohol much liked in Greece and usually mixed with water. It's meant to be taken before meals but many people seemed to like it at any time of the day. Konstantinos had been one of them, but not on the days that he had to cut hair – people got very drunk and loud on that stuff, sometimes.

So the old chap offered the lads some ouzo. Al and Mike were the only two to try it and both said they liked it. It had an aniseed taste and was strong is alcohol, making Al's head spin slightly. I had never experienced that before.

TURKEY

We left for Turkey the later that morning. It was March 24, 1972.

Keith was telling them that sometimes on the border of this place Turkey, the guards took people off and cut their hair, so Al was saying he did not like that thought and maybe he would not even go to Turkey if he had known that before, but now they were on the way.

"Don't worry, man", said Keith, "just put your hair up inside your new hat.

"Great idea," said Al, "good job that barber gave me Myhat!"

"Yeah man, cool," said Keith.

I felt useful, wanted, even maybe loved, elated enough to almost fly off my new head; I didn't of course, I wanted to fit well and be kept. I wanted to stay with these people, they seemed like fun, lots of laughter and good conversation to listen to.

It did not take a day before we arrived at the border, near a place called Ibala, and Al stuffed his hair up inside me with John doing the same with his own hair and hat. Marion, also with long hair, did not have to. Apparently border guards did not object to long hair on females.

The guards, however, simply looked at the documents, the passports as they were called and waved us through. No hat inspections, no hair inspections, no questions, just grins. As soon as we were through, the hair came down again.

I then learned something else new to me. I knew about money because men used to pay Konstantinos the barber back in Thessaloniki; the paper notes used to be called Drachmas and people had to work for them. It seems Drachmas were very important to people in Thessaloniki. That was how they were able to get their hair cut and get shaved

We were standing outside a door into a building that had the words "Change Money" written on.

I now understood through Al that Drachmas were not used to buy things in this country, Turkey. They used money too, and they called their paper notes Lira. The team had to change their Drachmas into Lira and Al also changed some notes from his home country, British Pounds.

It seemed strange to me when I realised that this may have to be done in different places if the people used a different sort of money. The lads also had to pay a commission, so every time they would lose out. I wondered if haircuts cost the same in Lira, but I never found out.

We headed for Istanbul, which Al said was the 'gateway to Asia'. Apparently some of the city was in Europe, then, across a river, the rest of the city was in Asia. Sounded strange to me, but then I already knew from what I had heard, the world was often strange.

Istanbul was a massive and busy city, hosts of people, much traffic. There were donkey carts on the roads along with cars, buses and trucks all tooting their horns. It was one of the noisiest places I had yet to visit. Fun though!

There were massive streets full of cars and buses, sounding their horns and weaving in and out of the traffic. There were tiny back-streets that looked unswept for years. There were people of many nationalities and eating places suitable for all tastes and pockets. Then there was the souk, the market, packed full of tradesmen selling their wares to tourists mainly, from huge circular brass plates to Turkish fine carpets, and rows and rows of massive water pipes called hookahs, used for smoking scented tobacco.

My group found somewhere to stay, a place called a hotel, and Al shared a room with John and Mike whilst Keith and Marion had their own.

"Man, I just need a smoke," said Keith, "but we'll have to wait 'til tomorrow. I'm not going out looking for puff at night, not here man– we'll go to the Pudding Shop in the morning, for a smoke!"

Pudding Shop for a smoke; sounded weird; puddings, smoke?!

ISTANBUL AND THE PUDDING SHOP

The Pudding Shop turned out to be just that, a shop, an eating place, selling dozens of different types of pudding, made mostly of rice – some sweet and some savoury. So my team ate.

On the walls were small notices asking for lifts to India, to London, or to places in between. Apparently Istanbul was on the "hippy trail" and the Pudding Shop was full of long-hairs and short hairs on their travels. People talked about where they had been and what they had seen, with both pleasant and less pleasant tales of their experiences in places called Iran, Kabul, Peshawar, Pakistan, India and Nepal. Mostly they were good tales but sometimes bad enough to put one off going anywhere.

I learnt that the Pudding Shop was really called the Lale Pastahanesi and had been opened in 1957 by two brothers, Idris and Namil Colpan. It was on Divanyolu Street in the Sultanahmet district of Istanbul, near the Blue Mosque. There was a great view of the Blue Mosque and the Hagia Sophia Mosque from the garden. People sat around eating and drinking, playing guitars and singing, and exchanging greetings and news – along with the occasional warnings. It seemed to be a place that attracted a wide variety of travellers. It felt good there. However, nobody was smoking hash and there was none for sale.

After we left the Pudding Shop, on foot, we had to cross a big bridge to Asia, across a massive river called the Bosphorus Strait. I had heard about rivers but never about the boats that floated on them, apparently made and guided

Heads, Hats and Tall Tales

by people, out for pleasure or business. It was one way to get around. I thought that if I ended in that river, I could get blown or washed away, so I clutched my head tightly. But that never happened. I stayed firmly on Al's head.

There were people walking and people driving across the bridge, and even a few men fishing from it.

John and Al separated from the others and headed along a busy street filled with shops and stalls.

Suddenly, I heard the word "Hasheesh!"

It was a local man and he seemed to be offering John and Al something "to smoke." I knew that some humans smoked something called tobacco. It did not smell nice to me. That included John and Al and the others, but this man was offering something else, trying to persuade them that they could trust him and go with him to get some but not to tell anyone and to smoke it only in the hotel. It didn't take much persuasion and John and Al were led down through some of the less busy back streets and eventually arrived at – oh no – another barber's shop! I did hope I would not be left there, forgotten again for months.

I also knew that Al and John had smoked hasheesh before.

The man told John and Al to wait inside where they sat watching the jolly barber sharpening his cut-throat razor. John and Al seemed worried and I don't blame them – but soon the man returned. They gave him some money and he gave them some hasheesh. "Keep it in your pocket, there are police about. Just smoke in hotel," he said. "I wonder if Keith scored," said John; I wondered if Keith was off playing some sort of game. I had heard about football.

John and Al went back to the hotel and it was not long

before there was a knock on the door which seemed to cause some panic. "Open the window." said Al. "You lean out and I'll open the door and if it's cops, you sling it."

It was Keith and Mike with Marion. "Any joy man?" asked Keith.

"Yes," said John, "look what we got."

John showed the others the small lump of greenish brown hasheesh.

"Aw man, that smells ace" said Keith. "Let's barricade the door and have a joint."

A joint was made by licking and sticking some small, thin sheets of paper together. They called them "skins" and using them to roll around a mixture of tobacco and hasheesh. A small piece of rolled-cardboard, called a roach, was inserted into one end. In was then sucked at from that end by one of the people and lit at the other with a match. It that way they inhaled the smoke of the burning mix and then passed the joint to somebody else.

As this procedure continued, it seemed like everyone started to relax and chuckle. To be honest, I was thinking I would gain something like that from the smoke too, but smoking is not for hats – you know, no mouth, no lungs!

It was a while later that there was another knock on the door which was barricaded again, and everyone sat upright – Keith jumped up and moved over to the open window, whilst Mike went to the door and asked who it was.

"Your friend from barbers," said a voice, "I bring you coca-cola."

A short conversation and the group decided to open the door, so Mike and Al moved the furniture away from it and let in the visitor. Al said he recognised him and the man entered and placed a few bottles of drink on the floor – I had seen people drinking that whilst hanging from my hook in Thessaloniki. Some humans seemed to drink a lot but others did not like it at all. Bottles were passed around, the visitor first opening them – with his teeth. It was called cola.

He told the group that he also had some hasheesh and would roll some joints.

His way of rolling these joints was different – he made a mix of tobacco, hasheesh and opium and emptied it into some papers he had put together and placed on the floor. The others had put the tobacco in first then added the hasheesh. But the ritual of passing the joint was the same – but the smell was quite different – it was sweeter. So they carried on smoking and drinking until suddenly Al jumped up and ran out of the room.

He ran straight to the toilet – with me still on his head.

The toilet was a hole in the floor and above the hole was a shower for washing. As Al vomited down the hole, water dripped all over me and I made sure some ran down the back of his neck too. He seemed to be trying to hold himself up between the walls!

It all ended well though. Al seemed to recover and the visitor left in high spirits and everyone breathed a sigh of relief.

There were now four men and one woman in the party, smoking hasheesh whenever they had the chance, wandering the streets of Istanbul, visiting the markets and eating houses. Then they decided to leave and head down into Turkey and maybe beyond.

With all the warning about hasheesh in Istanbul they were glad to be leaving – heading South.

AFYONKARAISHAR

The task of driving was shared between Keith and John and they were heading for a place called Afyon or Afyonkaraishar, which, Keith explained, meant "The Black Fortress of Opium". Keith added "I heard they make some great Turkish Delight there too, man, let's see if we can get some!"

Unfortunately though, it was evening by the time we arrived, so no sweets were on sale. Most eating places were closed. There were very few people on the streets.

We walked along a street with covered arcades either side and saw one man, alone, walking towards us. As he came closer, he smiled, and Keith said "Hasheesh?"

The man ran away across the road, saying "No! No! No!"

Yet, as we continued down the street, the man was following us on the other side of the road, darting from pillar to pillar. Then he came over to us again. He said if we wanted hasheesh, he could get some. We would have to drive around the town, drop him somewhere and pick him up ten minutes later. Keith agreed.

Keith drove him round the same route twice and then stopped so he could get out. "I will be back in ten minutes," said the man.

So Keith drove round the same route at least three times before we spotted the man and picked him up. "Quick!", said the man, "Drive out of town," pointing the way we were already heading.

About five minutes later he told us to turn off onto a track and stop besides the dirt road – we could see the town on one side and a small settlement of ramshackle buildings and tents on the other. The man said "I have hasheesh, but only to smoke, not to buy," and made some joints.

There under a beautiful clear and moonlit sky, he insisted that they all smoke "my way. Inhale deeply through your hand, throw back your head and blow the smoke at the moon." This produced fits of giggles and I ended up on the ground!

Some time later, we parted company with the man, who never gave his name, and Keith asked which way to our road South. He pointed up the dirt track, telling us to turn right at the end and off we went, with Keith driving again. I was in the other front seat, on Al's head.

After a short while the track became a road and we sped onwards. There was a turning to our right and Keith took it. Suddenly, we screeched to a halt.

It was a Turkish army camp and the two soldiers on the gates suddenly took down their rifles and pointed them at us, just as we came to a. halt. Keith shouted something to them and they relaxed and pointed us back the way from which we had just driven.

"Man, we must have fucked up and missed the turning," said Keith.

"And I'm glad we missed the bullets too," said Al. "I thought we were going to get shot, did you see their eyes?"

On we drove then, into the night. They were looking for somewhere to sleep. Keith suddenly pulled off the road, drove down a dirt track, as if he knew where he was going – and pulled up. This was where we were to spend the night, in an open area close to a shallow river. The lads set about building a camp fire.

Almost as soon as the fire was burning, we were visited by a group of young Turks, few of whom spoke any English, which was the language of my head. They had brought with them some bottles of alcohol and offered them around. Despite the lack of communication on a verbal level, there was much laughter. I sensed, however, some trepidation in my head.

The Turks were piling massive pieces of wood onto the fire which was burning away brightly and hotly – it was quite large. I heard Keith saying that he thought they needed to be told to stop, but there were now over a dozen of them. Slowly my travelling group was getting into their van saying they were going to sleep. Keith and Al went over to the group and told them we wanted to sleep now and asked that they keep the fire low and not to make too much noise. With that there were handshakes and "bye-bye" and they started to leave in groups of three or four. There were just two left, one of whom spoke English.

He walked over to the van where Keith and Al were sitting on the ground, and said "You want smoke some hasheesh?"

"Oh yeah man, you bet we do," said Keith and once again I

saw joints being rolled and smoked. The feeling of relaxation once again come into my head – and then the two Turks said goodbye and left.

I think my group was glad as there had been no trouble. We had already had rifles pointed at us by the Turkish army earlier that night!

The following morning my group was awoken by rumbling noises and shouting. As Al and the others sat up, I could see what looked like military tanks rumbling towards the small stream that was near-by. I knew about tanks as there had been pictures on the walls in Konstantinos' barber's shop in Thessaloniki and the customers there talked about them and the "army" and the "war". Tanks were meant to fire at people and buildings and other tanks, with the object of destroying them. It didn't make sense to me – why would people want to kill other people – surely not fighting over hats?

Then I could see that the tanks were just part of a long convoy of military vehicles and that some of the leading ones had been driven into the river and seemed to be stuck; hence the shouting. My group started laughing. It did look odd, with two vehicles half way across the small river and all the men running round shouting, trying to push and pull them to get them to move again. The tanks were just sitting there. I wondered whether they would just shoot at the other vehicles and blow them up and get them out of the way – or would they turn and fire on us! What a start to another day in Turkey!

A couple of the soldiers walked over to us and started speaking in Turkish but when they realised we did not

Heads, Hats and Tall Tales

understand them, they just shook hands and left. A while later the convoy was able to move on.

I liked that sort of adventure as it was exciting and different, then turned out to be OK.

The group ate breakfast and with John now driving, set off for the next place.

PAMUKKALE

It was some hours before we reached Pamukkale Hierapolis.

"Let's go take a look," said Al.

"Yes, maybe we can swim in the mineral pools, that'll be cool" said Keith.

So my group headed up the hill, stopping to look at these beautiful pools of water in their white basins. Higher up the hill we could see a hotel!

"I bet the warm pools are in there!" said Mike, pointing to the hotel.

"We'll have to sneak in, man," said Keith. The party blatantly walked into the hotel grounds and headed for the pool. There was nobody else to be seen anyway.

The sign on the front gate read 'Hotel guests only'. I suppose we were guests then.

So that's what we did. It was more of a blatant stroll than a sneak and we were inside the hotel grounds sitting besides a pool of steaming water where we could see what looked like broken statues at the bottom. "Look," said Marion, "I bet they're Roman. I'm going in for a swim."

Marion jumped in. "It's lovely and warm, warmer in here than out there," she said. Keith followed her into the pool but Al, John and Mike sat on the side watching.

That evening the group drove just outside of the town and stopped to camp by the side of the road. A few joints and they were all asleep. About the only time I left Al's head was when he was sleeping.

It was in the smaller towns and villages that we passed through that I began to notice how differently the people were dressed compared to those in Thessaloniki, although I saw few women there.

Marion was dressed very differently to most of the women I had seen and very different to the women in Turkey. She, like many European and American girls I had seen at the Pudding Shop in Istanbul, wore trousers that they called jeans, but in Greece many of the women wore black skirts and tops and were covered to their feet. Now, in Turkey, all the women wore black and it seemed that the more remote the village was, the more they covered themselves up. The men too, dressed very differently to the men I had seen in Greece, and many of the children wore little more than rags, often bare-footed. It was obvious that Turkey, outside of the big cities, was populated by people poorer than in Greece.

I had gleamed from conversation, that most Turkish people were members of a religion called Islam, which was quite strict on daily prayers – they had to pray five times a day – on dress code and on diet; they did not eat pork or pig products, believing it to be unclean. I did not see the lads or Marion eat much meat at all, and I knew that Al was a vegetarian.

The topics of conversation that I had witnessed in Greece were mostly football, weather or politics. The lads and Marion did not seem interested in either football or politics, hey seemed more interested in travel, music and laughter.

Whenever we stopped in a small village we were almost immediately surrounded by people, especially children, that just stood and smiled, staring at us as if in disbelief. To tell the truth I felt that they would each have liked to have had me on their head. The people were friendly enough, usually bringing somebody to us, such as the village schoolteacher who spoke English.

In one such village we were invited to play seven-a-side football, a game that seemed to be about kicking the ball around and trying to get it into a net that was guarded by a goalkeeper. Whilst the five in my party was joined by two local lads, on one side, the other team consisted of four young men, one old man and two children. They won.

EPHESUS / EFES

So, this time John driving, they packed the van and set off southwards.

Upon arrival, we drove directly to the ruins. It was quite a large area, by the looks of it, and would take some time looking around.

After walking down what looked like a wide street, called the 'Street of Heroes' with broken columns and statues on either side, grass growing through the cracks on the road, we arrived at the amphitheatre, which was quite well preserved with intact seating tiered in a semi-circle. The lads went down to the bottom area where the performers must have entertained many spectators.

John and Al started to shout lines from poems and then perform a spontaneous play as if they were ancient Greeks. I don't know what it all meant but from what I picked up from Al's head, neither did he but I sensed they were having fun.

It only lasted about ten minutes before they started swinging their arms as if fighting with swords, and John fell to the ground as it hurt. Al also fell to the ground and the two of them were rolling round, laughing!

Suddenly there was clapping and shouts of "Encore!", not from Keith and Mike but from a small crowd of what looked like tourists that had entered and were seated at the top row. I don't know whether they thought it was some sort of scheduled entertainment but they had seemingly enjoyed it.

Al felt a little embarrassed, I sensed that, but all ended in good humour.

We spent the rest of the afternoon hanging out amongst the ruins, not knowing what was what. Keith said he was surprised there were no locals standing round looking to earn baksheesh by showing tourists around. It was a pleasant day and I sensed great relaxation in Al. I was happy to be on his head!

That night the party slept under the stars and then we knew that it was time for Marion to start heading back to her own country – England. She was to fly to Istanbul and then go

Heads, Hats and Tall Tales

home by train. That was when I first learnt that people could fly, although I never knew how. It was only later that I realised they needed a machine called an aeroplane to enable them to fly and it took oil to fuel it. I had never even heard about flight before that, except with birds of course. We were all sad to see Marion leave. Although I had never been on her head, I had felt I knew and liked her.

John Sullivan on the Avenue of Heroes

ANTALYA

After Marion had left, we drove down to the southern coast of Turkey to Antalya and headed for a quiet beach where we were to spend the night. There was a friendly fisherman called Mustafa living in a small hut with his son, Zafer, and he invited us inside for tea. Mustafa spoke a little English and Keith asked him if he had any hasheesh. Very quietly the man said yes but he did not want his son to know. After sending the Zafer out on some short errand, Mustafa gave Keith a small piece of greenish hash. Mustafa also cooked the team some fish he had caught that day and told us that the next day he would take one of us to his village to meet his family. Also we could get some more hasheesh. Keith volunteered.

The party slept on the beach that night but in the early hours of daylight we were abruptly woken by a small group of angry looking Turkish policemen pointing guns at us and shouting. That was one of the few times that I felt Al panic, not knowing what they were shouting – but our new friend Mustafa soon came over and told us that the police wanted to see the passports and everyone, except me, had a passport – hats don't need them. The fisherman spoke to the police and then told us it was OK, he had told them we were his guests. The police started smiling and left. I sensed great relief in Al.

Later Keith went with Mustafa and Zafer and was gone for some time before returning with a big smile on his face and some more "smoke". We spent the day and evening on the beach, smoking and enjoying the warm sun. I was pleased that my brim provided shade for Al's eyes so he kept me on his head.

We were just outside the city and port of Antalya, the biggest place I had been to since Istanbul. It was a busy place, full of traffic, and along the port, many fishing boats of various sizes. I did not feel that Al liked it very much there.

JOHN SULLIVAN 1971

Keith announced that he was going to catch a boat to the East of Turkey and anyone who wanted to go with him was welcome. John said that somebody would have to stay with the van and it was going to have to be him. Mike and Al decided to "toss for it" and Mike tossed a coin into the air. Al shouted out "heads" and as the coin landed on the ground, Mike said "You win!" So it was agreed that Keith and Al would buy tickets and go by boat and that the four would meet up again in 6 weeks, back in Istanbul. Keith went off to buy the tickets. I sensed now that both Keith and Al had very little of that stuff called money: Al said he had just twenty pounds and that they would have to live on their wits. With no van or car of their own to travel in, they would have to hitch-hike. Keith came back with two tickets and said he was going to Beirut but the problem was, he said, pointing at a ship some distance out in the water which was the ship we needed to catch but the weather was too rough for it to come all the way into port. "No problem, man" said Keith, "I'm going to ask one of those fishing boats to take us out."

Well, the sea was indeed so choppy that Keith had to ask quite a few fishermen before he found one willing to take him and Al out to the ship.

Al had already packed his rucksack and also had a sleeping bag to carry. He kept me on his head. They said goodbye to John and Mike and climbed aboard the small boat. It was up and down in the water and I sensed that Al was not too happy about this: "I can't swim", he told Keith. The wind was blowing and as Al clung on tightly to the boat, I clung on tightly to Al's head. I knew that if the wind took me away now I would be taken far away out into all that water.

When we reached the ship, I felt Al's mood drop even lower and I realised that he and Keith would have to climb a ladder a long way up to board the ship. With both boat and ship going up and down in the water, I knew that Al did not feel it was easy to do, especially with his rucksack on his back and clutching his sleeping bag in his arms. I knew that Al had some experience climbing as he had spoken to the others about his adventures rock-climbing, fell walking and caving whilst at University, so I thought he'd make it up that ladder and I'd be OK so long as the wind did not catch me. Suddenly we were at the top and being helped aboard by a smiling crew. That was the first time I had ever been on a boat or on a ship.

ISKENDERUN, ANTAKYA, ANTIOCH

Keith said that it was an overnight journey to the Eastern part of Turkey to a place called Iskenderun, but they didn't have a cabin and so it was very cheap. The problem was, he said, that they had very little Turkish money between them for food, and not much other money either.

KEITH MARSHALL 1972

The journey was very pleasant but both Keith and Al were hungry so Keith said he would try asking some of the other passengers for some money to buy dinner. A short while later Keith came back and said he's asked a crew member and "he said we can go down and finish off what's left on the table after the crew has eaten, for free." I did not feel that Al relished the thought of what he called left-overs, but when we were called and went down to the eating area we found a long table covered with many different foods: fish, chicken and meats, vegetables, cheeses, fruits, breads, sweet cakes and the cook came out and said to eat whatever we wanted and take as much as we needed in our bags. What a feast! Of course Al did not eat the meats but he ate fish and many other tasty foods and I felt his mood improve.

Also during the journey Al and Keith met some other

travellers from somewhere called America and were chatting. Keith told them we were going to Beirut in Lebanon but the new friends said "It's terrible there, not at all worth visiting, we had a horrid time and glad to be out of it."

So Keith and Al chatted together and decided that instead of going to Beirut, they would head for Baghdad in Iraq. They would try to get lifts in cars or trucks, due to lack of money, but they could always catch a bus if necessary.

The next day the ship arrived in Iskenderun.

They hitched a lift to Antioch to see the cave that had once served as one of the first Christian churches

As Al and Keith walked up to the cave, we could see that there were other small caves in the hillside.

"We can sleep in one of those," said Keith, pointing, "We may have to pay to see St Peters' place but at least we'll get a free room!"

The cave of St Peter was about to be closed for the night but we did manage to go inside for a brief look. There was an English-speaking caretaker who explained that the caves had secret exit routes built in so that the monks inside could escape to safety if the caves were attacked. He told us that the cave was the first Christian Church outside the Holy Land, wherever that was I did not know, but I sensed that Al did. There was not much else to see except what the man said was an old altar.

Keith asked him about the other caves nearby and the caretaker said they were empty, so the two climbed the slope and found a cave that had a good view of the valley and then they built a small camp fire and made a hot drink and ate some food just as it was becoming dark.

Suddenly we were approached by a group of Turkish boys, five or six of them, all shouting "hello Mister, what is your name?" and "where you come from?" They were a jolly bunch and laughed when Al told them his name. "Are you Al-lah?" said one of the boys, and the others fell about. "No," said Al, "just Al." "Peace for you," said the boy.

Another boy asked "What you do here?" and Al explained that they were going to sleep for the night."

"No, no," said the boy, "bandits will see fire and come down and rob you – you must put fire out now!"

All the boys suddenly started throwing earth onto the small fire until it was out, making big clouds of smoke in the process, and enough noise to attract St Peter let alone the bandits. Then, as fast as they had arrived, they all left, leaving Al and Keith alone in the cave and within minutes it was pitch black.

"May as well sleep and make an early start tomorrow," said Al, which is what they did. Al put me on the ground near his head and within a short while, was snoring loudly – it seemed to echo up and down the alley. I could feel that Keith was moving about restlessly for some time. Then Keith jumped up and shook Al as though to wake him.

"There's somebody out there, fuck it man" said Keith, "climbing up the slope."

Al jumped up and put me on his head. I sensed his trepidation as he began to strain his eyes peering into the darkness, where nothing could be seen. Every now and then we could hear the movement of small rocks and rubble, as if somebody was slowly creeping towards us. Al tried to peer into the blackness of the night but could see nothing but the outline of the hill opposite us and a few dim lights in the distance down the valley.

Al stayed like that for what seemed like hours, staring and listening. Nothing happened until suddenly he heard Keith snoring! He had gone to sleep. Was it all a ruse to wake Al up and stop him snoring? Al himself climbed back inside his own sleeping bag and lay there listening for hours, unable to sleep, until it started to get light again when he finally dosed off. Keith, it seemed, had slept soundly.

When Al awoke, Keith had already made tea to drink and warmed some bread by the new camp fire. "Sorry about that, Al," said Keith, "I just couldn't get to sleep while you were making so much noise snoring!"

"So were you," said Al, "I think those goats down there

thought you were making a mating call to them. They were heading our way.

"At least there were no bandits!"

It wasn't long before the two men were scrambling back down the slope from the cave and standing besides the road waving their hands to try to get a lift. They had looked at the map in the guidebook and could see it was a long way to Baghdad and they would have to cross Syria first. Quite soon they were offered a lift all the way to the Turkey-Syria border.

Aleppo was just sixty-nine miles from Antakya.

When we reached the town of Silvegozu near the border crossing, we discovered that we would have to walk through the Turkish customs and passport control, then walk about five miles through "no-man's land", to reach the Syrian customs and passport control. We also had to change some of our money into Syrian money. We did not have much in terms of British money, I knew, but I sensed that both Al and Keith were pleased that it was worth a lot more in these countries.

Al was carrying his rucksack and I had a great view from from the top of Al's head. I could see we were following a rough road with fields and hills on either side. There were people working in the fields and also some animals. There was no traffic on the road at all, until suddenly a small camper van appeared. It pulled up beside the two men and the driver leaned out and said hello, in English

"Hi, where you from, where you going?" asked the driver.

"Hello, we're from England and we're on our way to Baghdad," said Al, "but we've got to get across Syria first."

"We'll we're driving to Aleppo, then back, we're Aussies, good luck!"

"Any chance of a lift to the border?" asked Keith.

"Nope, sorry, we don't give lifts!" answered the driver.

"Well any chance of some water?" asked Keith – I knew both he and Al were thirsty as it was not very hot.

"OK," said the driver, pouring two cups and handing one to each. "Sorry we don't have much left either."

Keith and Al drank the water and gave back the cups, and without another word the "Aussies" drove off. "Man, I hope they're not typical fucking Aussies," said Keith, "they could have fitted us in."

So on we walked and within the hour we had reached the Syrian border post, completed formalities, bought a three-day visa, changed money, Turkish Lira into Syrian Pounds, and quickly found a lift in a truck going to Aleppo. Even though the truck driver spoke no English and neither Keith nor Al spoke his language he seemed far more friendly than the "Aussies".

It was April 10, 1972. They had three days to hitch-hike across Syria to reach the Iraq border before their visa expired.

ALEPPO AND DEIR EL ZUR, SYRIA

Aleppo did not seem to interest either Al or Keith and after a night in a cheap hostel dormitory and bread, fruit and black tea for breakfast, we were soon back on the road and then inside another truck going close to our next destination, Deir

El Zur. Again the driver spoke no English. Keith said that the second most-widely spoken language here was German. Al said he had studied German in school but not been very interested and had failed the exam.

The following day, Al and Keith hitch-hiked from Aleppo to Deir el Zur, a distance of 213 miles.

It was quite a long time before the duo had arrived in the city of Deir el Zur and found a small hotel.

To get inside they had to climb three broken steps.

The room was small but cosy and Al could see the sign of a large hotel from the window, obviously much more pricey – the Hotel Continental. The hotel we were now in did not seem to have a name, just a small wooden sign saying "Hotel".

We also noticed that now most of the women were wearing black and covered their heads, some even their eyes, and almost all the men were dressed in typical Arab style gowns called Djellabas, of different colours. Some wore head scarves or turbans and most wore sandals. On the streets were stalls selling snacks such as falafel in bread, nuts and sweet cakes, others selling meat hanging from hooks, and fruits and vegetables. It was also much cleaner than most cities and for sure, people were smiling.

This was the last day of their Visa to cross Syria and Keith explained that they would have to leave early afternoon to try to get a lift to the border. If they were late they may have to pay a fine and they did not have enough money to do that. They could, however, take a stroll around the area near the hotel.

So after a cup of tea, the two decided to go out for a stroll, walking the streets just looking at the people. But it was not long before Keith said he wanted to go back to "get some kip," and Al decided to stroll around on his own. He suddenly found the Tourist Office next to a small park. He went inside the tourist office only to find that the staff spoke no English and after trying a conversation in German he picked up a map and left. He strolled into the park and sat on a wooden bench to look at the map of the town.

It was only minutes before he was approached by a couple that said "Hi!" and he knew straight away that they were Americans. They seemed friendly enough and after a couple of minutes the guy produced a small "joint". "Want to smoke some Turkish hash?"

Of course, Al wanted to do just that!

So they all sat about chatting and smoking the joint – I could sense that Al found the joint very strong. After about twenty minutes the Americans left and Al decided it was time to head back to his hotel. But where was it? He did not remember it having a name or the name of the street it was on – all he could remember was that it had some broken steps in front of the entrance.

So Al headed off up a street opposite the Tourist Office – at least, he muttered to himself, if it was the wrong street he could turn round and find the Tourist Office again.

It was the wrong street! Al did turn around and tried another street, then another street – he was stoned and lost!

Now he was back at the Tourist Office for the third time at least. He sat outside to rest and think and was then approached by a young Syrian man who said "Excuse me Sir, I think you are lost. I have seen you coming back here. Can I help?"

Heads, Hats and Tall Tales

Al thanked him and said he could not remember where his small hotel was or the name – but that from the window he could see the sign for a larger hotel called 'The Continental.'

The Syrian man, who said his name was Mohammed, said he knew where that was and headed off chatting, with Al following. Suddenly in the distance, Al could see the sign and then, just as suddenly, he spotted an elderly Syrian man waving from an upstairs window. Al's eyes fell to the entrance, spotted the broken steps and the small 'hotel' sign and exclaimed, "That's it!" I felt he was relieved.

As soon as Al reached the room, Keith said, "Come on, we're late, I've arranged a lift to Iraq! They're going all the way to Baghdad. Where the heck you been anyway?"

"I got stoned and then got lost and couldn't remember where the hotel was or what it was called. I was walking up and down from the Tourist Office anyway, then I remembered the Continental sign and a guy offered help. I only knew it was our hotel 'cos of the broken step."

"Anyway man," said Keith laughing, "stoned or not we gotta go."

They had to walk to the outskirts of the City where there would be a convoy of trucks arranged by the hotel manager, waiting to pick them up and take them towards the border. That was no problem. The trucks were waiting and eagerly set off, with Al in one truck and Keith in another, about five trucks in all. The driver of our truck spoke no English and very few words of German, so Al settled down to try to read. The countryside was very brown and hilly, very dry looking but quite beautiful. Then Al tried to ask what time they would reach Baghdad. Al pointed to his watch. The man held up three fingers and Al became confused. They could not possibly reach Baghdad in three hours.

So after trying a few words in German, Al realised it would not take three hours but three days! He had to try to explain that they only had about 8 hours to get to the border and out of Syrian because their Visas would expire and he had no way of contacting Keith..

Al managed to explain and found out that it would be over 36 hours before they reached the border and that they were heading for Baghdad via a place called Mosul. They were in fact, back on the road going towards Aleppo.

A short while later, the driver pulled into an area by the side of the road where other trucks were parked, and our convoy stopped for a break. The break consisted of bread, fruit and meat, and a drink called "Ouzo", an anise-flavoured alcohol that I had become familiar with back in Konstantino's barber shop. Al explained to Keith that they had a problem and were heading the wrong way and on a much longer route to the border. Somehow, he explained, much to Keith's surprise as he was oblivious to the problem, having been asleep, they would have to get back into Deir el Zur and find a lift to the border but it was now late afternoon and they had just 8 hours to get there. "Doesn't look good," said Keith.

Al's friendly truck driver came over with another driver who spoke some English and after the problem was explained the man said "No Problem, I take you to truck stop in Deir el Zur then I find you good lift right way! But first we drink!"

They did not seem to worry about drink driving in Syria – at least these truck drivers didn't and before long, Al and Keith had both drank enough Ouzo and water mix to start laughing and staggering slightly. It was going to be an interesting evening getting to Iraq.

True to his word, the driver introduced Keith and Al to the new driver and they climbed aboard and were soon passed through Deir el Zur. They pulled up at another truckers' picnic spot and then merrily on their way towards Iraq in yet another truck. This one had a music player and the driver seemed very happy to have company even though only he knew very few words in English.

They went for about an hour along a road with increasingly more pot holes, and as it was beginning to get dark, stopped in a small village. The driver, another Mohammed, said that he would be stopping and pointed into the village, so Keith and Al said their goodbyes and shook hands, put on their rucksacks, with me all the time on Al's head, and walked through the village.

Everybody they passed started waving and shouting greetings with big broad smiles. Not just that though, they started following Keith and Al through the village and out the other side. Few spoke English. Most of the men wore Arab style dress and most of the children were bare-footed in virtual rags. We passed various shops, stalls and tea-houses, where men sitting in the street. There was not a woman to be seen. By the time we found a place to try to get another lift there was a party of about 30, mostly children, behind us and as soon as a vehicle came along and Keith and Al started waving their hand asking for a ride, all the children and adults started doing the same!

Keith said: "Aw man, we'll never get a lift like this. It looks like we're at the end of a long line of people wanting a lift too, man," as he started trying to motion to some of them to move away. But as he waved them away they came closer.

Al laughed and said "I think that wave you're doing means

'come here'! I'll just go and tell them."

Finally Al walked over to one of the adults and asked if anyone spoke English. He discovered by chance that he had chosen the village schoolteacher who did indeed understand. Al explained that we were in a hurry to reach the border and needed everyone to go away so we could try to get a ride.

"No problem," said the schoolteacher as he walked away leaving everybody else standing there. I could sense the frustration in Al and could see it in Keith. I don't think the Ouzo was helping. Keith started walking further out of the village so Al picked up his bag and followed. The crowd, however, didn't.

As darkness fell and Keith and Al had walked onwards, they could see no lights ahead. There was no traffic on the road, there was nobody about. I don't think Keith or Al's mood was very good at that point.

Suddenly there was a car with no lights coming down the road behind them, honking the horn as if in a panic. It pulled up behind Keith and Al and the headlights went on. Two figures got out of the car and started walking towards them.

"Hello, hello, Sir," said a voice, "we have come to take you to next village." It was the village schoolteacher! He explained that the other man was his 'friend with car' and that they would be happy to take us some of the way on our journey.

The next village was about a ten minute slow drive away, carefully avoiding the many pot holes. It looked like it was going to be a long night. "We'll never get there by midnight," said Al.

"No way man. We're fucked", said Keith.

This was to become a pattern for the next few hours. They would arrive at one end of a village and walk through, gathering a crowd of followers along the way. In one place there must have been over 100 people, cheering!

From that point somebody would turn up to offer a lift in a whole variety of vehicles most of them new to me.

There were more trucks and another car, but also a horse and cart, a tractor and almost unbelievably, a motorbike with two men already on it. They sat, first the driver, then Al with his rucksack, then the other man and finally Keith with his rucksack hanging on at the back! We weaved in and out between the potholes for about twenty minutes and pulled into another village. The man said "Passport" and pointed further down the road, indicating with his fingers that we had to walk. "Al Bu Kamai," he said.

It was now 10.30, according to Al, so he said "We've got time for a cup of tea and some food?

"There's a place there, look!"

Keith agreed.

The duo drank tea and ate some bread and cheese, some sweet cakes and headed back out of town towards 'Passports'. "I don't like the vibe here, man" said Keith, "that guy didn't seem like he wanted to serve us. Heavy, man. Let's just get across the border before anything bad happens."

"I reckon so," said Al, "I felt a bit paranoid in there, they didn't seem like the other people in the other villages. Maybe it's because they know we're leaving their country. It's not like we're big spenders!"

So they walked about a mile and arrived at the border with its passport and customs control. The border guard spoke English. "We are closed for the night, good evening," he said, "you cannot go now."

Keith and Al showed their passports and explained that they had a visa but it expired at midnight. The guard kept looking at me, I thought I would end up with a new owner tonight. Maybe he would ask for Al's hat before he let them go through!

"No problem," said the guard, "you sleep here outside and in the morning I give you tea and then you go through, walk to Iraqi border."

AL QU'IM, IRAQ

It was April 13 1972.

At that time Iraq was governed by President Ahmed Hassan and the al-Bakr Ba'ath Party.

"Another walk through no-man's land," said Al. "I wonder how far that's going to be. The last one looked like people lived there and they go back and forth freely to markets and things – if they're in no-man's land they may not even have passports. "We'll take some extra water this time, as it's gonna to be hot walking if it's a long way."

Al and Keith took out their sleeping bags and lay down on the wooden balcony outside the custom's post; the guard brought them some strong and sweet coffee. As they relaxed drinking the coffee, all they could hear were crickets and flying bugs.

The bugs were massive. Neither Al nor I had ever seen anything like them before. They flew around madly targeting the bright lights that were on at all four corners of the custom's building, often crashing into a wall or post. Then they fell to the ground, often landing on their backs and started trying to flip themselves over with their wings. Few seemed to manage that.

As the numbers of bugs increased, the noise grew louder and louder and sleep was retreating. The guard came out with a broom and brushed away the bugs – some took off again and presumably ended up crash landing again, because numbers did not decrease. The guard said "Flippers!" and laughed. This carried on throughout the long sleepless night, every time the guard shouting with glee "Flippers."

The next morning Keith and Al rose quite early, left the border post and walked several miles across no-man's land, where they spotted several small houses and people working in the fields. Keith told Al that they were neither Iraqi nor Syrian people and I figured out they must be no-men and no-women if they lived and worked in no-man's land. Or maybe he meant Norman's land – I had met somebody called Norman once but I did not know if this was where he was from or not.

After an hour or so we arrived in Iraq, presented their visas, changed their money again, this time the money was called Dinars and walked on into a small village.

"I wonder what this place is called," said Al, "the only sign I saw was in Arabic."

As we arrived in the village we were greeted by several smiling young men dressed in what I realised was typical desert costume of djellaba and sandals.

Heads, Hats and Tall Tales

To say that the village was dry would be an under-statement. It was parched! There was very little vegetation in sight, lots of dust and sand and many of the buildings seemed to be made of dust and sand too. The main road which led eventually to Baghdad went straight through the village and as we arrived along that road, we saw a tea-house. We headed straight for it, accompanied by some of the young men.

The men were all very friendly and smiling and kept offering Keith and Al cigarettes and black tea. They would not take no for an answer. They wanted to talk and talk in English – as they were all studying English at school.

Al asked one of the men what the village was called.

"Al Qa'im," he said proudly.

Al asked whether there was a way to get to Baghdad cheaply. He knew that it was about 330 miles from Deir el Zur to Baghdad and they were not half way yet.

One of the young men, called Mohammed, a very common-place name and not just in this village apparently, said that the bus was in the early morning and had already left that day, but maybe a truck would pass by. "But," he said, "you have to pay driver same as bus fare – we all pay for lifts in Iraq."

He offered to show Keith and Al around the small village before sharing some food. I sensed some reluctance in Al. He said to Keith: "What about our bags, I don't want to be carrying a rucksack round the village. I am a bit worried if we leave the bags here and one gets nicked, what chance would we have of getting it back?"

Mohammed immediately said "No problem my friends, there

Heads, Hats and Tall Tales

are no thieves here. In Iraq we cut off a hand of a thief. You can leave bags here, nobody touch."

"I guess so, man", said Keith.

When Al opened his bag and took out his camera, immediately there was a small crowd eager to get their photos taken. Mohammed organised them in one line and led Al over to join them, whilst Keith took the photo. It must have looked odd with about 15 local lads dressed in djellaba and sandals, some with head-scarves, lined up with Al wearing a donkey jacket and jeans and ME perched on his head! There was a lot of movement until suddenly Mohammed shouted "Cheese". They all shouted "Cheese" and froze perfectly still. Keith took the photo. It would be along time before that film was developed.

Mohammed and a couple of his friends or brothers walked

Keith and Al around the village and took them to their little school. There were few people about, those that were had donkeys and one or two carts laden with figs or dates. Some children, some dogs, a few cars, not a woman in sight!

It was not a large village so the tour took just about half an hour and they returned to the tea house where they were immediately served with couscous and spicy beans with vegetables, dried and fresh figs, goats cheese and unleavened bread, yoghurt and black tea, followed by more black tea, coca cola and endless cigarettes.

Mohammed had asked questions about where we were from, where were we going, why, what we did at home, did we have wives and children and why not? They wanted to know what life in the UK was like and did we have televisions and telephones. "Have you been on aeroplane?" asked Mohammed.

Suddenly Mohammed turned to Al. "Do you like the

Zionists?"

I felt some hesitation in Al before he answered. "There's good and bad in everyone," he said.

"Very good answer," said Mohammed beaming. "You are right, but here in our village, only good!"

Later in the afternoon, Al asked if there was a small hotel or lodge to stay the night. Mohammed said "You both stay at my father's house. I take you now?" So this time with their bags, the duo followed Mohammed down a few narrow dusty streets, around a few corners, and eventually stopped at a small one-level house with a few chickens, goats and dogs roaming around outside. Mohammed's father was called Mohammed!

Mohammed senior asked many of the questions that Mohammed Junior had asked and Mohammed Junior translated both ways. It wasn't long before more food arrived. Couscous with spicy beans and vegetables, bread, goats cheese and yoghurt, dried figs and this time olives. There was also chicken that Keith tucked into. As much as Keith and Al ate, more arrived. Nobody else was eating.

Eventually both Keith and Al said they could not eat any more.

Then the others at the table started eating most of what was left.

At this, Al said to Mohammed junior "I hope we have not eaten your dinner."

"No, no," said Mohammed, "you eat first and we eat after, that is our tradition for guests. What is left is for women."

That night as the sun set they went to bed. Fine embroidered quilts and cushions were provided.

The toilet was a small shack down near a tiny stream about fifty yards from the house. One had to take a candle and a bottle of water at night. It was a crouch down toilet, a hole in the ground with a run-off to who-knows where and would not cope with toilet paper. The idea was to use one's left hand to wash oneself with water from the bottle, then wash one's hands afterwards, of course. It was a tradition that everyone kept, to wash or do dirty stuff with the left hand but to eat or shake hands with the right hand. To offer the left hand to shake is a powerful insult and to eat with the left hand is considered dirty, almost obscene. That makes having one's right hand cut-off for thieving even worse. There are probably few with only one hand in Iraq.

In the morning after a breakfast of bread, yoghurt and figs, Mohammed junior led us to the place where we could catch a bus to Baghdad. It was to take almost all day and we passed through the desert. They carried several bottles of drinking water each and some bread, goats cheese, figs and olives for lunch.

"Great people there," Al said to Keith, "this is the first time I've ever been across a desert."

"Yes but it's very hot man and not much to see except sand. Fucking hot," said Keith.

He was right; it was hot, and I spent several hours on Al's lap instead of his head.

BAGHDAD

They reached Baghdad as it was getting dark and soon found

a cheap dormitory near the bus station where they could spend the night. It was cheap enough, even for Keith and Al neither of whom had much money left. It was upstairs above a small eating house where we were told we could eat for free.

The dormitory consisted of two rows of about twelve beds and a few tables and chairs. At one end of the room were gathered about 8 elderly men

"They look like Ali Baba and the thieves," said Al.

"Hey man, I don't think they're thieves," said Keith; "they've all got two hands."

"Maybe they're clever thieves," said Al, "I am going to tie my rucksack to the bed."

Al kept me on his head all night. Sometimes, tossing and turning, I would slip off, but Al would stir and pull me back on to his head. It seemed like a long night.

When Al finally decided to get out of bed, I sensed his relief, for not only was there no bad incident, no attempt at stealing his rucksack, but when he looked around, I too could see that those men were not the 40 thieves after all. It was a small group of smiling men that soon offered Al and Keith some black tea to drink and some bread and cheese to eat for breakfast. There was no conversation between Al and those men, as it seemed they did not understand Al's language, English, and he did not understand theirs. Yet somehow I felt a great sense of friendship between them.

After breakfast, Al and Keith decided to go out into Baghdad and do some exploring.

They strolled down a dusty road filled with people that mostly ignored them. There were men dressed either Arab-style or Western-style, women in black, some with faces completely covered and just a criss-cross pattern to look through, others showing their eyes, scruffy children, donkeys, cars, buses and trucks.

"Look!"said Al, "There's a sign saying 'Youth Hostel'. Shall we take a look?"

It was a short way up a side street, even more dusty than the main street, but, surrounded by a wire fence,; it looked spacious and clean.

"I'll nip in and see if they've got rooms and how much," said Keith. "Might be cheap, man".

Within minutes Keith was back out with big grin on his face: "It's even cheaper than the dorm, "he said, "a twin room with a toilet and shower and we can use the kitchen and it's clean too and they sell food and have table tennis and darts and games."

Keith was really excited so Al went in to take a look and sooner said than done they had booked a room for three nights and moved their bags in.

"Let's not hang about", said Al, "It could be a good day, let's go explore!"

Al and Keith started walking up a wide but dusty street. Al felt very hot. The men he saw were dressed in various ways, some in jeans and T-shirts like Al and Keith, others in flowing robes of various colours and some with cloth wrapped around their heads; others wore suits with or without ties. Then there were what Al assumed were the women underneath what looked like heavy black bundles from head to ankle. He thought they must have been very hot and wondered why they dressed like that. Was it out of choice or was it forced upon them.

We passed shops and stalls selling food and clothing, bits and pieces, a butcher's shop with meat hanging from hooks, shops selling books, tools, kitchen items. And there was a barber or two. There were lots of small Tea Houses and small eateries and plenty of stalls selling tobacco and newspapers.

It wasn't exactly clean, with a lot of litter and animal droppings, and the dust was made worse by many trucks and buses, and as we progressed up the street there was more and more crowds of people and suddenly we found ourselves in a fruit market.

"Wow!", said Al, "Look at that! Fruits! I'm parched, I want some blackcurrant juice!"

Al and Keith spent the next hour or so wandering up and down the first section of this long street market, trying all sorts of fruit juices and then milkshakes: I remember there were so many different tastes; fruits called raspberry, strawberry, apple, pear, orange, mango, melon and a juice made from carrots. Many of the juices were offered with ice and Al was a bit doubtful as he had been told not to drink tap water, but since the locals were drinking the juices with ice, the lads did too.

We also bought some bread, dates, cheese and olives for later, and some soft cakes.

As it was now even hotter, we headed back to the hostel.

The following day Al and Keith spent many hours alternating between sitting outside in the sun and laying on their beds inside, drinking copious amounts of black tea, water and cheap soft drinks loaded up with ice.

"Baghdad is a really old city", said Keith.

After a few days in Baghdad that both Al and Keith seemed to enjoy, a couple of visits to the market and an afternoon spent in a museum, we planned an early morning bus to the Iraq-Iran border. That had meant a visit to the Embassy to buy a visa and another change of money.

Iraq and Iran were fighting at some sections along their border but we were told by an information officer at the Tourist office that it was OK where we were going. Iran did not want Iraq money so the plan was to change it at the border.

We were heading for Tehran, about five hundred and sixty miles away.

The bus took ages and was crammed to capacity with people wearing all sorts of clothing from complete head-to-toe burkas to T-shirt and jeans. There were just another two Europeans on the bus. When we reached the border town it was almost dark, most places were closed and there was nowhere to stay. Al felt very uncomfortable as soon as they alighted from the bus and people scattered. The streets looked empty and shadowy.

Trying to cope with a strong feeling of impending disaster, Al and Keith entered a saloon-like eating house that had lights on and an open door. Inside sat a small group of older men watching football on a tiny black and white TV. Near the counter sat a small group of young men drinking Fanta and smoking cigarettes. The place was indeed smoky and run-down. Although everyone seemed to turn to look at us as we went in, nobody said a word or even made a gesture.

We went up to the counter and the aged man sat behind it seemed to look straight through us.

"Hello, we would like something to eat please, and some tea", said Keith.

Nothing. It was as if he had not spoken.

Al tried gesturing that he wanted to eat and drink.

The man shrugged and pointed towards the door. I felt Al's strong feeling that we needed to leave.

"Maybe they don't like that we are leaving Iraq," said Keith quietly.

"Well Iraq and Iran are at war in the South if you remember – we're lucky they're not shooting at each other here. Let's go", said Al.

So we left the building and turned left heading again towards the border crossing point that was just a few miles away, Al knew from a sign post with Arab writing and the number 2 pointing that way.

About fifteen minutes later they passed another café.

As we approached, a young man in jeans came out and ran towards us.

"Welcome, welcome, my friends, you are most welcomed here. The border closed now, you go tomorrow."

"Hello," said Al, "is there something to eat here?"

"Yes, yes, please come, we have food and we have room to sleep and for you my friends no money."

So with thoughts on whether he was once again risking his safety Al followed as Keith headed towards the low door and into a shadowy interior.

There was low music playing and what could have been an extended family with young children crawling or running around. They were almost all dressed like westerners, although the women were mostly covered they did show their faces.

Several people at once gestured to empty chairs and Keith and Al sat down. Everyone was looking at them – and smiling. Immediately glasses of black tea were served up, with biscuits.

Al was sat next to a young man on one side and an elderly man on the other. The young man pointed to the older man and said "My fadda!"

Al turned his head and was met with a massive toothless grin and outstretched hand. "Very pleased you are here now", he said, "You are our guests this night."

Whilst they sipped tea Al and the old man chatted and Al learned that this was indeed a guest house but they had few guests as they were a big family already and because they were Christians many people passed by. But they were also farmers and were able to grow food for the markets and, said the man "God gives what we need."

The man said his name was Abdullah and he had come to Iraq with his father and mother many years ago, from Turkey. Then they did farming.

Suddenly a steaming hot bowl of soup was put in front of them, with bread, olives, figs, beans and green vegetables.

"Eat, eat, my friends, this is for you", said Abdullah.

As it turned out few of the family spoke English and over the next hour or so many left. Al was keen to avoid talking politics and anyway he did not know the politics of the area. Abdullah was keen to learn about the places Al had been, asking a lot of questions about his home too.

Close to midnight now, Abdullah showed Al and Keith to two straw mattresses at the one end of the room, where they could sleep.

Next thing I knew it was morning, April 18 1972, and we were sitting outside at a wooden table with Abdullah and a few others, eating yoghurt and bread and figs with cheeses and pickles – and marmalade!   Abdullah's son came out with a camera and happy photos were taken. Al never got to see them though.

TEHRAN, IRAN

Al and Keith left and walked for about half an hour to the border where they changed money, went through formalities, and then boarded a bus to Tehran in Iran. The small village where they caught the bus, not far from the border, was the opposite of the town Al had hated the night before.

The street and its buildings were clean and almost modern, people saying hello and smiling,   It looked quite busy with cars and trucks and quite welcoming. Al wondered why it was so close but so different to the other place he realised now that he did not even know the name of the place. He thought for a moment that Abdullah and his house may have been a dream.

But almost a soon as they found the bus station office, it was time to get on the bus to Tehran which would take all day again.

Iran was being ruled by Shah Mohammed Reza Shah Pahlav,

basically a king.

This time there were no Europeans but there was a Russian man on the next seat and as soon as he found out that Al and Keith spoke English he started talking loudly to them and did so for most of the day. He had food to share, fruit and bread and cheeses, so everyone was happy.

We arrived in Tehran just as it was getting dark again and immediately spotted a hostel near the main bus station and booked into a dormitory which already housed several Europeans on their way to or from India.

One of them was American John whom they had last seen in Greece before Al and I met – he was the guitar player that they had picked up in their van.

Although they seemed to see each other, the meeting was brief, and Al being tired, went to his bed.

Next morning when Al awoke and put me back on his head, we went outside into a large courtyard and Al joined Keith who was already sat at a table drinking tea and eating bread and fruits. Al sat down and almost immediately a young teenage boy brought him tea, bread, fruit and yoghurt.

Later we went out into the busy street outside the hostel in order to get something to eat. We walked for about half an hour towards the city centre before we found a small eating house. It was a very noisy street and the eatery was just as noisy inside as outside. But inside, everyone seemed to be shouting at everyone else, so Al and Keith decided to sit outside at a wooden table with a plastic table cloth.

There was a menu printed on card but nothing in English, but luckily the waiter spoke English and was able to direct them to some vegetarian food. This consisted of falafel wrapped with flat bread and served with spring onions, bowls of hot and spicy noodles, bean and vegetable stew, a dish of hot broad beans and salads and dips with more bread. They ate their fill. Al felt pleased to get so much food and thought it cheap. Most of the eating places they had passed seemed to be serving mainly meats in bread, or meat in rice. Afterwards they ate a sticky cake with strong black coffee.

"Actually, I wouldn't mind a beer, it's been months!!", said Al.

"Iran is alcohol-free," laughed Keith, "Fuck, you've picked a bad time to want beer man, all these countries are alcohol free and you can get sent to prison for being drunk"

"I guess I'll have to wait 'til we get back to Istanbul then," said Al.

"We'll have to talk about that, man," said Keith, "I know we said we would meet up with Mike and John but that's still weeks away, and I think we should head east across Iran and spend a week or two in Afghanistan it will be a fantastic place with great hash!"

Al and Keith discussed that on their walk back to the hostel. I could tell Al was really keen on getting out of Tehran but at the same time thinking more of an adventure in Afghanistan – which he knew nothing about except they grew cannabis and made strong hash in the mountain areas and yes they did have enough time.

"I haven't got much money left," said Al. "I don't want to end up stranded somewhere I don't know anything about, it could be like getting stuck 2000 years ago!"

"Well the best thing is to get some money sent to American Express in Kabul, the capital. If you write a letter now if should be there by the time we get there. It should take a few days.

"We could get a bus to the outskirts tomorrow. We can get a visa in the morning and be hitching a lift by about two o'clock."

So it was decided, that is what they would do, and the next morning we made an early start with out bags and walked into the city. It was more like a Western than Asian city, with streets full of people, cars, trucks and buses. There were no donkey carts and few bicycles. Many of the men were dressed in western styles, either jeans or suits, and the women wore colourful cloths and showed their faces.

Al was surprised that the Embassy was easy to find and the queue to apply for a visa to cross Afghanistan was short. The visa was for up to four weeks. But they had to buy them in Mashhad.

They very quickly found a cheap bus to the city outskirts and the road heading east – they would aim for another large town, called Mashhad, much closer to the Afghan border, if they could get a lift. It was 625 miles by road from Tehran to Mashhad.

Al was wondering what sort of adventure lay in front of them, hitch-hiking with so little money in a country where they knew not one word of the language and was probably going to be very different from Tehran.

It was!

As it turned out a car with two young men wearing jeans and shirts stopped within minutes. They spoke English. They were not going all the way to Mashhad and said they planned to sleep that night on the edge of the Caspian Sea and carry on next day to their village.

"You can stay few days in our house", said one man, "we have morphine."

THE OPIUM FARM, IRAN

"We don't take morphine," said Al.

"Well stay with us any way," the man said.

Later we learned that these two new hosts-to-be were called Atash and Nouri and were brothers.

The car was driven by Atash into the night so by the time they reached the home it was dark.

By that time Al and Keith had chatted to their new friends and learned that the lads' father was in fact the village and area policeman and that he had a license to grow poppies to make opium. It was opium that the brothers had offered, not morphine itself – morphine was the name they gave to it though. Al asked if opium was legal in Iran.

"Oh no no," said Nouri.

"It is not permitted without special permission to grow and my father has that and anyway he is the police. If you like you can smoke some opium tomorrow. My father will give some for you but only if you want."

"I've smoked opium before, man, it's cool" said Keith; "I really dug it, made me feel relaxed and dreamy. I'd like to smoke some tomorrow. How about you Al?"

I felt that Al was both enthusiastic to try something new and reluctant to take any risk with it. I knew that Al had taken an interest in experimentation whilst at University studying chemistry, after all, that was what science was about and Al was a scientist. Al wondered whether Mike and John whom he had left in Turkey would also try a smoke and thought they probably would – they were chemistry students too.

Al's interest in chemistry had started when he was about 13 and had been given a "chemistry set" by his father, Jim. From the first time Al had mixed two chemicals (sodium bicarbonate and citric acid) and watched them effervesce, Al's imagination and interest in chemicals had been awakened. Al had thought it was like the two substances had become aware of each other in a "chemical way" and that awareness, he thought, was a form of life.

It was about that age when Al lost interest and belief in any form of god.

So chemistry had come along and Al thought that maybe there was some answers in science as to what the universe was, what life is and why he was here at all.

To tell you the truth those thoughts, not part of Al's memories but also his behaviour pattern. His need to search and explore, try new experiences and experiment. It was that burning that had taken Al onwards to study chemistry and science at university, but also what had first led him to want to try cannabis – and now he was thinking of trying opium.

Keith, Al knew, was very different in that respect. He had told Al that he did not believe in any gods or any secrets to life and for him, life was just to enjoy and that was why Keith took drugs. He enjoyed them.

The car pulled into what looked like a large courtyard.

"We eat now", said Nouri, "then we sleep and tomorrow you meet father and maybe smoke – for you my friends, no charge."

The next morning Al awoke to find Keith studying the map in his guide book.

"We can get from here to Mashhad easy I think," he said "and from there we can get a visa stamp and go to Afghanistan. I'll send a letter home and ask Marion to send us some money to Kabul – maybe you can get some sent out too."

There was a knock on the door and Atash came into the room. "First little food and tea, then to smoke."

"After smoking pipe only little black tea, no food as it will upset stomach and make sick", he said.

Breakfast was short and sweet. Sweet black tea, eggs and bread and sweet breads, and fruit.

Soon enough Atash led Al and Keith into a large room full of cushions and some of the cushions had men laying on them. Al, Keith and Atash went to one side and sat on some cushions. There was no conversation at all in the room.

In the centre of the room was a man putting a light to the end of what looked like a very long pipe and on the other end was a man laying on his side and sucking on the pipe. Al could see that the man at the lit end seemed to be prodding what looked like a small black ball – and knew that must be the opium.

Atash pointed at the man lighting the opium. "Father." he said, "He speaks no English but good man. He will make pipe for you. Remember, no drinking or eating, only little tea."

It was not long before it was Keith's turn to try the pipe. Keith smoked three pipes as did everyone else in the room and then went back to his cushions.

Then it was Al's turn.

Al noticed how the pipe was smoked through small wooden mouth-pieces and each smoker had their own so that lips did not have to touch the pipe. The room was clean and Al was pleased to see that and the mouth-pieces. It was nothing like the dark and dirty opium dens Al had read about.

Father, policeman, opium farmer, called Mohammed, took up a small piece of the black opium on a small metal rod which he them placed on the end of the long wooden pipe. Father lit the opium whilst Al sucked gently but consistently until his lungs were full. Mohammed seemed to know exactly how much Al needed, for it ran out of smoke just as Al's lungs were full. Al sucked on three pipes and went back to his cushions to relax.

It carried on like that well into the late afternoon. Al was feeling pretty good, in a dreamy state, not asleep but euphoric. Al did not feel that opium, when used in situations like this, was a bad thing – none of the other smokers seemed anything like the poor decrepit addicts he had read about in the press in his home country. But he was aware that opium was very different to manufactured heroin or morphine. And taking it for a day may be very different to taking it day after day.

Al was feeling very warm and cosy, laying down on the cushions and drifting into pleasant dream-like chains of thoughts. He had smoked about nine pipes!

Mohammed the father had left the room as had most of the other men, when Al opened his eyes and looked around. It was then that he realised that Keith was missing, so he scrambled to his feet and went outside into the courtyard first, to see where his travelling companion was.

To his surprise Al found Keith in a corner by a tree, being sick into a bucket! He asked Keith: "You OK,? Doesn't sound too good."

After getting his breath back, Keith stood up: "Aw man, I drank some fucking 7-Up fizzy drink and had some bread and cheeses. It must have been that."

"Well they did tell us not to eat or drink between smoking," laughed Al.

"Yeah, that too, man" said Keith.

Al and Keith went indoors and Al took me off his head, a rare occurrence, and I knew nothing until the next morning.

Whilst Al was eating breakfast, he told his hosts that Keith had been sick all night and was still asleep, asking if they could stay another day.

"But," he said, "We won't be smoking today."

"No problem my friend," said Nouri, "We are hoping you will stay and it is our honour to have you and Mr Keith in our house. No smoking, no problem.

It was late afternoon before Keith arose; Al had been spending the afternoon in a shady spot in the courtyard, reading, drinking tea and making notes. He had been looking through Keith's travel guide book, reading a little about Afghanistan, the next country they would visit. They would need to go first to Mashhad and buy a visa, then go by bus to the border. He was thinking just how different everywhere was compared to his home country, Wales, and England where he had been living whilst at University. He was thinking how different University life had been to his younger years at home in his parents' house with his sister and Aunt.

Al's last school as a teenager had been boys only. It had been like that since he was eleven. When he was eighteen, he went to University in a city called Norwich, a day's travel from his parents in Wales. As a University student Al suddenly had complete control over his life, having to pay his rent and buy his food, books and beer out of his money from a government grant. And there were women at the University too.

Here in Iran, Al thought, he had hardly ever seen a woman except western or American travellers.

What women there were, were covered head-to-toe in black clothing. In the village there did not appear to be any at all. It seemed unlikely that many girls or women had much of an academic education. He wondered if there were any at Iranian Universities – were there qualified female doctors or teachers or lawyers? He did not remember seeing any women working in shops or offices, except maybe a few in Tehran. Al thought just how isolated in their lives those women were, probably hardly going outside of their homes or the nearest market. He wondered how much even the men knew about his country and how different it was, especially from this village-come-opium den.

Towards the end of the afternoon, Al spotted Nouri and Atash and asked them if he could take their picture, and they agreed. They stood on a porch outside of a door and put their arms round each other's shoulders and Al took one photo. He had only one film with just about eight shots left.

Nouri asked if he could take one of his brother Atash with Al and it was done.

(Now I can tell you that a while later, when the film was developed and printed, to Al's big surprise, whilst his back was to the door and he was facing the camera, and couple of quite young looking women had opened the doorway, and stood in the background with some small children, one in arms. So there had been women in the village after all? But sadly I was not on Al's head for that photo.

The following day, Atash took Al and Keith by car to a bus stop where they boarded a bus to Mashhad. It seemed like a journey that would never end, a long hot and dusty road in a bus crowded with women in black, men in a variety of garments, and a few live chickens.

MASHHAD, IRAN

Mashhad was well over seven hundred miles from Tehran the way we had travelled – but just one hundred and twenty miles from Afghanistan.

Yet we reached Mashhad in the late afternoon, found a small hotel and were already out for dinner in a cheap eating house. It was hard to find real vegetarian hot food, so Al resorted to rice with nuts and sultanas called Kabuli rice, and salads. But that was plenty after a hot day on the bus. The next day they would find the Afghan embassy and get their visas.

The streets were either dusty or muddy. On their journey to Mashhad they had noticed many small settlements or villages that seemed mostly composed of mud huts. But now, despite the mud, the building were of stone. Many were clearly quite old and badly in need of repair.

They found the Embassy first and quickly they had their passports stamped for entry to Afghanistan and permission to stay for up to four weeks. They had to pay for that, but despite shortage of cash it was very cheap, they thought, just pennies.

So after the Embassy they headed to the bus station to find out how much it would cost for a bus the next day, to Herat, a town in Afghanistan about two hundred and thirty miles from Mashhad.

The bus station was awash with mud. They had to literally wade through it, to reach the office, but once inside it was clean and it did not take long to learn that the bus left in the morning and was cheap. First they would have to go to a small border town called Tayebad, in the morning.

By that time the lads were tired of walking and hungry and decided not to visit the Shrine. We went back to the hotel.

AFGHANISTAN, HERAT AND KANDAHAR

The bus journey to Tayebad was incredibly bumpy, often on more of a muddy track than a road, and every time we passed another vehicle there was a great hooting of horns. Definitely not a comfortable ride.

The bus stopped there for an hour or so and then amidst what seemed like total chaos with people loading massive piles of luggage on to the roof, we left for Afghanistan, where the bus would stop for the night in the tiny border village and passengers could find somewhere to sleep, something to eat, and complete the formalities.

Al and Keith were the only Western travellers on that bus – everyone else was from Iran, Afghanistan or Pakistan.

Al and Keith took their rucksacks from the roof of the bus and headed into a wooden shack labelled, in English, 'Passport and Customs'.

This was close to a small town called Islam Qala.

It was April 24 1972.

Inside the shack were wooden tables and chairs and in the corner a window to a small office. At the window stood a line of ten or so people waiting to get their visas stamped. It was all done speedily and efficiently, so there was not too long a wait. Al stepped to the window first, passport in

Heads, Hats and Tall Tales

hand, dragging his rucksack. A sad-looking official sat at the window, but as Al approached, he smiled.

"Ah, you from Inglant, why you come to Afghanistan?" said the official.

"Just to see the country and the people," said Al; "We're travelling to India."

"You smoke hasheesh in Inglant?"

"No I don't!". Al thought in this instance it may be best to simply say no.

"Okay, good. You no smoke hasheesh. You no buy hasheesh in Afghanistan. You buy, you smoke, big problem, prison, very bad."

"No, no, we won't smoke it".

With that the official stamped Al's visa and told him he could go through without his bag being searched.

Then it was Keith's turn. Al stood nearby waiting and listening to almost exactly the same conversation again. At the end, Keith asked if there was somewhere to sleep.

Following the officials suggestion, we left the shack and walked a short distance down a rough road to find a guest house offering "dirt cheap" accommodation, sleeping on rough mats on the floor, in their own sleeping bags. The only facilities were a shared hole-in-the-floor toilet and a shared wash-tap and drain-away sink. But despite his initial impression and appearance, the man on reception smiled and tried to help, although he spoke little English. He was indeed a very large man, at least 6 foot eight, and wore a long black beard and turban-like hat. He was dressed in a blue suit and white shirt without a tie. He held up a card with the price per person for one night. They handed over some of the Afghan notes that they had bought earlier at the border – the currency was the Afghani. How imaginative, Al had thought.

The room was surprisingly large with space for maybe six people to sleep on the rough dirt floor, which is why it was so dirt cheap, thought Al.

But Al and Keith were the only two to sleep in that room that night.

They sat on the thin mats and were both reading their books, when there was a knock on the door.

Keith jumped up and opened the door to see the reception manager grinning at us.

You no smoke hash here, big trouble with police!" he said.

"No we are not smoking, we are reading," replied Keith.

"OK said the man, "Do not buy outside."

With that he bowed and walked out of the room, slamming the door behind him.

"Fucking hell, I'm not sure I dig this place," said Keith. "Not sure we'll get a safe smoke if it's all going to fucking be like this."

But within minutes the door opened again and in walked the giant grinning and carrying a large colourful water-pipe hookah. He placed it on the ground and said "I give you some tobacco so you only smoke that, OK. You happy men? Welcome."

Without more ado, he walked out again, this time closing the door more gently.

"What's going on?" said Al. "Seems a weird chap. We said we weren't smoking!"

"Well, we may as well smoke the tobacco," said Keith, "Looks like he may have left something in that newspaper."

Somewhat gingerly was how Al was feeling, as he unwrapped the newspaper, wondering in fact what strange thing he was going go find. It was in fact tobacco, chopped up and extremely dry. It was dark brown in colour.

As they had both smoked plenty of cigarettes including the dry rolling tobacco in Turkey, the only new thing here was the hookah itself. It was about three feet high, a round clay bulb and clay neck with a flexible tube to suck on attached, and the smoking bowl at the top of the neck, made again of clay. The whole thing was painted and decorated with short strings of tiny beads of many colours. Al felt it was more of a precious ornament than tobacco pipe.

Keith poured some of the dry tobacco into the pipe, put his mouth to the tubing and a lighted match to the bowl, and sucked – one long, slow but deep suck.

He sat upright holding the smoke in his lungs a while before blowing out a massive cloud of smoke.

He doubled-over, coughing. His colour changed from tanned brown to dark green. He looked like he was about to explode.

But he didn't. A bout of coughing later and he was passing the tubing to Al to try.

I sensed that Al was a lot more wary than Keith had been, as he sucked gently on the pipe. He inhaled and immediately blew out a small cloud of smoke and coughed.

"That's bloody dreadful," shouted Al; "It tastes foul and just made me feel bad, not good. I am not bothering with that."

Just then, once again, the door opened without any knocking, and once again in strode the giant from reception – this time followed by the grinning official from the border control post.

They looked at the hookah and sniffed the air. "Ah, not smoking hasheesh?" said the official with a massive grin. "Very good.

"Now we smoke good hasheesh. You want to buy, you buy from me OK. It is safe now."

With that he threw his bag to the ground and pulled open the zip. He started to pull out some discus-shaped lumps of black hash.

"I have 100 gram, or quarter or half kilo good hasheesh from Mazar. I give you some to smoke, you want, you buy. You not buy, no problem". He bit off a lump of about ten grams from the smaller block and passed it to Al. Al looked at it and then lit a match and warmed the corner of the piece. It smelled fantastic. He passed it to Keith, who took one smell, laughed out loud and proceeded to replace the foul tobacco with some of the crumbled hash.

They smoked a couple of pipes whilst the customs man and reception giant rolled and smoked joints made with American cigarettes.

"You want buy some?"

"No thanks we enjoyed the smoke but we don't want to be taking any with us and don't want to go to prison,." said Al.

"No problem, very good very wise," said the official. "In

Afghanistan drugs very bad but it is OK here with me but when you go, do not buy drugs."

The official and the giant left the room. Keith and Al moved a cupboard across to place in front of the door.

"Hopefully that'll stop them barging in. I'll roll a joint."

The last cannabis that the lads had smoked was in Turkey, except for the one time with the Americans in the park in Syria, and I can tell you Al was very "high" and enjoying the experience. The two lads spent some time giggling at nothing. They ate bread, cake and fruit that they had bought from a shop on the way to the hotel. Washed down with bottled water.

Al stretched out on the mat, which seemed to be much more comfortable now he was laying down.

He fell asleep.

The following morning there was a banging on the door that woke the two travellers, and a shouting from outside:

"Mister come quick, bus to Herat going soon."

So they scrambled to their feet, stuffed their rucksacks, grabbed the remains of their supper, and got out of the hotel, walking fast to the bus stop.

There were a few old cars on the street, and bicycles, as well with the men leading donkeys laden with crops. What was really noticeable was the trucks.

There seemed to be lines of trucks going in each direction, throwing up dust, honking their horns – but it was the way in which the trucks were decorated that was amazing to Al.

Each was painted in bright colours and in unique styles, showing depictions of buildings, people, animals, mountains and lakes. There were trees and flowers, birds and even insects.

Al spotted a truck with an elephant painted on the side, with the trunk going to the cab and then as if raised to the roof. There was one with a lion. There was one with people that looked like men and women dancing together. Several had large birds painted on.

Others were painted brightly in lines and patterns; reds, blues, greens, well almost every colour.

Most of the trucks had a box-like section over the cab, Al thinking that was probably where the driver slept for these would surely involve overnight stops. All the trucks seemed laden to the limit.

Al thought the drivers must be very proud of their trucks; maybe even named them.

When they reached the bus station, it looked like chaos. There seemed to be at least two bus loads of people with a massive amount of luggage. Huge cloth bundles were being passed up to the roof to be tied down.

Keith walked off and came back a couple of minutes later.

"God man, it's ridiculous," he said, "they reckon that yesterdays bus never left so people had been here all day yesterday waiting, now they want to get on this one..

"Look they're getting bags back down off the roof. The driver said we should get on. I showed him the ticket, he just pointed inside. But I reckon it'll take hours sorting this out. There's still only one bus. Some guy told me this is today's bus and yesterday's bus has broken down so they have to get another one from Herat and that won't be here 'til tonight. Come on let's get on – you get two seats and I'll get the luggage onto the roof. I'll climb up and tie it myself."

So that is what they did. They claimed two seats, put their coats on them. A while later they got off the bus again, for a smoke. Keith had some of his joint from the night before so they went up away from the people to smoke it. It was now about 9 o'clock. The bus should have left at 7.30.

In fact it was almost 11 o'clock before the bus left. The journey was along what seemed like one long straight road through desert, the occasional small village with mountains in the distance.

The bus made several stops at tea houses and once in the middle of nowhere all the men got off for a piss. Keith too. The men lined up and all crouched down, pissing from under their gown-like clothes, mostly grey or white, some with stripes, and a few in blue. Looking out of the bus window, Al laughed. About thirty feet from the road on the sandy ground, in the middle of the long line of crouching men was Keith, standing up with his back to the bus, presumably pissing: dressed in jeans a T-shirt.

It was just then that Al heard an American-sounding voice. "High man."

Al had not even noticed any non-Asian looking people in the queue or on the bus, but soon learned that sure enough the guy was from the US. He explained that he had arrived from Mashhad had three nights ago. He had missed his bus, bought another ticket only to find the next day that bus was broken down. So then this morning he had turned up late but managed to swap his ticket and some money so he could get on this one. From the general conversation, Al gathered that the American was travelling alone and was hating it. Almost everything he said had the word filthy or the words nuisances or stupid in. Al was actually quite glad when the guys started getting back on board and the American went back to his seat.

There was a stop for refreshments, at what were basically a shack with charcoal stoves in the street outside. It was all pretty dirty looking and smoky. People from the bus crowded round barging each other about as if there was a limited supply of gourmet treats.

In fact there was only one choice, a set menu, a watery-looking soup and a meat and rice dish, and bread.

Nearby was a tiny stall selling vegetables. Al bought bread and spring onions and a few bottles of Fanta orange drink. That would have to do.

And both vegetable stall and shack café were hassled by flies. Several donkeys in the street, a few dogs, probably open hole-in-the ground latrines. Hardly hygienic. In both the shack and the shop the bread was charred looking, unleavened, covered with flies. The locals did not seem bothered. Al wondered if he should eat anything at all.

The men here were mostly wearing head-coverings that looked like puffy pancakes, flat hats of grey, white or black wool, called Pakols.

Other men were wearing scarves of varying colours or what looked more like a towel, thrown over their heads.

What women there were wore black garments from head-to-toe and were always seemingly carrying baskets, buckets or bales.

I felt that all the men, seeing me on Al's head, shading his eyes from the glaring sun, wanted me.

Almost all the men wore beards, many quite long. They looked weathered.

Al wondered what the American thought of this, but he was still on the bus.

Al was surprised to see the size of all the vegetables and fruit on sale. The spring onions, red and green peppers, tomatoes, apples, melons, onions, carrots were all massive. Two or three times the size he had seen before. There were nuts and open pots of yoghurt sitting in the sun, and bunches of various green leaves. Cans of fizzy drinks and packets of American tobacco were also on sale

The bus stayed there in the heat for about two hours. Everyone seemed irritated in the heat with nothing to do but wait, but the driver was not going to move. Al fell asleep.

Al was awakened with a bump. The bus was speeding down the new road which was said to have been built across Afghanistan through deserts and paid for with Russian, American and British money. But there was nothing to keep people or animals off the road. Apparently the bus had hit a dog. That was it. The dog was left in the road and the bus carried on.

There were also plenty of Bedouin tents close to the road and sometimes small groups of men leading camels.

Eventually and none to soon, they pulled into Herat just as it was starting to get dark.

It once again looked dusty and ramshackle, the roads far worse than the highway. There were a few cars about, trucks as well as donkeys.

"Hey man, Al, let's get our gear and find a place to stay fast" said Keith, "Before all the rooms get taken.."

To Al's amazement their bags were already off the roof of the coach before they got outside, and they immediately spotted a sign across the road that said "Hostel".

They went in; the receptionist spoke English and was pleasant. He said there were many Westerners staying there. He explained that tomorrow many would go on buses to the border or to Kandahar and Kabul. They served an evening meal and breakfast. It was remarkably cheap and looked clean so they booked a room that turned out to have two beds.

The receptionist explained that the bus to Kabul left at 3 o'clock each afternoon and would take almost 24 hours, stopping in Kandahar. He said he could buy their tickets the next morning. Keith and Al gave him the money, about two hundred Afghanis, worth about one pound in British money.

The lads decided to drop their rucksacks into the room, lock the door and go for a walk before it got too dark. The room had two beds. These would be the first beds they had slept on since Tehran. The beds had sheets and thick woollen blankets. In the corner was a table and two wooden chairs, and another small table with a wash basin and large jug containing water. They could see the street from the window.

Al told Keith that he had hardly any money left.

That was when Keith first told Al that he had fifty British pounds in travellers cheques that could be cashed at a bank or maybe sold for more on the illicit market on the street. So really they had no big money problems if Keith would give Al a loan until his money arrived. Al had left Turkey weeks earlier and travelled many miles on less than £20. Surely they had enough to get to India? Fifty pounds was about two weeks wages in Britain. Al had lived on his 'grant' of £10 a week for three years, four pounds of which went on rent and the rest of books, bus fares, food and beer. Then he had worked on a building site erecting fences for twenty pounds for five days work. Here in Asia so far, it seemed that £20 was worth more like £500.

It was getting dark now and the temperature was dropping quite quickly. They walked up the main street that the bus had stopped on, past tea and coffee houses, small eating places, shops selling foodstuff or with butchers meat hanging as if a feast for the flies, hardware shops with piles of metal and clay cooking pots outside, a baker's shop with a window full of chocolate brownies and other cakes, and shops selling cloths.

They bought some bottles of water, chocolate brownie cakes, rusks, soft cheese, yoghurt and tobacco, and headed back to the hotel.

"Well I can't see there's much here," said Al, when they were back in their room. "What's it say in your book?"

"Aw man I'm hungry, I'll read some later, let's see what they're serving up."

So they went to the dining room in the hostel and to their surprise it was filled with western men and women. Some were sitting at tables eating and others were sat on large bean-bag cushions on the floor. Some of the men had long hair, but some short; same for the women. Some were dressed in jeans and T-shirts or sweaters, some in Indian garb, white pyjamas, and a couple in orange robes. There was a girl sitting on a cushion singing and playing her guitar.

Songs by Bob Dylan and Joni Mitchell, as Al recognised.

Al sat at a table and a few of the other diners said "hi".

The man from reception appeared at the table holding a small blackboard with a list of food for sale, in English. Al was amazed to see Pizza, Burgers, Fried Potatoes and Milkshakes listed. But he and Keith decided to try the vegetarian goulash and yellow rice with beans and salad, and a milkshake each.

"Bloody hell, it's cheap," said Keith.

He turned to one of the others and said "Hey man, is the food OK?"

"It's actually very good,"said a chap with a very English accent, "best we've had since Athens." The guy explained that he and his girlfriend were going to Nepal and had left the UK six months earlier. They had chosen to go across Turkey to Iran, rather than the route taken by Al and Keith, but had got stuck in eastern Turkey due to a bad storm and landslide. They had had to wait weeks whilst the road was cleared.

They were correct in that, the food was superb and the two ate their fill to the sound of peace songs from the girl on the cushions. Al thought she looked very pretty with her long black hair and smiling face and wondered if she was going to same way as he and Keith.

After dinner and after most of the others had left, Al and Keith went back to their room and Keith rolled a joint with some of the hash he had left. He shared it with Al.

MIRIAM

Keith and Al smoked another joint. Al decided to go to see if they could get a cup of tea, so he left the room and headed to the reception area.

At the reception was the happy friendly man that seemed to be manager, waiter and maybe even cook and the guitar-playing girl from the cushions in the dining room, chatting. From her accent, he guessed she was Canadian.

Al ordered two cups of tea with milk. There was no sugar, just hard boiled sweets to suck on whilst the tea was sipped. Apparently, according to the man, there was often a shortage of sugar but never a shortage of sweets and cakes!

"Hi, I'm Al." He smiled at the girl.

"Hi, I'm Miriam," she said, smiling back. "I'm from Vancouver on my way east." she said.

"I'm going to India," said Al, "at least that's where we're heading now. We left England in a van and we were just going to Turkey and back. There were five of us. But I decided to head east with my mate and the others stayed in Turkey. We're going to meet them later. Well, that was the plan. Now it looks like we're going to India instead."

"So did you come through Turkey and Iran?" asked Miriam.

"Yeah and Iraq and Syria. We were going to go to Beirut but we were put off, so we went to Baghdad instead. We've been on the road a few months now. "Actually, it's the first time I ever left the UK".

Al felt good chatting to Miriam and they exchanged a few travel tales. They talked about the Pudding Shop in Istanbul and how bad it was in Tehran. Al did not mention the opium village though. Miriam did not look the sort that he thought would take opium.

In fact, Al was so busy chatting and sipping his tea that he completely forgot to take a tea for Keith.

Keith suddenly appeared saying "Aw man, where's my fucking tea? I made another number."

He smiled at Miriam and Al introduced them.

"Get some more tea and come and have a smoke," said Keith.

"That would be nice," she said.

So the three went back to the room with tea and smoked a joint, then another. Miriam sat on the bed next to Al. I could tell he liked this girl and wondered what would happen. Would Al leave Keith and go with Miriam? I knew he was thinking of it. Plus it turned out Miriam was catching the same bus to Kandahar the next afternoon.

After an hour or so, Miriam said "Good night, see you!" and left, presumably to her own room.

Now Al was looking forward to the bus journey and maybe chatting with Miriam again and maybe more. With the pleasant feeling from the cannabis and from the girl, he got into bed and soon fell asleep.

Next morning Al was out of bed and quickly down to the dining room for breakfast, hoping to see Miriam there; but she wasn't there.

Breakfast was a big surprise, there was masses. Porridge, eggs, boiled, scrambled, fried, pancakes, sausages and pieces of lamb, which Al did not eat, toast and jams, bowls of massive fruit and even cold pizza, with tea and coffee and fruit juices.

After breakfast, Al and Keith went outside to see what the place was like in daylight. Al was secretly hoping he would see Miriam.

The city was dominated by a fifth century citadel known as Herat Fort. Very impressive but it did not draw Al and Keith to it. Neither did they visit the mosque. Instead they amazed themselves simply by walking the street. It was like going back in time a couple of thousand years.

The street was quite busy, with just a few cars and trucks, a lot of donkeys with or without carts, and a camel or two.

Stalls were set up along one side of the road, offering mostly fruit and vegetables, meat, bread, clothing and kitchen utensils. What traffic there was had to drive past this market on the other side of the road.

There was also quite a large number of elderly men dressed in long robes and turbans, holding out hands or gesturing to eat. Al did not have money to spare for them if he had wanted to give. Many seemed to be given food from the stalls.

Strangely, although it was dusty and hot and looked like something out of Biblical times, obviously not wealthy but mostly unchanged for probably centuries, the place felt really calm and in a way idyllic. Only thing was, no Miriam!

They spotted a sign in English which read 'Bus Tikkets Here' (sic).

Luckily the man selling the tickets from a small booth spoke English and they were able to make sure that their two tickets would take them all the way all to Kabul..

"Yes yes," said the man, "but you must pay five Afghani extra to reserve seats, five each, You go first Kandahar and then the bus stops for night – you can sleep on bus or get hotel, or stay one day and get another bus to Kabul. But you say now so we keep you seats."

It was two hundred and eighty miles from Herat to Kandahar and another two hundred and ninety to Kabul.

Al and Keith quickly agreed that they would stay two nights in the city, the night they arrived and one full day.

"May as well stay, man, if it's where the weed grows," whispered Keith.

So that is what they did. Soon enough they were out of their hostel and it was 3 PM and the bus was leaving on time! Apparently the road to Kandahar, once out of the city of Herat, was in good condition until they entered the city of Kandahar itself.

Miriam was not on the bus and Al felt the journey was disappointing despite the views across the desert to the distant hills and the small groups of Bedouin tents. It went on and on. They arrived in Kandahar when it was dark. The driver pointed them to walk up the street they had just driven down and said "Sleeping there."

Sure enough, there were several hostels and Al and Keith soon found a cheap room with two beds. But there was no food and it was a very different atmosphere to when in Herat. So they dropped their bags and went into a small restaurant near the hotel. It was maybe that they had never heard of vegetarians. Al tried saying "No meat, carne no, nicht Flesh!" wondering if that was Spanish and German at all. The guy with a long black beard, black headdress and grey gown, just shook his head.

Al signalled 'two' and said "Kabul rice no meat' and "two tea." Everyone else seemed to be eating kebabs. Al spotted what looked like omelette; he pointed and said "two"

The food came almost instantly.

It was pretty dreadful. The omelet was cold and oily and quite stale; it came with hard crusted bread.

The rice was yellow with specks of black and warm. Al wondered if it was black rice or burnt bits. He could see there were nuts and raisins in it.

But before Al could even taste the rice, Keith spurted out quite loudly "Man it's fucking horrible, cold and soggy and fuck me look at that. It looks like bits of some animal. It's lamb. You said no meat man, that's no good, I can't eat it."

That put Al off as he pushed the plate of rice aside. He struggled through the omelette.

The waiter brought the tea, black with boiled sweets. He looked at the uneaten food and said something in his language. Keith and Al shrugged and said "I don't understand."

With that the restaurant seemed to come alive. All the other customers seemed to want to take part in a debate. Some quite loud, waving their arms and gesturing at their own plates and at Keith and Al.

"What the fucks going on now, man,"said Keith, "Sounds like they're gonna lynch us!"

But no, suddenly the place went quiet and one man stood up and said "Excuse me mister, you are speaking English?"

"Yes we speak English," said Al, wondering if it would have been had better if he had just said no.

"Very good Sirs, he say to you ask if food no good. You no want?"

"No we don't like the rice," said Al, "Because it's cold and has meat in it and we said no meat – we don't eat meat."

The man appeared to translate that into a local language and once again the restaurant erupted as everyone wanted their say.

After what seemed to be along debate, the man turned again and said "OK mister no problem, That Kabuli rice with lamb. Only the poor people eat rice with no meat so he think you not have big money and give you meat as gift. No problem mister, you no pay."

"That is very kind but we can pay for the eggs and tea," said Al. "It's because we do not eat animals, no lamb or beef or chickens."

The man translated again and half the restaurant started laughing, smiling and nodding at us.

That done, they went back to their hostel wondering if they had made the right decision to stay a day in Kandahar.

That night was quiet; Al wrote letters ready to post the next morning, to some of his friends back in England, asking them to send him some money. Keith had told him to ask people to send it through American Express and to write to "Poste Restante' and the name of any town, and that Al could pick up mail using that at the main post offices. So Al asked for some to be sent to Kabul and some to be sent to Delhi in India.

The next morning they ate bread and curd cheese with fruit for breakfast in a small café next to the bus station, and were soon on the bus on the way to Kabul. They never saw fields of cannabis, as they had hoped for, in Kandahar.

KABUL

The bus journey was again, unfortunately, not inspiring Al despite the distant mountains. He was glad when they pulled into the bus station in Kabul, a journey of another 280 miles.

Getting out of the bus, Al and Keith were immediately set upon by a group of men offering cheap hotels. Suddenly a man appeared with their rucksacks, asking for money as he had independently climbed to the roof of the bus to get them down. One of the other men said "Take your bags and come, I take you to good cheap hotel Mustafa. Do not give money, he not official porter."

So that is what they did.

They walked for about ten minutes and arrived at Hotel Mustafa. It looked clean and was convenient to get to the bus station and the city itself. Inside on reception there were two young men with big gleaming smiles and bright shining eyes beneath their pitch black hair. They were both wearing jeans and shirts.

Al had noticed that there was a greater range of style of clothing and hats than elsewhere so far since reaching Afghanistan. Many men wore long coats over trousers. Some even wore suits and shirts but open-necked.

They booked a room with two beds for twenty Afghani per night. Al knew that was very cheap. He had been working forty hours for twenty pounds in England, and twenty Afghanis was worth just a few pence and that was for two beds.

They paid for seven days in advance. That was almost all of Al's money so he was going to have to depend on Keith.

When he told that to Keith, his friend replied: "No problem man, I have an idea with the travellers cheques. We should be able to sell them on the street and get more than from the banks.

Inside the room, Keith rolled a joint. There was a small shared balcony but nobody there. So they sat on some chairs at a rickety old table and lit the joint.

Almost immediately one of the guys from reception appeared asking if they wanted tea.

"Yes please," said Al, "With milk!"

Minutes later the man appeared again with a large metal pot full of tea, a jug of milk, some sugar and three cups. He pulled up another chair and sat down.

"Where you from my friends?"

"England," said Keith.

"Wales," said Al.

"Welcome to Kabul," he said, "my name is Abdul. My brother is Rafi. We are here for our father's hotel and you are welcome. You want to smoke some good hasheesh. I have chillum."

Al and Keith both knew that a chillum was a clay pipe through which cannabis mixed with tobacco could be smoked and inhaled deeply. They had both, in fact, smoked chillums in England..

So they heartily agreed to share the pipe.

Abdul took a cigarette from his pocket and emptied the tobacco on to his hand. He took a small piece of black hash from his pocket and warmed one end with a lit match before rubbing it into the tobacco and pouring the mix into the chillum. As if by magic a young teenage boy appeared with three cups and another pot of tea.

Abdul told them that if they wanted more hash, he would buy for them, or they could buy from "boy in street with cigarettes".

Al enjoyed the smoke. He and Keith laughed at nothing once they were back in their room. Al lay on his bed and was soon asleep.

He awoke some hours later. Keith was snoring, but awoke soon after Al started moving. Al went to reception to get some tea and when he returned, Keith was making another chillum.

They smoked the chillum and drank the tea, joked and laughed for a while, then fell asleep again.

When they woke up it was the next morning. They left the hotel and went to a small eating house where they ate fried eggs and bread. Nearby was a small shop selling what seemed like almost everything. They bought bread and cheeses, brownie cakes, dry bread rusks, jam, strawberries and yoghurt out of Keith's money.

I noticed a type of hat I had never seen before. Al knew it was called a Jinnah Cap", made from the fur of a breed of sheep, often from the fur of aborted lamb foetuses. The triangular hat is part of the costume of the native people of Kabul which has been worn by generations dating back in Afghanistan. The hat is peaked, and folds flat when taken off of the wearer's head.

They went back to the hotel, smoked, laughed, slept and woke up a couple of hours later.

They ate some snacks that they had bought and decided to go out for a walk. Outside the hotel they saw a boy of maybe 14 years in the street near the hotel. He was selling cigarettes. One could buy a packet or just a few. Keith bought a few and the boy offered a small piece of hash, which Keith also bought. The boy said "Mister, be careful, only buy hasheesh from me. It is very good. Others selling bad hasheesh and maybe big problem for you."

Al and Keith went walking down the street and soon reached the river. Looking back at the town behind them it seemed like a building site – pills of rubble, holes in the road, buildings tumbling down.. On the other side of the river there were many houses built on the hill.

The streets this side were busy with people, many carrying baskets and some of them on heads. Why put a basket on a head, I thought, when they could have had hats. But the baskets contained their wares. Others were carrying massive bundles on their backs.

As we had strolled down this busy street we also saw men sitting on carpets laid out in the street; presumably selling carpets! Others had piles of fruit for sale. Oranges and melons were everywhere. Some stalls were offering slices of melon, with the vendor constantly fanning off the many flies.

Tiny stalls were selling a range of food cooked on small fires or stoves on the ground. Al had no idea what they were selling, but sitting and cooking on the ground like that did not appeal to his sense of hygiene. The place was also littered with trash and animal droppings.

We spotted a man sitting on a wooden chair in the street; behind him was a man who was cutting his hair – a barber. The cut hair fell to the ground and was blown away by the breeze, Next to them was another man giving his customer a shave with a long cut-throat razor.

There were low, covered stalls with rows of meat hanging from the roof – live chickens for sale outside.

Other stalls offered cooked lamb kebabs or pieces of chicken, baked potatoes, eggs, breads. Most of them were busy with customers.

There were small stalls selling flowers, shoe-shiner boys, knife-sharpening and stalls with piles of crates of cheap fizzy drinks.

The women were all covered head to toe in their long burkas, as they were called, even their eyes were covered with a cross-lattice. Some wore blue, some wore brown and some wore black. Al assumed they were women. Al saw two women walking together dressed in blue burkas; later he saw another two. Or were they the same two? He wondered how they would recognise each other in a crowd.

That was of course the local women. The Western women wore either jeans or knee-length dresses showing their legs.

There was a whole range of styles of clothing that the men wore. Some wore long robes and turbans whilst others wore rough-looking jackets or waistcoats over cotton shirts with dark cotton trousers below. Others wore dark suits, and some even wore jeans similar to Al's. There were more Westerners than Al had seen for months. Al wondered briefly if he would see Miriam, but he didn't.

There was also a variety of hats: flat hats, hats made from scarves of white or grey, as well as many different styles of turban, Almost all the older men sported beards.

Most of the male children seen on the streets were either dressed in rags and bare-footed, or like smaller versions of the men; the girls, however, wore dresses, not burkas.

There were many brightly-coloured trucks, buses, cars, bicycles, heavily laden donkeys and even robed men driving sheep or leading a few camels.. There were low-backed trucks filled to overflowing with men, and many buses seemingly filled to capacity too, sometimes with men hanging on at the doorway.

Men were pushing large laden or empty barrows. It was hot, dusty and, in places, smoky or smelly.

Occasionally we saw a couple of police or military dressed in khaki, just strolling round like everyone else, but with batons. A couple of times they were shouting at someone.

There were plenty of men and children whose clothes could only be described as dirty rags.

But the view of the mountain was better. There was what looked like a fort on the top.

Beyond the river they could see the beautiful hills. It was a great view and they found a place to sit away from people, and Keith rolled a joint. As they looked down to the brown water of the river, they could see women washing clothing and children playing in it.

Al and Keith spent almost a month in Kabul and smoked a great number of chillums and sat at that spot many times..

Al enjoyed discovering the city. But Keith was paying his way. There were no letters at the post office, 'the Poste Restante' and no money to collect at the American Express offices,

Keith had mentioned several times that he wanted to sell his cheques on the street so the two of them could go to the Afghan Government building to apply for visa extensions.

Keith sold some travellers cheques, without problem. They

simply went closer to the big hotels and waited for a street money-changer to approach them.

Keith gave Al the equivalent of ten pounds in English money, but Al did not feel that would get him very far on public transport and with hotel bills, albeit that it was all so comparatively cheap here. It certainly would not get him to India.

He had a couple of cotton shirts that he sold to the two brothers at the hotel. And a compass set on a plastic base..

Al went out with his compass and, seeing a small shop that seemed to be selling junk and second-hand clothes, he entered. Inside was an old man dressed in a brown gown, sitting behind a counter, Al said hello but it was obvious that this man spoke no English.

Al showed the compass and tried to explain its function. He took out a map of Kabul that he had been given by the hotel, and showed it to the man, pointing to the North on the map and to the compass needle. He thought that the man had no idea at all what this was about, but sensed he was fascinated that the needle always pointed the same way, however the compass was turned, pointed to the door to his shop!

Al knew the symbols for the numbers by now, and gingerly wrote on the back of the map "2000" and said Afghani. The man immediately went to a drawer and came back and gave Al a few bank notes – it was 1200 Afghani. He took it happily, although it was only about six pounds in English money it would last for ages here. He could give Keith some money and still have enough to get by for a while – and strangely enough six pounds was what the compass had cost back in England.

CHICKEN STREET AND SIGIS

By now Al and Keith had found Chicken Street, a street known to be popular with Western Travellers. There were small hotels and eating houses that sold food such as pizzas and burgers, milkshakes and a range of herb teas. Most of the places played Western music, including from Bob Dylan and The Band to Jimi Hendrix, Janice Joplin, Joni Mitchell who made Al think of Miriam, The Doors, The Animals, The Byrds, The Beach Boys, Jefferson Airplane, Captain Beefheart, Frank Zappa, Cream, The Rolling Stones, all the music Al liked and of course The Beatles and Elvis Presley.

Heads, Hats and Tall Tales

There were several with cushioned rooms and young people smoking joints. They chatted with many of them – some going East and some going West, and heard many strange tales of their experiences, some good and some bad. They heard of a woman supposedly a psychic, at the Pakistan – India border, who seemed to know who had hash and where they had hid it, as people went from one country to the other. They heard bad stories of how those caught smuggling were mistreated until they paid hefty fines. But they heard worse about the Afghan – Iran border where anyone caught with a kilo could be taken out and shot on the spot. Al had thought how strange that was if the Afghan Customs Officer was selling it!

They spent many hours sitting in those places.

BOILED EGGS

On one occasion they had smoked a chillum and gone out wandering and had found a small restaurant and gone in to

Heads, Hats and Tall Tales

eat – they both wanted boiled eggs.

It was an upstairs restaurant, quite a large room filled with wooden tables and metal chairs. They sat near the open window with an excellent view of the street below: there were several stalls selling melons and fruits and vegetables, and a couple opposite with smoke blowing across the street, selling cooked street snacks. The ground in between was rough and unsteady and the whole place was busy with men and women, many carrying bundles or pushing wooden carts with big wheels, several riding or leading donkeys and even one man driving sheep, maybe for slaughter in the deeper parts of this street market. Beyond that corner they could see the main street with its various forms of transport.

A boy who looked about fourteen approached them and spoke. It was apparent he spoke very little English but was asking them what they wanted. "Tea with milk" That seemed to be understood.

"Two soft boiled eggs and toast," said Keith.

The boy looked dumbfounded.

Al decided to try to communicate through sign-language.

He knew the local word for water was "Pani".

So he made a shape like a saucepan in the air with his hands, pointed into the invisible top and said "Pani."

The boy nodded.

Feeling good about that, Al took out a box of matches from his pocket and made like to strike one and hold it under the imaginary now pot of water.

The boy smiled.

Al made a shape like an egg in the air and pretended to place the imaginary egg into the imaginary pot of imaginary hot water – he signalled with two fingers and pointed to himself and Keith.

Meanwhile Keith had come up with his own idea of how to order eggs.

He was crouched down and started flapping his arms and making a noise like a chicken clucking. He pretended to lay and egg and pick it up, then a second egg. Then he pointed at Al and showed four fingers.

The boy smiled and bowed and walked off.

Keith shouted after him "And toast!"

A short while later the boy returned. He motioned to Al to follow him.

Well Al already knew that often several eating houses would share a kitchen and that it could be even 100 yards away.

Heads, Hats and Tall Tales

So he followed the boy feeling confident he would see eggs and bread in the kitchen.

Down the stairs, turning right out of the door, up the market street passed stalls selling cloths, about 50 yards or so.

The boy stopped and pointed up a short alley. Al could see that it opened on to some sort of yard, but he felt a little uneasy about this. So he motioned the boy to go first, which he did.

When they came out of the alleyway, Al saw that it was a courtyard with closed wooden doors all around and two sets of wooden steps leading up to a wooden veranda with more closed wooden doors. Al looked at the boy and shrugged.

The boy smiled and pointed at one of the doors up the stairs.

"Strange place to have a kitchen!," said Al; the boy obviously did not understand.

Heads, Hats and Tall Tales

The boy waved Al towards the steps, so he ascended and walked along to the door and knocked.

There was no answer. He knocked again, with greater force.

Still no answer. The boy was shouting something.

When Al looked down he saw the boy seemed to be motioning Al to go in, so he slowly opened the door.

He was expecting to see a number of cooks at hot steaming stoves.

Instead he saw a hole-in-the floor toilet!

Al laughed out loud, so much for his eggs in hot water act. So much for Keith's flapping and clucking!

So much for boiled eggs on toast.

He resigned himself to going back to the restaurant with nothing. He didn't even feel the need to use the toilet.

But as he and the boy were walking back up the street passed the stalls selling cloth, the boy shouted something at the stall-holder and gestured towards Al.

The stall-holder motioned for Al to approach and suddenly produced a telephone, on which he spoke. He handed the phone to Al.

A voice on the other end said "Hello, Kann ich Ihnen helfen, was Sie wollen?"

Al recognised that as German. Something like "can I help what do you want". They had tried to teach him German in school for two years but he had had no interest and failed the exams. But he inevitably knew some words and that included the words for four, eggs, water and bread.

"Er ... vier Eier in Wasser mit Brod, bitte" - meaning 'four

eggs in water with bread, please.'

"Yah, gut!"

Al handed the phone back to the stall-holder who then listed and told the boy.

The boy laughed and pointed back up the street to the alley where the toilet was again, then at Al.

As they walked back to the restaurant the boy kept laughing. He was making a clucking sound!

As it turned out, after Al had returned to Keith and they had laughed about the adventure, they were pleased to see the boy return with tea along with four eggs and a pile of toast. Albeit the eggs were hard boiled but the lads did not care.

Most of their time in Kabul they ate meat-free Kabuli rice, pizzas, pastas and the lovely baked and spiced potatoes from the street stalls, and plenty of bread and onions and fruit and yoghurt.

They had been in Kabul for three weeks when they heard about the opium den. One evening they decided to try it. Apparently they did not allow cannabis or tobacco to be smoked inside, just opium pipes.

It was a rather dingy looking place off a small courtyard off a dirty back street. There was a man on the door that simply said "Twenty each" and let Al and Keith inside. It was quite dark but Al could see men sitting or laying round on cushions. In the centre of the room was the pipe-maker, sat on the floor, applying a light to the opium on the end of the long pipe that another man was sucking on. The sickly sweet smell of smoked opium reminded Al of that time in

Iran and he thought once again he would enjoy it.

Here, however, there was no friendly feeling. It was just a commodity they had to pay for.

They smoked two pipes each and left. Little did anyone know the consequences that were to come weeks later, but I will reveal that at the right time. For now you can only guess.

Instead, they went to Chicken Street to meet friendlier people and smoke some hash.

Chicken Street consisted of stalls and two story buildings occupied by cheap westernised restaurants and shops selling trinkets, clothing wall hangings and mats, Afghan coats, breads and pancakes, even antique guns and swords – and hats and head scarves – it was where people went to meet and eat or to buy their souvenirs.

"Sigis" was a popular eating house that we visited many times. It had a courtyard with a giant chessboard.

Other restaurants we visited and sat about in were the Marco Polo and the Khyber.

At the end of Chicken Street was Flower Street where one could buy flowers, fruit and vegetables.

In the restaurants and so-called hippy bars one could meet people with advice on where to stay and they learned of the Hotel Rainbow in Peshawar, in Pakistan, their next planned stop.

We also learned that the Pakistan – India border was closed due to fighting but there was talk of it re-opening soon,

With all those chillums the days passed quickly and before we knew it Al and Keith had bought tickets for a bus through the Khyber pass into Pakistan and Peshawar. That region of Pakistan was called the North-West Frontier and was populated by tribes very different to most Pakistanis.

THE KHYBER PASS AND HELLMUT

It was 180 miles from Kabul to Peshawar, across the Khyber Pass.

On the bus, they heard a voice with a German accent belonging to a man that sat opposite us.

"My name is Hellmut. You want smoke some joint?"

He had lit and was offering them a joint – on the bus!

Well, I could tell Al liked the smell so he quickly accepted it with a "Danke" (thank you in German, Al thought). He took three rapid puffs and passed it to Keith who took three puffs and passed what was left back to Hellmut.

Al was feeling quite self-conscious about smoking on a bus heading to Pakistan. He thought everyone was looking.

He turned round to look back down the bus.

Almost every seat had a man leaning out and looking back up the bus at him!

And, Al noticed, they were all grinning and smiling and nodding, as if to say "You are stoned now, as we are stoned too."

Al thought those men probably did not smoke cannabis but it must have been in their blood, handed down over the centuries.

Heads, Hats and Tall Tales

He relaxed, chatted with Helmut a while. Helmut said he travelled that route every year for ten years. Then as the calming effect of the lovely hash took over, he sat and started to enjoy what was to be an incredible journey through the Khyber Pass.

The over-laden coach trundled on, struggling up hills and rounding bends with sheer drops, then down and up again. At the end of most down bits there was a small waterfall. At the end of each up bits there was a beautiful view, often including the same road below them, winding around the boulders in between the fields.

At some places there were what looked like caves in the sides of the hills.

We passed small groups of men that seemed to be just sitting and looking; we saw young boys driving herds of sheep or goats or camels and several times we had to stop to let them pass us.

Occasionally we saw groups of women carrying baskets, bundles or clay pots on their heads, trailed by urchin-looking children – her children always waving at the coach.

The women here were dressed very differently and, Al thought, more practically than those in Burkas. These showed their faces beneath head-scarves decorated with beads and chains and quite colourful too. These must be tribal mountain women, Al thought.

The coach was moving quite slowly and Al had a chance to take a couple of photographs through the window, of the valley below. He wished he had more film, but thought he would not be able to afford it.

Hellmut was quite jolly company and did lot of talking. They smoked another couple of joints.

He explained that he travelled this same route for years and the border post guards knew him. He always gave them a little money and they left him alone. He also said that every year he visited Afghanistan and Pakistan, India and Nepal, and arranged for shipments of hash to be sent back to London where his partner lived. He travelled for six months, then went back to London and his partner did the same. They were paying off customs everywhere, including the UK, and they were making a lot of money. But, he said, he preferred to stay in cheap hotels, not the big ones, and then he met people.

So Hellmut too, was heading for the Hotel Rainbow.

"Very very cheap", he said, "But it is OK for a few days, but do not eat their food – it is better to go out to eat in a secret local restaurant that I know, it is good and clean."

Hellmut said that after Peshawar, he was heading to Lahore and then would fly to Amritsar where the "Golden Temple" was and where travellers could sleep and eat for free, courtesy of the Sikhs. The same plan as Al and Keith's, they used to call it the "Hippy Trail."

PESHAWAR, PAKISTAN

It was quite a journey until they reached Peshawar, but once there, with Helmut leading the way, they soon found and booked into the Rainbow Hotel. Reception gladly changed Afghani money into Pakistani Rupees.

The room for Al and Keith was small with two beds, but the view out of the window into the street below was good.

It was May 5 1972.

The street looked like a chaotic mishmash of tumble-down buildings with broken or torn flags hanging everywhere. The road was pot-holed. It was crowded with people. There was a restaurant across the road. Al took a photograph; not many left.

There was no toilet in the room. In fact, there did not seem to be one visible at al. So still with me on his head, he went to the reception to ask.

"On roof," said the small man sitting behind a desk reading a newspaper. He did not seen interested.

Al climbed two flights of stairs to find a door that opened onto the roof.

In the middle of the roof was a wooden structure with three doors, a couple of steps up and inside there was a hole in the concrete floor and a jug of water. The water was to wash instead of the Western toilet papers we had seen in some cities.

Below the hole was another level of concrete, piled with human shit. It was smelling real bad even though the day was cooling fast as the light was beginning to fade. The whole place was, of course, swarming with flies.

Later Al learned that the place was emptied once a day, the shit shovelled into wicker baskets lines with rushes and leaves, to be carried down through the hotel and into the street. Al could not imagine what they did with it after that. Those poor women deserved a reward. But he had nothing spare to even offer.

A while after returning to the room, there was a knock on the door. Keith jumped up and opened it and there stood Hellmut, grinning and with a smoking joint in his hand.

"Hello my friends, you want to smoke some hash with me and I buy you dinner?"

So they puffed on the joint, their spirits again lifting. Al had been wondering where he was. Absolutely everything was so different to his home city; in fact it was so different to anything else he had seen even in the places we had passed through.

Al was thinking, what is different: well for starters the smells and the air, the people and their costumes, the language and the script, the food and the drink, the streets and the buildings, the transport, the health care, the hygiene and safety rules and protection, life expectancy and family life, politics and religion, even the ways in which business was conducted. People argued over the prices.

And, thought Al, what is the same? Well I guess I am, he thought. I guess everyone, well most people, have two arms, two legs and two eyes; we're all breathing; we probably all want the same thing, We all want to achieve something and to find fulfilment, peace, love, freedom. We probably all wonder at some time what life is all about or maybe their religions satisfy all that.

Al began wondering why he was travelling. What was he looking for. Religion and science had failed him, now he was feeling like he was wandering far from home, maybe risking his health and safety, taking risks in a dangerous part of the world and with very little money. "Am I nuts?" he thought.

But so far this adventure had gone well, and in any case there was only one direction to go and that was India. Al thought that it was said people could find answers in India. That was where The Beatles had gone to their Guru called

Mahesh Yogi. It was a land of many beliefs, supposedly with enlightened beings willing to impart the truth. Or so he'd read. Probably not like that at all. And, thought Al, I probably don't have enough money to buy enlightenment.

Outside in the damp street, the women were dressed in black Burkas again, or colourful cloth wraps, except the Westerners of course. Some of them were well covered too and many wore head scarves. Almost all the Western men wore blue jeans, some with hats of varying sorts, and one even looking quite like myself.

The local men were of two distinct types. One lot were quite short in height and slight, dressed in what often looked like dirty pyjamas with white caps or wrapped in sheets of cloth. The other lot were massive, thick set giants over 6 feet in height, wearing turban-like headgear and armed with rifles and long swords.

Bicycles, three wheeler Rickshaws, and beasts of burden, were the main form of transport here.

Al spotted a sign above a doorway. It was a drawing of a set of false teeth.

There were three-wheeled street stalls with massive piles of apples, oranges, lemons and yellow and green melons for sale. Dirty-looking streets stalls offered strange looking food in huge pans cooking over charcoal or wood fires.

"You know, my friends, Peshawar is called the 'City of Thieves' – you can buy guns here, be careful with your bags," said Hellmut.

"Fucking great, man," said Keith.

The street was filthy.

"Two nights here, then I am going to Lahore on the train, if you want, my friends, I will tell the manager at the hotel and he will buy us tickets," said Hellmut.

"How much do the tickets cost?" asked Keith.

"No problem my friends I am paying, you are my guests.

LAHORE, PAKISTAN

The morning after that, they took the train to Lahore, direction India.

In comparison to the bus rides, the train journey was boring. It was about three hundred and twenty miles but it took many hours.

When they reached Lahore, Hellmut took a taxi to a hotel he knew and they soon booked in. It was another hotel for mostly western travellers.

It was the Hotel Eden!

A small hotel with about a dozen room surrounding a small open garden with small shady trees, potted flowers and a pool in the centre!

The hotel also had a games room and Al looked inside; it had a pool table, table tennis and darts board.

He went to their room, small but comfortable, with two beds, dressing table with mirror and another table with one chair. On the way in he spotted a machine offering fizzy drinks and bought two for a few rupee coins.

Hellmut arrived at their room and they smoked joints.

Heads, Hats and Tall Tales

The following morning, breakfast was provided by the Hotel. There were eggs, cheeses, breads, fruits, yoghurt and tea or coffee with sweet and spicy cakes.

By the time they had finished eating, Al was thinking it was already far too hot to move. We sat in the courtyard under the shade of a tree and Al took me from his head and placed me on a nearby table.

Hellmut appeared again and invited Keith and Al to share a "Bhang".

Al knew that Bhang was a cold drink made from cannabis and spices, ground together with milk, clarified butter called ghee and water.

The Bhang in fact did not taste very good this time, so Al drank his glassful quickly.

About half an hour or so later and Bhang! The drink lived up to its name! They didn't even go outside of the hotel grounds that day. They spent the day reading and chatting and laughing and eating snacks with tea. Apart from the effects of the Bhang, it was over 100 degrees Fahrenheit by noon.

At one time Al decided to go to the games room.

When he entered it was quite dark but he could see what looked like a light switch on the wall half way along, so he went to switch it on.

Al put his hand to switch on the light and as he touched it there was a loud bang and a flash.

Al seemed to be flying backwards through the air. He had received an electric shock, first time for him and first time for me. Very strange feeling.

As Al went backwards, time seemed to slow down. Al seemed to have plenty of time to think about what had happened, how stupid he had been in the dark, whether he was about to hit his head on anything and how he would cushion his fall and even what would happen and how people would react back in England if this was going to kill him.

As he landed backwards on the floor, he realised he had not hit any tables or anything and thought about how to best protect his head, so he did his best to keep his head forward and try to take the force of the fall on his back and shoulders.

He bent his head forwards as he hit the ground I flew off his head, unable to protect him. Lucky for him his method worked and the back of his head hit the ground quite gently.

But he was pretty much shook up.

He returned to the garden and told Keith what had happened.

Keith seemed like he was in a world of his own, very stoned on cannabis – he did not reply, as if he had not even heard Al, who felt lucky to be alive.

"Hey man," Keith suddenly said, "it's almost four thousand miles direct back to London, we must have done six or seven thousand the way we came."

The next day after breakfast in the garden, Hellmut asked Al and Keith if they would like to join him on a flight to India.

"A few days time," said Hellmut; "They have opened the border with India and there will be flights from here to Amritsar, I will buy you the tickets, I just need your names and passport numbers. If you want we can fly in a few days after I have done business."

So Hellmut went off in a taxi to buy the tickets. Al and Keith decided to go out and look about the city.

It was about as different, as Al thought, from Peshawar as it is different from Norwich – or maybe less different from Norwich.

The streets were now dusty, not wet, but with less litter and animal droppings.

There were far more cars, taxis, trucks and buses as well as bicycle rickshaws, and far fewer animals of burden. Quite a few bicycles too.

Most of the men were dressed either in one-piece djellabah's, loose-fitting cotton in white or grey, or two-piece cotton garments that looked like pyjamas. A few wore suits, some western-style, others high-buttoned jackets over trousers.

The women wore feminised versions of the same, often with lose scarves draped over their heads, some dressed quite colourfully.

Children were dressed pretty much like the adults!

Some men wore the Afghan Jinnah Cap made from sheep's wool, with it's peaked shape and favoured by Pakistani politicians. Others wore oval hats that sat in the middle of their heads not covering the eyes at all. Others wore turbans.

Al and Keith found along street with stalls on each side, selling just about everything except the guns we had seen in Peshawar. The buildings were three story and had decorative balconies, many with sheets hanging from them.

Most of the signs were in Arabic writing but some were in

English, many offering Pepsi or Seven Up drinks.

There were stalls selling 'lassi', a drink made from crushed ice with milk and yoghurt, with sugar or salt to taste, or fruit juices. The ingredients were scooped up from various aluminium bowls; the ice was piled up behind the vendor who sat cross-legged as he worked. He would lean over, grab a lump of ice and smash it between what Al thought looked like rags. But they were thirsty so they bought and drank some out of aluminium mugs.

That evening they met with Hellmut again at the Hotel Eden, smoked some joints and drank some tea. Hellmut had bought the air tickets for the next day.

"Then tonight I invite you to film studio," said Hellmut. "I am giving some money to make a film. We will have dinner there, it is gut. Also you may meet the top singer in Pakistan and a famous actor.. We leave in half an hour when the taxi is coming."

It was a modern-looking building with a couple of guards outside and they just waved us in.

Inside the big doors, Hellmut told a receptionist who we were and we were shown through some corridors to a large room decorated with glitter and lights, with pictures of people around the walls, presumably film stars and sponsors.

After a while two young men approached us – they were dressed immaculately in suits and ties.

They shook hands with Hellmut who introduced us simply as "Keith and Al". Obviously in such a place, Al had removed me from his head and I had been placed on a table, so nobody mentioned me.

I simply watched, listened and learned.

A waiter came and asked us if we wanted to drink; beer was available, so everyone ordered that. It was American beer.

The conversation was mainly between Hellmut and the two Lahore lads.

Sure enough he was going to give them hundreds of thousands of rupees to make a film. They were saying that the industry had suffered. They said they had a top actor and one of the best known pop singers. There was some talk about what the film was about. It sounded that it was mostly about a man and a woman that met and wanted to be together but circumstances always interfered.

After about half an hour, several waiters came in carrying plates and trays of food: bowls of dahl, flat bread, a spicy lamb dish and more pieces of lamb and of chicken, a dish made with chick peas and spice, vegetable curries and rice, yoghurt and fruits. And a massive cherry tart! And creamy rice pudding. There were five of them eating with enough food for twenty.

Whilst they were eating, suddenly a group of about ten people entered and headed towards them. They were all men except the two women they were surrounding. Apparently one of the ladies was the pop singer.

As they approached the others stopped eating and stood up. Al and Keith did the same. One of the Pakistani hosts at our table spoke, introducing only Hellmut. Smiles were exchanged, but no words and as rapidly as they had arrived, the group left.

"So much for pop stars, man, "said Keith quietly.

After the dinner, we headed back out into a wide corridor.

As Al, Keith and Hellmut headed down the corridor, Al

noticed something in another wide corridor off to the left.

There was a group of about ten young men that seemed to be surrounding a girl that Al thought was European. Al thought that did not look like a good situation so decided to look closer.

She was certainly not Pakistani. She wore a headscarf. She looked familiar. She looked a bit like Miriam.

Al started to push his way through the small crowd.

It *was* Miriam!

"Miriam, hi!", he shouted.

"Al!" she answered and stepped towards him and they gave each other a hug.

All felt good about that hug.

"You OK, what's happening?" asked Al.

Miriam replied: "I'm OK, great, it's just this lot, they think I'm a rock star!"

"Well I guess you are!", said Al, "Shall I get rid of them?"

Al turned to the crowd of youths and said "OK, that's enough, now fuck off!"

And, somewhat to Al's surprise, they did!

Al told Miriam that he had better go to the exit to tell his friends what he was doing, so they went down the stairs and back towards the long wide corridor that led to the exit.

Suddenly a group of about twenty men were approaching us, all huddled together but still filling the corridor so all Al and Miriam could do was to stand close to the wall as the large group passed by.

Al could see that in the very middle of the group crammed so much that he had to go with the flow, was Zulfikar Ali Bhutto, the President of Pakistan.. Al had the idea he was not entirely popular with people. "Apparently," Miriam said later, "he is on his way to do a TV broadcast, in English as that was the language shared by most of the people rich enough to have a TV."

Miriam told Al that Bhutto had managed to get the release of thousands of prisoners and some territory from India, after signing an agreement with Indira Ghandi, the Prime Minister of India.

When Al and Miriam reached Keith and Hellmut, Al told them he was going to stay a while and drink some beer with Miriam and he would make his own way back to the hotel later. Hellmut passed Al a small paper bag. "It is blues, speed," he said quietly, "Take a few and they will keep you awake and give good buzz".

Al swallowed three tablets and went back to Miriam. They drank coffee instead of beer and chatted for a while. I learned that Miriam had been invited to the studios for dinner by an American but he had not turned up. He also discovered that Miriam had a ticket for the same flight as he for the next day and that she too planned to stay at the Golden Temple in Amritsar.

After a while Al started to feel the effects of the pills. He was talking a lot! Miriam did not seem to mind, she seemed like a good listener. But Al felt it was time for him to get back to his hotel. Miriam would get a taxi but it was in the opposite direction to Eden. Al saw her into the taxi and was about to order one for himself when one of the young men that had met Hellmut appeared and he offered Al a lift on the back of his moped.

Quite a ride. The 'speed' in the blues had kicked in and they seemed to be speeding ever so fast in and out of the busy traffic along poorly lit roads. I thought that I was going to blow off Al's head several times and land in the road and get crushed by a car. Gladly I was OK and we soon reached the Hotel Eden, Keith sitting in the garden smoking a joint.

So this "speed" drug seemed to make everything go faster whereas the electric shock in the hotel games room and the backwards fall had seemed to make time go more slowly.

"I didn't expect you back tonight. I thought you'd be with Miriam, What happened man?" said Keith.

"No I thought I'd better come back and get ready for tomorrow," said Al, "and anyway I don't like those pills, I wanted a smoke."

Several smokes later, his rucksack mostly packed, Al lay on his bed for hours tossing and turning. He just could not get to sleep. Keith was snoring. Al was thinking about Miriam and the flight to Amritsar.

AMRITSAR AND THE GOLDEN TEMPLE, INDIA

As it turned out the flight was only about half an hour and a stewardess gave everyone a fizzy drink and biscuit. It was a small plane but larger than the one he had been in with Steve of course. Every seat was taken. Al was in an aisle seat so did not even get to look down.

The high point of the flight was that Keith had sat next to Hellmut and Al was sat next to Miriam. She told Al she was going to stay at the Golden Temple a couple of days and then try to get a free lift to Delhi and asked Al if he would accompany her. He said yes straight away.

Customs and immigration formalities both sides of the trip were fast, just a stamp in the passports and they were through to collect their bags and get a taxi to the Golden Temple – all four of them squeezed in. Al felt good squeezed in next to Miriam.

It was May 28 1972.

At the temple, they were met by a friendly Sikh in a turban, who showed them to the shared room, "Boys and girls separate," he said. "You must smoke only outside the rooms. You are very welcome here and please come to big dining room for food, it is given by us to travellers. Maybe tomorrow if you want, go to see Temple?"

Inside the room were four beds. It did not look like any were being used.

The following morning, Al decided to visit the Golden Temple. It was already very hot, approaching a hundred degrees Fahrenheit. Keith was not feeling so well so decided to stay in the room and sleep.

As Al approached one of the Temple entrances, he spotted Miriam. They greeted each other with a quick and discreet hug and walked together towards the entrance. It was free to go inside.

Heads, Hats and Tall Tales

They had to take their sandals off and wash their feet in a small pool of water.. Then they had to cover their heads – scarves were provided for free: there had been street hawkers outside trying to sell scarves but Al did not buy – at that stage he did not know that he had to wear a head covering.

Al took me off his head and put me into his shoulder bag. By this time I had built up such a level of telepathic contact with Al that I was still able to see what he saw:

Inside the complex, Al saw an incredible marble and golden building set out in the middle of an artificial lake joined by a walkway to the surrounding wide marble pavement and beyond that, white buildings. There were individual and small groups of Sikhs walking around the complex.

The upper part of this ornate rectangular marble structure was covered in gold.

As soon as Al's feet touched the marble pavement he

regretted it. Now about 100 degrees, the marble was almost unbearably hot. There was little shade, little relief. He headed for the water in the lake, sat on the edge and put his feet into the cooling water – Miriam did the same.

Within minutes they were approached by a Sikh wearing a bright orange djellabah's over white trousers and an orange turban.

"Mister and Madam, I am sorry, but please take feet out of holy water."

Al and Miriam immediately removed their feet from the water, the Sikh said thank you and walked off.

Al said "I thought people bathed in this, I thought it was supposed to purify, like the Ganges."

"Maybe we should just jump in and immerse ourselves," said Miriam.

"Could do," laughed Al, "It's so bloody hot my feet are burning. Oops I forgot, not supposed to swear either!"

The two of them stayed for a couple of hours, just chatting quietly and feeling the good feeling. They went back to their separate rooms.

That evening, Al decided to go to find the room where the food was provided, Keith saying that he would join him later.

The large dining room was packed with hundreds of people. Miriam was in the massive hall and sat with a bearded young man. As Al approached, Miriam motioned to him to go and sit with them. She had kept two places for him and Keith. Everyone was sitting on cushions on the floor with cloths laid out in front. Some people were already eating.

Al said hello. He learned that the man, called Sher, was in fact a Sikh who was living as a student in Germany but his home was in India, in Amritsar. Sher told Al that although here he wore a turban over his long hair, when in Germany he took off the turban and let his hair lose like Al's, saying that he seemed to get better treatment there as a hippy rather than a Sikh.

It wasn't long before food arrived. That evening they ate dahl, rice, chapatti and yoghurt with sweet Indian sweets and cool water. All lovely vegetarian food.

Miriam said "I've got us a lift to Delhi if you want to come."

"Yes, I'm into that," said Al.

"Sher's father is a mango merchant and tomorrow he will take us to taste his mangoes and then take us to a man that will get us a lift on a truck through the night."

"That's far out," said Al. "I wonder how long that will take, it's about two hundred and fifty miles, I think. Keith's going to try to sneak on a train without paying but I don't fancy that. I was wondering about hitching a lift."

Miriam told Al that after she had left Herat, she went direct to Kabul and stayed there two weeks. She must have been there for a least some of the days that Al and Keith had been. She said she had been to Chicken Street and Sigis and had even played her guitar and sang there. But she had stayed on the outskirts. Then she had met up with some Canadian friends who had been driving overland from Europe in a Land Rover. Miriam had travelled with them across the Khyber Pass and down to Lahore. They were staying in a city close to Lahore, and when the border was open and they completed the formalities and repairs to their vehicle, they would drive through to Delhi and then up to Kathmandu in Nepal. Miriam was to meet them in Delhi and go with them to Nepal.

Al and Miriam left Sher having agreed that his father would meet them in that same place the next afternoon; they strolled around the streets for an hour or so, chatting. Al told Miriam the story of getting the boiled eggs in Kabul and she laughed for a long time.

The following day Al was up early and went for breakfast and bought some bread and fruit and water for the journey. He was now really hoping that there would be some money waiting for him at American Express in Delhi.

Al felt that he had been a burden on Keith, and Keith had not been too happy about it. He didn't want to end up being a burden on Miriam. He had thoughts of picking up money and going to Nepal with her.

Mid-afternoon, Al had said cheerio to Keith as Keith headed off towards to railway station. He met up with Miriam near the dining hall and soon Sher appeared with an older man, his father, the mango dealer. They called for a three wheeler motor rickshaw with seats for three and waved goodbye to Sher.

THE JOURNEY TO DELHI WITH MIRIAM

Father took Al and Miriam across town, where they tasted yellow mangoes, then across town again to taste green ones, and then back across town to try red ones. Each time he gave them a few in a bag, so now they had about ten of them. But they were all delicious.

Then he took them to the outskirts of town to what looked like a truckers' stop. He took them to a small building and introduced them to all old man with a long white beard.

It was some sort of religious groups. There were many old-looking books and pamphlets, including one in English. Al read it – it was some sort of Ashram, a shelter for practices of Yoga and read that the Universe was made by an all-powerful God called ParaBrahman. He realised that the old man was some sort of priest, teacher or Guru – he was very pleasant, constantly smiling – he had a symbol painted on his forehead.

The old teacher chap told Al and Miriam that he had arranged for them to go to Delhi but the truck was not leaving until midnight. He invited them to dinner and soon another delicious vegetarian meal with Nan bread arrived, followed by the Lassi drink flavoured with mangoes!

It was late into the evening before the truck was ready to

leave, and Al did not know or care how long it would take to reach Delhi. He had a bag of food, lots of mangos, enough water for a couple of days, and Miriam to keep him company.

When they reached the truck they discovered it was laden high with large rope-tied bundles – they were shown to climb up and found enough space for them to comfortably sit or lay down, in front of the bundles. They set off into the night.

Of course, there was not a lot to see at night but they did pass some lit areas, maybe small towns or villages. They chatted on, shared some joints using hash that Miriam had, and felt good. When it got too cold, they huddled together under Al's sleeping bag.

But suddenly after a few hours the truck halted abruptly and some of the bundles shifted so there was a danger of them toppling down on top of the duo. The truck carried on and every now and then the bundles shifted again. Their space was restricted and Al began to worry for their safety.

He began to try to bang on the roof of the cab to try to get their driver's attention but to no avail. So he thought to try to climb up so that he could dangle something down in front of the cab window so the driver would stop. He used a dress that Miriam took out of her bag.

After a while the truck stopped. The driver got out and Al motioned to him that the bundles were about to topple down. Climbing up, the driver tried pushing up the bundles with Al's help, but they hardly moved. They tried repositioning the ropes. In the end they had made little progress so the driver jumped down and straight away they were on the move again.

Al was still worried about the bundles but the advantage was that Miriam huddled up closer.

So on they travelled until daylight and on into the day, which got hot very quickly.

They made two stops and the driver bought them Chai (sweet milky spicy tea). Each time they tried tightening the ropes.

At the third stop, Miriam bought a hot meal for Al and for the driver. It was now late afternoon.

As they were about to climb up to their space on the back of the truck, the driver handed Al a small black lump of what Al now knew to be opium, motioning for him to eat it. Al broke it into two small pieces and he and Miriam ate one each.

DELHI

It was a few hours later after the opium had induced a sort of slowed-down dreamy state, that, now dark again, the truck was passing through lit-up areas. They were on the outskirts of Delhi and soon the truck pulled up at a large roundabout that Al later learned was called Connaught Circus. They climbed down and the driver motioned across the busy road and made a gesture meaning sleep.

So Al and Miriam tried to cross the road – the effects of the opium did not help. The traffic seemed to be speeding past, trucks, coaches, three-wheeler motorised rickshaws, cars and even donkey-pulled carts. It was taking ages. The traffic seemed non-stop. There was a great honking of horns.

Well, they did eventually get across the road and headed off in the direction that the truck driver had pointed, soon to find a street with several guest houses on. They selected the second one that they were passing. It had dormitories, some for boys and some for girls, no mixed rooms. The dorms were set around a small courtyard with tables and chairs and a water pump. Inside the dorm that Al was shown to there were six beds, and it looked like three were taken, so he chose one saying hello to his fellow travellers and sat down. One of the other lads started speaking to Al in English: he was German and told Al that he was on his way back to Germany after travelling around India for six months dressed like a Sadhu, in robes with just a begging bowl and chillum. Al knew that Sadhu's were supposed to relinquish all their possessions and their homes and families, worshipped a god called Shiva and smoked lots of chillums.

There was a Spanish guy there. He spoke English. He told Al about an 'Ashram' called Prem Nagar, in the foothills in the town of Haridwar on the Ganges, the Holy River, where they accommodated people free of charge. Then he told Al about the symptoms of Infectious Hepatitis, a yellowing of the whites of the eyes and the finger nails, how urine would look dark yellow to red, and stools would look pale. Al thought it was strange to be told that.

Then Al went to the courtyard and found Miriam sat drinking fizzy orange. Not having slept a lot the previous night, it wasn't long before Al said goodnight and was asleep.

The following morning when Al awoke, Miriam had already

left but she had left her bags so she would be back! Al had a light breakfast from the food and mangos he was still carrying and headed off to find the American Express office to check for money and then the Post Office to check for mail. He was pleased to find ten pounds waiting from Australian Paul and at the Post Office a letter from Paul and his wife.

With that he went back to his dorm and received bad news.

Miriam had made contact with her friends and they were planning to leave Delhi to drive to Nepal the next day. She invited Al to join them.

Al told Miriam that he had so little money and wanted to wait for more, but when he had more he would maybe travel to Kathmandu and leave a message for her at the Poste Restante, hopefully meet up again.

Connaught Circus and the immediate area was quite built-up, with roads off the roundabout in many directions. There was an incredible amount of traffic. It was a busy commercial area and the streets had large buildings, offices, shops and street stalls, some selling strange-looking concoctions of coloured pastes spread onto leaves and sprinkled with Betel nuts. Apparently the vile-looking leaves had to be chewed and spat out, and gave an exhilarating effect. Al could see the stains red around the mouths of some of the men and he could see where it had been spat out on the pavements.

The number of three-wheeler rickshaws was incredible, and any without passengers always seeking work, slowing as they drove past, offering lifts. There were also larger rickshaws carrying eight or more passengers and many overcrowded buses. Just off the big roundabout was the Indian Coffee House, in Mohan Singh Place. Nearby was an indoor market where Al found a many Sikhs selling their wares, one with cheap vegetable triangular pasties called samosas. Al visited that indoor market many times for samosas or dahl and chapatti and fruit-flavoured lassi drink lunches. That was where Al sold his camera, a week or so later.

The walk between Connaught and the hostel was of just about ten minutes but passed an incredibly smelly public toilet to be avoided at all costs. Al learned that water was only available through mains taps for part of the day, so the toilet was seldom cleaned.

This was India and the contrast between rich and poor was striking.

Many of the men wore white Indian Pyjamas, some just rags, whilst others wore western suit and tie. There were many westerners and Japanese-looking people, many in jeans and shirts, others India-style clothes and others dressed more richly.

After Miriam had left saying she hoped to see Al again soon, and Keith had not appeared, this was the first time that Al was travelling alone.

He spent about a week in Delhi, checking for mail or money every day, to no avail, but during that week he was out and about every day, visiting New and Old Delhi sights such as the Red Fort and the Astronomy Gardens off Connaught Circus.

Heads, Hats and Tall Tales

AGRA AND THE TAJ MAHAL

After a few days, Al took a train to Agra, to see the Taj Mahal, the world famous white mausoleum built by Mughal emperor Shah Jahan in memory of his third wife in 1632. Mumtaz Mahal, a Persian princess, had died during the birth of their fourteenth child.

Al had arrived at Agra railway station only to find it pouring with rain – the first real rain he had seen since leaving Europe. He took a bicycle rickshaw to the Government's Tourist Bungalow Accommodation and booked a room to three nights – it was very cheap and clean, but the downside was the number of small lizards that were running up the walls and upsides down across the ceiling, and the crickets that seemed to find their way into his rucksack, even his trouser pockets and what is more, inside me, at night. The first morning, Al was constantly surprised when he found them hidden away. After that he looked before he put on his trousers and before he put me on his head.

The next morning Al had a quick breakfast of eggs and toast, unlike in Kabul it was easy to order and took a rickshaw to the Taj Mahal. He picked up a pamphlet from a stall outside that was selling postcards.

Al stood up and absorbed the pleasing view of this incredible white building reflecting in the pool of water that was between the two walkways leading to the marble miracle. On either side there was green grass, bushes, flowers and trees.

There were quite a few tourists about, Indian-looking as well as Japanese and Westerners, and many people taking photographs of their friends in front of the Taj. Al waited for an opportunity and took a photograph. He had just two photos left in his camera and knew that at the moment he did not have enough cash to buy another film.

Al spent about an hour walking round the building and took a look inside – it was all sparklingly clean and well decorated with various types of writing and symbols that we did not understand.

It was a peaceful place to be, unlike many places that we had visited, Al found he could sit without being approached or disturbed by anyone.

When he left, his driver insisted taking Al to some souvenir shops even though Al stressed he did not want to buy anything. He drank tea provided by merchants whilst they showed their wares. He kept telling them that he did not want to buy, and when he left without buying anything, they did not seem to mind. He saw gem stones, cut and uncut; there were stores crammed with brass ware, from ashtrays of various designs, candle-sticks, goblets and trays and pots small and large. There was a shop selling beautiful marble boxes and table-tops inlaid with slices of semi-precious stones. They also passed many shops selling small models of the Taj Mahal, others seemed to be offering lamps and shades of all types, brightly coloured clothing, beads and jewellery, bags and other leather goods, sacks full of spices and herbs, fruits and vegetables, sweets and breads and several barbers shops – and a stall selling all sorts of hats! We even passed by a beer shop.

To Al's surprise he spotted several cows just standing in the streets buzzing with bicycles and bicycle rickshaws and

Heads, Hats and Tall Tales

mopeds. Al knew that Hindu's considered the cow to be Holy, did not eat the meat and more or less left the beasts free to roam and munch on whatever they could find to eat.

FATEPUR SIKRI

The next day, Al decided to take a twenty-five mile taxi ride to 'Fatehpur Sikri'.

The walled palace was mostly a pink red sandstone and quite massive. Al had to pay an entrance fee. There were several levels to explore. Al soon found the magnificent Tomb of Salimdelicate carvings.

There were many other buildings to see that he did not read

about and also some magnificent views over the walls and across the plain. Al enjoyed the place and vowed to return. He enjoyed the tranquillity, with very few tourists wandering around.

A couple of days later and Al was back in New Delhi by train. He checked the post office but there was no mail. He checked at American Express. There was no money for him.

He decided to sleep in the small local park and save money.

The next morning he went again to the Poste Restante. This time there was a letter from a friend back in Norwich promising to send some money in a "few days."

HARIDWAR AND RISHIKESH

So Al decided to best use what money was left and buy a train ticket to Haridwar to try to find that Prem Nagar Ashram that he had been told about, where he could sleep and eat for free, on the Ganges riverbank.

He had now run out of film so immediately went to the Sikh indoor market and sold his camera.

He bought a big bag of samosas and another bag of fruit, and sooner than imagined was on a packed train to the foothills of the Himalayas. Talk about a crowded train, there were people riding on the roof.

Al actually now had very little idea where he was heading or how long it would take. It took almost twenty-four hours. The train seemed to be taking a zigzag route, a steam engine pulling us one way then the other, as it travelled up and down the valleys, through places that Al had never heard of. It was supposed to be about 150 miles but with all that zigzag was probably closer to two hundred and fifty.

Haridwar, Al had learned, meant 'Gateway to God' and was one of the Hindu holy places in India and a centre of Hindu religion and mysticism for centuries. It was on the banks of River Ganges and attracted a large number of Hindu pilgrims from all over the world.

When the train arrived, it was not long before dark. Al slept that night on a wooden bench at the railway station.

When Al awoke it was really early in the morning. He left the station and found a small café where he ate some breakfast. Whilst he was in there, the waiter recommended that Al go by train to Rishikesh, another of India's sacred Ganges cities. He headed back to the station and yes there was a train in an hour. By now Al had just less than one hundred rupees and his ticket back to Delhi. He wanted to stay at that ashram for a week and then felt sure that money would be in Delhi when he got back.

All he had was a few dirty rupees notes and a fifty rupee note. The fare to Rishikesh was just five rupees return.

Al queued for over an hour for the tickets which were sold just before the train arrived. When he finally reached the ticket office window and presented his fifty rupee note, he was told that it was no good because it was torn. He was told to go to a bank to change it. Of course that would mean we would miss the train.

So he decided to board the train and he could show the ticket inspector his ticket from Delhi and pay the extra few rupees.

It was not long before the inspector arrived, the train chugging slowly onwards.

Al showed his ticket and explained the problem back in Haridwar.

The ticket inspector said that as Al had no valid ticket, he would have to pay 100 rupees fine on top of the fare. Of course he didn't have one hundred rupees and said so.

There was a short argument between them and suddenly the inspector turned away and pulled the emergency cord. The train stopped.

The petty official ordered Al to get off the train and feeling that there was no alternative he did.

He climbed down, heard the blowing of a whistle and watched as the train pulled away up the track towards Rishikesh. All around seemed like jungle! Al imagined monkeys in the trees and then thought about tigers.

All he could think to do was follow the railway line.

"Bloody petty bureaucrats!" thought Al; "Here I am between two of the most holy cities on the Ganges and I get kicked off a train by an official without compassion."

After walking for about ten minutes and enjoying it, the track crossed a road. As Al reached the road he spotted a car heading towards the direction of Rishikesh. He waved down the car and it stopped.

There was a man and woman and two children, presumably a family, and the man speaking English asked Al if he wanted to go to Rishikesh and offered a lift. The man, told Al that he was a Hindu and his name was Ashok. He told Al that he was very happy to meet him and that, if Al wanted, he could spend the day with them. They were planning to visit the ashram of the Maharishi Mahesh Yogi near Rishikesh. Al quickly agreed.

Al could hardly believe his luck. Travelling with this family could be far better than on the train.

Ashok told Al a few things about Rishikesh.

Al already knew that it was a special holy city on the Ganges, but he was surprised to hear that it is also known as *'The Gateway to the Garhwal Himalayas'*.

Apparently the name means means Lord of Senses or Lord Vishnu.

Ashok explained that the Maharishi taught meditation to rich foreigners that paid for their courses. It was called Transcendental Meditation. The ashram was just outside Rishikesh surrounded by trees. Ashok said that normally Westerners were not allowed to look around but Indians could do so, and he thought Al would be allowed inside with them. "John Lennon and George Harrison and the Beatles and many pop stars from UK and US have come here to learn," He said.

The ashram was within a complex of lecture halls and sparse concrete cells where paying students stayed. The contrast between the luxurious lecture halls and the cells was shocking, as is the contrast between rich and poor throughout India. There were pleasant gardens with many trees where people could stroll or maybe meditate.

It did not appeal to Al at all. He felt he wanted no part of that. How could anyone charge money to supposedly teach peace?

After leaving the Maharishi's ashram, Ashok drove first to a small restaurant for a delicious vegetarian lunch. Ashok told Al that Rishikesh was vegetarian by law. That suited Al.

Ashok explained to Al: "Legends say that Lord Rama did penance here for killing Ravana, the demon king of Lanka; and Lakshmana, his younger brother, crossed the river

Ganges using a rope bridge."

Now there was anew bridge for locals, tourists, cows and monkeys.

Rishikesh was quite full of people in all sorts of styles and colour of clothing, Many women dressed in bright coloured *sarees*. There were also the *sadhus* and babas that had renounced worldly goods and wealth and lived beside their holy river Ganges. At this point where two rivers met it was the origin of their holy waters.

The sounds also bells and chimes was everywhere.

It was almost like a supermarket for the occult and spiritually-minded, offering courses on well-being and some form of enlightenment, as well as services like palmistry, massages, healing and yoga.

The streets were lined either side with stalls and shops offering, as well as food and drink, amongst other things, gems and semi-precious stones, sarees, all sorts of clothing and shoes and boots, kitchen utensils, wooden goods, books, sweets and cakes. There were street-side barbers, dentists and pharmacies, travel agents and shops offering to tell one's future.

The streets were full of the smells of incense and wood fires, mixed sometimes with the smell of cooking or unpleasant drains.

The most astounding site was the thirteen-story red temple, called the Tarah Manzil, believed to have been built over five hundred years ago.

The bridge itself, built where Lord Rama's younger brother Laxman was believed to have crossed the Ganges by a rope bridge, was a narrow and swaying suspension bridge. It was used by rickshaws and bicycles as well a pedestrians. At the entrance to the bridge there were monkeys ready to grab what they could from unsuspecting travellers.

The plaque there read:

"Lahshman Jhuala Bridge - first Jeepable suspension bridge of U.P.

"Span - 450 feet; Carriageway - 6 feet.

The views both from and of the bridge with the beautiful mountain backdrops were stunning.

After a pleasant afternoon with Ashok and his family, they drove back to Haridwar and Al was dropped off back near the railway station where, once again, he slept on the wooden bench.

The following morning after a breakfast of fruit, yoghurt and bread, Al took a stroll around the town. It seemed very old. The streets were crowded with people going about their days amidst the cows.

After a while he found a bridge over the river Ganges. It looked greener on the other side, with trees to sit beneath and watch the powerful currents pass.

So he crossed the bridge and turned right to follow a rough path running besides the River.

He spotted an orange-robed elderly and bearded man sitting cross legged beneath a tree, a semi-circle of younger people sitting facing him.

Al knew that they were called Baba's, as he himself had been called a few times.

"Maybe he's one of those guru teachers," Al thought.

Back in England Al had read about the pop group The Beatles who had taken up with a Guru called Maharishi Mahesh Yogi who had taught them how to meditate and himself gained great publicity and popularity. Maybe it was something to do with that?

The orange-robed 'teacher' shouted something and motioned to Al to go over and join them and sit down. Al complied.

The elderly teacher smiled and asked Al where he was from and why he was in Haridwar, in a broken English with an almost German accent.

Al explained that he had travelled overland from the UK, simply on an adventure and that he was here because he had met a Spanish man in Delhi who had recommended it as a good place to stay for a while.

The teacher laughed and from under his robes produced a chillum. The chillum was prepared, wrapped in a "safi", a small piece of cloth that served as a sort of filter, the tobacco hash mixture poured in and the lit chillum passed around so that everyone including Al had a good puff.

The teacher-come-chillum-maker, the "Baba", asked Al if he had a few rupees for another chillum. Al handed over a small note. A young boy suddenly appeared from amongst the nearby thickness of trees, took the note, ran off into the trees to return seconds later with a small lump of black hash which he passed on and which was instantly made into another chillum and smoked.

Al stayed a short while and as nothing was being said and he was quite high on the hash, he said his goodbyes and left, carrying on in the same direction as before.

Within minutes he was sitting with another group under another tree, smoking, buying, smoking again.

"This is the good life!" thought Al, so high that he was beginning to feel like he was in a Holy city in India.

"By the Ganges!"

He left the second group and walked some hundred yards before he had the idea that immersing oneself in the Ganges was supposed to purify the soul.

"Well," he mumbled under his breath so only he (and I) could hear, "Why not, it's hot and I'll soon dry off."

Across the river he could see a long walled building complex with steps going down to the River.

As he got closer he could see steps going down on this side too. A few steps, "I should be OK."

A DIP IN THE GANGES

The water was moving very fast. Al thought maybe he would not immerse himself, just splash himself all over.

"After all, I can't swim."

So he put down his bag, took me off his head and put me on his bag, took off his sandals, and stepped down and into the water.

With some hesitation, one step, second step, third step – then his feet were swept from under him. He felt himself falling backwards into the water which he knew would sweep him away. Too high to feel real fear, he envisioned the situation if he was to be swept down the Ganges he would have to try to float. He had to hope he would be saved, but who would swim in this? How many bodies had ended up like this. Was this *really* Holy Water?

As he fell he reached out and somehow managed to grab a chain that was attached to the land, maybe for mooring a boat. He grabbed the chain but the force of the water was now tugging at his body like a hungry monster and now splashing his whole body with his head about to go under. As his head went under he felt a wrenching on his arm but he pulled stronger, now his head was out, now his body, now he was clambering up the steps, drenched and coughing up Holy Water. He made it to the grassy bank and collapsed on the ground.

I felt so many emotions and thoughts and images flooding Al's brain.

"So fucking stupid! I could have died."

"Am I cleansed? Am I saved? Don't feel any different."

"God I'm stoned! I shouldn't have done that. What would have happened if that chain wasn't there?"

"Glad I took Myhat off!"

Heads, Hats and Tall Tales

So was I.

Had I been in that water I would surely have been swept away for ever.

But it wasn't long before Al was dried out and sitting with yet another group smoking another chillum.

After a while, that particular teacher said that they had seen Al go into the River and now his soul was clean. That was about all he said, except he asked Al if he wanted some chai and said that "Mahatma is coming, he will take you for chai." Al liked the spicy milky tea drinks.

Al wondered if this was the Maharishi Mahesh Yogi or maybe some local lord or lord's son, a rich man probably. Everything was so strange that Al did not know what to expect next. I was wondering about who this "Mahatma" was - maybe he made hats?

After a while a man in orange robes accompanied by a small group of Indian-looking people approached. Apparently he was the Mahatma. He exchanged words with the teacher under the tree and said to Al: "OK, you come now for chai and this evening we will do our 'Arti' parade through town and then you join us and come to Ashram maybe?"

They walked a while, crossed a bridge and entered a small chai shop where the Mahatma said something to the owner or waiter – who did not look too pleased. He was pointing at Al and the chai was seemingly somewhat disgruntled. He delivered to his table with "no charge Sir" and the Mahatma and his entourage left, saying "Join is for Arti parade."

There was still a few hours before evening so Al decided to go and wait on his bench back at the railway station.

That was when everything changed.

I sensed that Al's head was spinning, not like it had been after drinking alcohol and nothing like the hash or opium he had smoked or eaten; not even like the blues that he had swallowed in Lahore.

This was different, not at all pleasant.

Suddenly Al jumped up and ran to the edge of the platform. He vomited onto the ground. He started to sweat profusely. He felt the need to rush to the toilet which he found just in time and his bowels emptied over the hole in the ground. He was sick again.

A while later he cooled down and felt a little better.

He returned to his bench. He was thinking that he had so little money and so few possessions but he had never set out to be a Sadhu, and people called him "Baba" too!

Now he was ill – he had no idea where Keith was and Miriam was probably in Nepal. He had little or no contact with anyone in the UK. He didn't even really know where Haridwar was. He didn't know where Prem Nagar was. He would have to miss the "Arti" parade.

Was it the holy Ganges water that made him vomit like this, or the reluctantly-given Chai?

Now he was sick. He would have to try to get the train back to Delhi and hopefully, some money.

And that is how I, Myhat, felt, like the head, Al, that I went with.

And felt I did as felt was part of my fabric.

THE JOURNEY HOME

It was the "Hippy Trail" and it was 1972. Al was twenty-two years old, I was about the same age as far as I know.

My story restarts with a long and uncomfortable train ride back to New Delhi.

We had just left Haridwar, North India. On the railway station Al was vomiting and had diarrhoea. He had very little money, no companionship, wondering where he really was and would he get home.

HOSPITAL IN DELHI

When we reached Delhi, Al went and stayed in the same small guest house, Mr Jain's, on Janpath Lane, that he had used before.

Every time Al ate or drank anything, he was sick.

He began noticing that his urine was a dark yellow colour and his stools were white.

Al thought these were the symptoms of Infectious Hepatitis, so the first thing the next day was to go to a local clinic not far from where he stayed.

When he explained to them his problem, they sent him straight to a Delhi hospital. We were to spend two weeks there, thankfully free of charge, giving Al plenty of good vegetarian food – boiled vegetables, chapatti, dahl and yoghurt, so he stopped being sick and began to build up some strength.

The hospital was clean and the staff friendly. A male ward orderly that delivered meals befriended Al and always gave him extra to eat.

Whilst there Al met an aged Indian Hindu man who said that he was dying. But the man had a deep calmness and joy about him. Something Al remembers to this day.

On our travels, Al had come across several people that seemed to have that joy about them. An elderly Sikh teacher, a Spanish hippy, a Hindu priest, a "Mahatma" in Haridwar on the banks of the Ganges, and now the old chap in the hospital.

He was thinking that maybe there was some sort of answer, one that neither religion nor science had provided him, some sort of key to the meaning of life that would bring peace and joy such as those men had emanated.

Also during his time there, Al had received a visit from a pleasant lady from his embassy who had given him ten pounds. So when he was released, at least he had some rupees.

Two weeks after being released from the hospital and arriving back in the city, Al went back to his dormitory room at Mr Jain's and booked in for a couple of nights.

Then he went to the American Express offices, as he had written to friends asking for money to be sent there. There was two lots of twenty pounds and one of ten pounds from his friends, waiting for him; a massive boost.

He now had fifty pounds at his disposal, enough to pay his bills and maybe even get back to England. After all he had initially left his home with little more than that, and everything was comparatively cheaper in Asia than Europe.

But, determined to save money, he slept for some nights in a small park close to Jain's hostel, and went each lunchtime to the India Coffee House near Connaught Circus, where, he had been told and it had proved to be true, rich Indian businessmen went for lunch and would buy Al food simply to be able to practice their English. That worked!

When he had left the hospital, the doctor had told him that no way was he to drink alcohol, and should avoid fried, oily or heavily spiced foods.

DIANE

Al had discovered a cheap Chinese restaurant near Connaught Circus, where he could eat simple boiled rice with boiled vegetables, so he frequented that.

Early one evening, whilst he was sitting on wall smoking before his meal, he was approached by a pretty young girl. She announced herself as "Diane, from Cambridge" and told us that she had no money and was hungry and said that she had been abandoned in India by her English boyfriend.

"Can you help me please?"

Al said to her "I won't give you money but I am going over there to that Chinese restaurant and I can never finish my plate of food, so you are welcome to come with me and share, just rice and boiled vegetables though."

Diane immediately said yes and that was the start of another relationship.

That night they huddled together under Al's unzipped sleeping bag in the park and at that time Al told Diane that he had been ill with Infectious Hepatitis so they had better not get too close in case he infected her. He told her about some of his adventures so far and that he had just a little money, so if she wanted, she could travel with him as he planned to leave in a couple of days, by train to Amritsar.

Diane said that she had already phoned her parents in England and they were going to send her some money to Islamabad in Pakistan.

So Al had a new travelling companion, some money and was feeling a lot better. Maybe the Infectious Hepatitis had gone; certainly the vomiting and running to the toilet had stopped.

The following evening they moved into a room in a cheap guest house called Mrs Colako's and the following day, Al and Diane went to the Poste Restante to check for mail.

There was a letter from Keith saying that he had been kicked off the train that he had "jumped" He had not bought a ticket but had reached Delhi after a few days by hitch-hiking. He wrote that he had stayed in Old Delhi but had not seen Al so he had headed off to the Kulu Valley for a while.

Al had read the letter and left the Post Office and walked up the street for about one hundred yards. He spotted Keith!

They greeted each other;

"Far out to see you again man," said Keith; "Where you been, I got here a few days after I left Amritsar, got kicked off the fucking train and had to hitch for bloody miles, ha! But here I am, how are you?"

Al replied: "What! I got kicked off a train too, in the middle of the jungle up between Haridwar and Rishikesh a couple of weeks ago. I had a ticket from Delhi to Haridwar but not to Rishikesh. It was only a couple of rupees but the bloody conductor wanted me to pay a 100 rupee fine. He pulled the emergency cord and stopped the train and made me get off. It was just jungle."

"Bloody hell man, at least they stopped at a station before I got the boot! What happened then? Where you been since?" said Keith.

"Yeah, it turned out OK, I followed the railway track and then there was a road and a car stopped so I had a lift to Rishikesh and back to Haridwar with a great Indian family – they took me to see the Maharishi place, you know, the Transcendental meditation guru guy the Beatles had."

"Where you going next? I'm off to Nepal tomorrow, by bus, fuck the trains, man!" said Keith.

"God I've been really ill. I got dysentery and Infectious Hepatitis. I came back here and I was in Delhi hospital two weeks," explained Al. "I'm going to Amritsar in a couple of days, with Diane. This is Diane. This is Keith" introducing them.

Keith shook hands with Diane. "I've got to go get some stuff done – maybe we can meet up later, where you staying?"

"At a guest house called Madam Colako's on Janpath Lane. We got a room there. She's got about fifty cats! Come tonight, it's easy to find."

Keith had a map of New Delhi and Al showed him where the guest house was.

It was so hot that every time that Al drank tea or a fizzy drink and by the time he managed to cross the main road he was thirsty again.

But Keith never showed up.

That evening, Al and Diane met a group of young English guys at the hostel. They had chatted for a while in the courtyard where there was a water pump that guests tended to gather round, covering themselves with cool water when the heat of the day had gotten too much.

One of the boys, Graham, was telling Al that they had come from England overland through Iran and Afghanistan. He had Infectious Hepatitis. He thought he had caught it in the opium den in Kabul!

Al said: "Wow, I went there and I got 'hep' too. I've been in hospital for two weeks. I got dysentery too. They told me not to drink alcohol and not to eat fried food."

"Yep me too, we cook our own now. Why don't you two come to eat with us tonight. Just some boiled rice and boiled veggies, safer than eating round here, I think."

So, a couple of hours later, Al and Diane went to Graham's room. They smoked some joints with them, then Graham started pulling things out of his rucksack to get ready to cook.

Al spotted a compass very similar to the one he had sold in Chicken Street in Kabul.

"Hey, I used to have a compass like that!" Al exclaimed, "I had to sell it in Kabul – funny thing was I got what it cost me in England, and the guy in the shop didn't seem to know what it was! I think he thought it was magic!"

Graham laughed out loud and said:"Bloody hell man, that's where I bought it, in a shop in Chicken Street. Yeah I don't think he knew what it was. Weird innit? He kept showing me how it pointed up the street. How strange!"

Al looked more closely and for sure it looked exactly like the one he had sold.

Graham cooked a meal of green peppers stuffed with onions and carrots and rice. Al thought it was delicious.

They ate with Graham the next day. They hardly went out of the hostel at all that day. "It was well over 100 degrees Fahrenheit. When they did go for a stroll round Connaught Circus, browsing the shops and trying to avoid the hawkers and the pools of red spit out by the Betel Nut chewers, suddenly the sky opened and it rained really heavy!

As Al and Diane darted into a shop for shelter, lots of Indian men and women ran out of the shops into the rain and started jumping for joy. So Al and Diane ran back into the rain, became soaked and joined the celebration. Apparently it was the first rain that year. The road became a little flooded and the traffic slowed, amidst a great honking of horns and ringing of bicycle rickshaw bells.

The rain stopped as abruptly as it had started.

Al and Diane, now soaked, headed back to the hostel, but the heat had dried their clothing even before they got there.

Al looked out for Keith, but did not see him.

The following day, July 14 1972, Al and Diane went first to the Iranian Embassy in Delhi to get a visa, then to the main railway station, which was about a mile from Connaught Circus, to buy tickets to Amritsar.

There was a queue of about fifty men at the one counter that seemed to be staffed and service was slow, even for India. Al and Diane queued for about and hour and then they were approached by a well-dressed and middle-aged English lady.

"Excuse me" she said, "do you know there is a lady's queue?"

"No," said Diane, "I can't see it, where is it?"

"Oh you can't see it my dear because there are so few women buying tickets, but you can go straight to the front of this queue and they will serve you next my dear."

So Al gave the money to Diane, and, sure enough, when she went to the counter the man serving went straight to her and she bought the tickets without having to wait at all.

Next day, they took a tut-tut – a three-wheeler motorised rickshaw – to the railway station, negotiated the crowds and found the correct platform and immediately boarded the train.

The train was just about to leave when Diane jumped up saying she needed to buy some food and water and rushed straight off the train, taking her bag with her, and ran down the platform.

BACK TOWARDS KABUL

Al waited a few minutes, and, as the train was obviously about to leave and Diane had not come back, he quickly hopped off the train and looked up and down the platform.

Diane was nowhere to be seen!

Al didn't know whether to wait in case she missed the train or get on the train in case she had got back on into a different carriage.

The train started to pull away.

As it began accelerating, Al decided all he could sensibly do was get back on. He spotted an open carriage door and ran and jumped aboard. An Indian voice said in English "Well done Sahib!"

Al found a seat and sat and enjoyed the journey but he discovered it was not possible to go from one carriage to another whilst the train was moving, unless, as some men seemed to do, he climbed out the door and onto the roof. He wasn't going to do that.

The train journey from Delhi to Amritsar was about two hundred and fifty miles and took over ten hours with several long stops at stations. By the time they arrived it was dark. There were plenty of Europeans and maybe Americans alighting from the train, but no sign of Diane. Al went directly to find free accommodation at the Golden Temple. It was signposted in English and a walk of about a mile.

After he found a bed in a room, he headed straight for the food hall. Inside, sitting with a small group of European travellers, was Diane.

Heads, Hats and Tall Tales

After dinner of rice and dahl with chapatti, provided free to travellers by the Sikh Golden Temple donors, Al met with Diane and they agreed to try to catch a bus all the way to Rawalpindi in Pakistan. This would involve crossing the border but no visas were needed. Then in Rawalpindi they could go to nearby Islamabad to collect Diane's money and get visas for Afghanistan.

The next day, July 20 1972, they met up and went to the bus station – there was a bus leaving that afternoon and it was due to arrive in Lahore in the evening. They would stay one night then get a bus to Rawalpindi. They bought tickets.

Al had been in India almost seven weeks.

A few hours later they were back at the bus station with their bags, had boarded the bus and were on their way to the border crossing at Attari – Wagah along the Grand Trunk Road. It was just about 20 miles and they arrived to be told that the bus would stop long enough to see the daily ceremonial lowering of flags at dusk.

This was one of the strangest military displays Al had ever seen. On each side or the border there were troops dressed in costumes and hats.

On the Indian side the troops wore black with black fan-like hats; on the Pakistani side they wore khaki with red fan hats.

It was like some sort of game, a flag-lowering with synchronised shouting and stamping of feet, with soldiers doing fast goose-step marches and high kicks with a waving of flags and shouting of orders, as if a show of one-upmanship, a battle of wits without bullets being fired with a great waving of arms, salutes and gestures. Crowds had gathered to watch this display. The gate was opened and closed and opened again, and the two country flags lowered simultaneously.

When the prancing and parading was over, Al and Diane walked through the customs and passport control and re-boarded the bus that took them towards Lahore.

Not long before they arrived, a young Pakistani man asked if they needed somewhere to stay. He had a house in a village just outside the city and they could stay for free.

Al and Diane agreed and got off the bus with the young man. He led them through a small village to a small house. They entered the house. It was completely devoid of furniture. Not even a chair or a bed.

The man explained that he had only just rented the house and was yet to move in, but if they waited then he would bring them blankets and a rug to sleep on and some tea and food. He left and had not come back.

Instead other young men started entering in groups of two and three, saying that they only wanted to speak in English to practice for their school. They were all talking. About half a dozen with Al at one side of the front room and others to Diane at the other side.

Suddenly Al heard Diane shouting - "No, get off of me, leave me alone!"

Al could see that Diane was looking very uncomfortable and up against the wall with about eight young guys in front of her. It reminded him of the similar situation in the Lahore film studio corridor with Miriam. But, he thought, that was in a public place, this is in a village.

He needed to act fast, so he did exactly what he had done before.

He pushed through the small crowd in front of him and crossed the room. He started shouting; "That is enough, stop it and go away!"

Some of the guys backed off.

He shouted again "Fuck off or I'll stab you!"

With that they started pointing at Diane and shouting at each other. Within a minute or so they had all left the house.

"Come on," said Al, "let's split before it gets dark and they come back."

As the light was fading, they walked back through the village to where the bus had stopped. People were shouting at them and it sounded like it may have been abuse. A woman threw a bucket of what looked like dirty water into the street in front of them.

"What's up with this fucking place?" asked Al.

"It's really aggressive here isn't it. Let's get into Lahore."

Just then a bus came along and they jumped aboard.

Al knew exactly the place to stay, the Hotel Eden, where he had stayed with Keith a couple of months earlier. But the staff were different so he did not ask for Bhang, the cannabis drink that he had tried last time. After all, he thought, we want to make an early start tomorrow.

So it wasn't long before they had eaten dinner and were in bed.

Diane asked Al if he had brought any hash.

"No," he said, "did you hear the tale about the customs

woman there that is supposed to be psychic?"

A couple of days after arriving in Lahore, Diane told Al that she needed to go to the UK Embassy in Islamabad to collect the money that she hoped her parents had sent. They decided to go to Rawalpindi, a town connected to Islamabad and they would go by train.

So they went to the Lahore railway station and bought tickets to Rawalpindi, about 160 miles, estimated to take 5 to 6 hours. The journey was uneventful, the views of no interest.

They booked into a cheap hotel near the station.

The following day, Al and Diane went together to Islamabad, a few miles away, to the embassy for Afghanistan to buy visas, and then Diane went alone to the UK Embassy to collect her money, whilst Al sat and ate one of the hottest dahl dishes he had ever eaten. It did cool him down though, it was about 100 degrees outside.

When Diane came back, she said she had to wait a few days.

Rawalpindi and Islamabad, although essentially two parts of one big city, were incredibly different.

Rawalpindi consisted of old and dilapidated buildings. The streets were crowded and congested with an array of vehicles and people. It was all quite dirty.

On the other hand, Islamabad with its big hotels, embassies, Government buildings and business offices, seemed to have wider and cleaner streets, pavements to walk on, and was all-in-all seemingly more orderly if less pleasant than Rawalpindi.

So they stayed three days in Rawalpindi, which, despite the dirt, they enjoyed. They were able to buy some very cheap good black hash which they spent the days smoking on the hotel balcony, looking down onto the street and enjoying the view of the local life..

Diane went back to the Embassy and when she came back she was smiling – her money had arrived. And it was in English bank notes. She counted out just over £100 and gave half of it to Al. They decided to go straight to the bus station to get tickets to Peshawar the next day; a journey, they were told, of about 4 hours.

So they took the bus to Peshawar, stayed at the Paradise Hotel and bought tickets for a bus to Kabul the next day.

Peshawar had not changed, it was still dirty and smelly.

KABUL AND HOSPITAL AGAIN

The following day, July 29 1972, was the day of the bus ride back through the Khyber Pass to Kabul, the journey that had so impressed and inspired Al on his way to India a few months earlier.

They journeyed past trains of laden camels that occasionally blocked the road, fields with sheep and cattle, the strange-looking men wrapped in blankets even in the heat of the sun, standing or sitting is groups seemingly in the middle of nowhere.

There was an incredible movement of people across the border and back. Many were walking in groups. Many of the men were dressed in garments the light-brown colour of the earth. Others were dressed in coloured tunics with waistcoats over light trousers. Most wore turbans.

The women were dressed in colourful outfits or entirely in blue, black or coloured burkas and many carried large pots or bundles on their heads. The children waved at the bus.

The bus itself was a rickety old machine that chugged along up and down the hills. As well as Al and Diane, there were several other western-looking travellers but sometimes it was hard to tell as they were tanned brown and dressed in clothes seen in India. In any case, they all kept themselves to themselves. There was no sign of any cannabis smoking.

As the road zigzagged upwards, sometimes passing over bridges built over what looked like small streams, Al noticed the many tent cities below in the valley, all with herds of camels and donkeys. Higher were the remains of the many forts originally built by the British. In the distance were snowy peaks.

High on the pass were fortified buildings that were the homes of the locals, each with its own watchtower.

In places the road had a simple and crude stone walls separating it from a sheer drop – in other places there was just the drop.

Then we arrived back in Kabul.

Al and Diane headed straight for a small hotel in Chicken Street, called the Peace Hotel. Diane told Al that she had stayed there before and that it was cheap and had good food.

They had been there for about ten days when Al started to get sick again. I knew he was feeling worse each day, unable to eat or drink without being sick, until one day he realised that he could not stand straight without his head spinning and the feeling that he was about to black out.

He told Diane that he was going to a clinic and she found the address from reception and arranged for a taxi. Al left his bag but was sure to take his passport. Diane went with him to the hospital reception but had not stayed. She took the same taxi back into the city.

Al had to wait about half an hour and then a doctor approached him, saying "Very sorry Sir, very few people here speak English – they had to fetch me from my home. It is a holiday for me today, but I come to see you."

He took Al into a room and asked his problem, which he explained briefly. The doctor called and a male nurse arrived and, without a word, took Al by the wrist and led him out of the room. As he left he spotted a poster that was warning against smallpox!

Al was led into a very large structure, the walls were made from corrugated-looking tin and the roof was canvas. It looked like it had well over a hundred big steel beds, most of them empty.

Al was led to a bed and given a bottle of water and the nurse gestured for him to stay. He got on the bed and instantly fell asleep.

It was some time later that Al was awoken. The same male nurse took a sample of his blood.

A remarkably short time later, the nurse returned with a blood transfusion kit. They gave Al a pint of blood, into his arm, and when that was done, several pints of plasma. The nurse motioned to Al so he understood to drink water.

Al just kept dozing off. Several times somebody woke him and gave him sugarless black tea, then the evening meal arrived. It was rice. Just soggy white rice. But Al was hungry and ate it all.

It was two days before Diane arrived for a visit. She had waited, she said, for Al to come back, then tried unsuccessfully to phone the hospital for information, then decided to get a taxi.

Al spoke to somebody for the first time in two days. Diane told him that the taxi-driver had helped her find him and that he had translated for her, Al had been at such a point of dehydration that his life was at risk. She said that the doctor here had said there was nobody to speak in English but in another two or three days an English-speaking doctor would come and until then, Al had to stay!

True to that, the English-speaking doctor that Al had first met at reception, appeared three days later.

Al had been there for five days.

The doctor said that he was surprised that Al was still there; he should have been there for just one day but nobody knew. He said Al could go now.

Al then realised that he did not have any money and told the doctor – his money was at the hotel. The doctor gave Al some few Afghani notes and told him that he could get a bus outside that would take him to the city centre. From there a short walk took him back to the Peace Hotel in Chicken Street.

Diane was there. She was not happy. She told Al how she had met an English woman whose husband had been in prison for drugs for two years and she had given her most of her money.

The she said "And I've lost my passport!"

"Oh no, how did that happen? Are you getting a new one?"

"I don't know," she said, "It was in my bag and then it was gone. I went to the embassy and they are getting me a new one in about a week, they just gave me a temporary document for ID in case I need it. They told the police. I've got to go back in a week."

"Wow, that's not too good, we've got to get out of here next week, our visa's run out and I've not got much money left!" said Al.

"I've got none either, well not much," said Diane.

"Bloody hell that all went quick!"

"And," she continued, "When I get a new passport I've got to go back to the border to get an entry stamp, then we got to get our visas extended."

"Well that's not too bad, it was a brilliant bus ride, I don't mind, I'll come with you. Got to get some money too, somehow."

"I'm not going to go back to the border," said Diane, "I don't see why I should, it's obvious I'm here so I must have come into the bloody place. They can stuff it. I'll get my passport but I am not going back."

Al decided not to argue. He just explained that it was all formality and if Diane wanted to cross into Iran she would need an entry visa and it was only at the Pakistan border that they probably have a record of when they had come in.

That didn't work.

Diane said rather loudly: "Look, I'm not going back, right. They can phone up or do it in the post I don't care. It's just stupid."

"Well anyway," said Al, "we've got to get some money or I'm going to die here. I don't have much energy. I'm going to go to the embassy and see if they will lend me some money or something. I've got a bank account but there's no money in it, maybe they will give me an overdraft.

"I reckon if I can get one hundred pounds it will get us both home.

"If we can get to Istanbul, I know the Pudding Shop. We may be able to get a cheap lift to UK or Germany or somewhere from there - they have a noticeboard where people can ask for a ride."

"I'll do that tomorrow. We might get some money before you get your passport. I've got enough to last a while, it's cheap here.

"Here, you better have some."

He counted out some notes that were part of what he had left out of what Diane had given him. It was ten pounds.

"Don't give it away," he said.

That evening they went to Sigis just down Chicken Street, sat ate, chatted with other travellers some going one way and some going the other, drank milkshakes and smoked joints. All for less than one English pound.

The following day Al went to the embassy for the UK. He was sent in to see an English official who asked lots of questions. Then he said that the embassy could not contact a bank and asked was there anyone that Al could ask for funds to be sent, what about his parents, where did they live.

Al provided the information. The official said it would take about a week and if there was no other way, they could not give Al a loan but they could fly him back to the UK.

Al told him about Diane.

The official said that when she got her passport and entry visa stamped into it, she should come to see him or she could come in sooner, they would have to see her before he could say how they could help.

Al went back to meet Diane at Sigis and told her what was happening.

"I'm still not going back to the border though," she said.

They had lunch and smoked a couple of joints of hash.

TRIPPING IN KABUL

Suddenly Diane said "Hey, you want some of these?"

She held out her hand and in her palm were four or so small squares of blank paper.

"What's that?" asked Al "looks like paper!" he laughed.

"It's acid," she said, "LSD, you know, Lucy in the Sky. I got some from a French guy. He reckoned they're really good! Want to try?"

Al found her manner too seductive to resist.

"How many do we take? How strong are they? How long do they last? I've never done it."

Heads, Hats and Tall Tales

"I don't know," she said "I've got four. You take two and I'll take two."

"I think I'll just take one first time," he said.

With that Diane popped one small square of paper into Al's mouth. "Suck it and see," she laughed.

Al laughed and then frowned as he watched Diane put the other three squares into her own mouth.

She washed it down with a fizzy drink.

"So this is going to be a trip", thought Al.

He thought about the books he had read: "Aldoux Huxley and Timothy Leary, about LSD and other psychedelic drugs: there was that book by the guy that gave acid to dolphins and then took it himself and put himself into an "isolation tank" and had met beings made out of light. What was his name? Oh yeah, John Lily's Eye of the Cyclone. Oh and the Carlos Castaneda's tales about a Shaman that took psychedelic plants to make contact with beings on other levels.

"The Beatles of course – was that before or after they had gone to Rishikesh with the Maharishi Mahesh Yogi?

"The whole hippy thing was a lot to do with LSD and love and peace and flowers, so that is obviously what it's about, a good time, a spiritual time, just probably stronger than hash."

He looked up from his thoughts and started to look around the courtyard.

It looked different!

Al thought that he hadn't noticed the bells hanging from the edge of the roof, or the bright red flowerpots that held the small trees. And there seemed to be more flowers than before. Yet he'd been there several times before.

Some of the people there, the Westerners, started to look quite funny the way they were dressed. Bandanna's! He hadn't noticed them – in Kabul – they looked really out of place!

Funny how so many were wearing blue jeans, including the two guys serving, and they had short hair, the customers all had long hair.

Weird that people came here to Sigis to eat food they could get back home.

Some of the people looked like people Al had known, or like mixtures of two of them. Several times he felt like shouting out to them, but then they moved and turned into themselves again. How strange, how funny.

He started to laugh and turned to Diane to tell her his thoughts – she was looking at a colourful bird, some sort of canary, that was standing on on top of a small green shrub, almost motionless, as she was. She looked mesmerised, so Al kept quiet, laughing again in his head.

Al turned back to look at the people again.

That guy looked familiar.

As he looked at the guy, the guy stood up and walked over.

"Hi!", he said. "Are you Al?"

Al felt a little uneasy at that – how did the guy know his name?

"You from Norwich? I'm Pete, remember me, Pete Roscoe?"

"Wow," said Al, "You *are* Pete Roscoe, yeah, I remember

you of course, I thought you were somebody that looked like him, I mean you!", he laughed.

Al had known Pete Roscoe back in Norwich but had had no idea that he too, would be heading for India. Pete had also known John and Keith.

"How you doing man?" said Pete, "How long you been here, where you going?"

Al answered: "I went to India with Keith and then I got sick, Infectious Hepatitis and dysentery, nearly died, had no money, on my own, in Haridwar in the Northern Foothills. But I got to hospital in Delhi. I've been in hospital here too. Just waiting to get some money to get home. I'm with Diane. I want to get her home too."

He turned to introduce Pete to Diane. She was staring into a glass of fizzy drink and quietly giggling.

"Hi Pete!"

Al knew that Pete had known John and maybe Mike, so he asked: "Have you heard anything about John and Mike? Keith and I left them with the van in Antalya in Turkey and caught a boat to Iskenderun. We hitched from there across Syria to Baghdad. I haven't heard from them. We were supposed to meet them back in Istanbul but decided to carry on to India. Are they back in England yet?"

"God what a drag about John. You don't know what happened, do you?", asked Pete.

"No," said Al.

"Wow man, I hate to tell you this," said Pete, "John was killed in a crash the night you left them in Turkey. Mike had broken his legs and some ribs and was in hospital there for several weeks. I heard they crashed into a parked truck on a bend at night – John was driving. He swerved out and probably saved Mike's life but was killed himself. Everyone was real sick about it, man."

It may have been because Al was still in some doubt that this was actually Pete Roscoe. Maybe that cushioned the blow for him. He was tripping on acid and just been told his best friend John had died hours after he had last seen him.

So Pete and Al chatted a while longer, Pete was on his way to India. Al gave him some advice about being really careful about what he ate and drank, to keep hydrated, and not to drink the Ganges.

Then it was time that Pete said he would have to go as he had people to meet. They agreed to meet in the same place at lunch time the next day.

Al ordered another two teas with milk. It tasted weird. Different. He didn't drink his.

Then he felt it time to go and explore the streets.

"Come on Diane, let's go for a walkabout. I want some of those spicy potatoes and corn on the cob I've seen.."

So they went outside to see the street.

"Where are we?" asked Diane.

"Sigis, Chicken Street!" said Al.

"Or is it? Hang on, it's not Chicken Street, we must have come out of a different door!," exclaimed Al. "Wait a minute, there's that Kabul restaurant place, it *is* Chicken Street. Wow, it looks different, I never noticed all those ribbons and flags. Hey be careful where you walk, there's holes all over the place. Hey look at that donkey, it's only got three legs!"

"Hey this is great, let's go look at Flower Street!"

"Okay," said Diane. She wasn't saying much but she had a big grin. She took hold of Al's arm.

"Don't let me fall down a hole, it's really tricky up here with the wind." she said.

Al couldn't feel any wind and we were not high up at all, from the road – well I guess if we're 6000 feet above sea level we must be "up here".

"Six thousand feet and climbing!" he said for no real reason.

So they strolled down Chicken Street towards Flower Street, looking in the shop windows and at stalls that Al thought he had never seen before. Everything except the road itself was much more colourful and shiny than he remembered, except the road had many massive piles of dung on it. As he looked, he saw a donkey adding more to it!

All the local merchants seemed to be nodding and smiling at them today! Al thought they all looked like – well they were on something. They were tripping too! Well, thought Al, I guess you've got to be on something to live here, it's like magic.

They reached the end of Chicken Street where it joined Flower Street.

It looked really busy with people that obviously weren't tripping.. It didn't look magic at all. Dark and damp with too many hidden spots, thought Al. Despite the flowers it was not inviting. Noisy too. Chicken Street had seemed very quiet – probably all the shoppers were down here.

"Let's go back or down by the river, we could see the

Mosque," he said.

"Yeah let's go that way, to the Mosque," laughed Diana. "It doesn't matter where we land, we'll be OK."

It seemed like hours before they reached the Mosque and Al had to sit down.

He sat on a low wall outside a building where he could see the Mosque and got lost in thoughts about the good and bad of religions and how the bad side made it hard to believe, yet so many had fallen for religions, as if it was some sort of spell to control people. Al did not want to be a part of religion. He wanted to be apart from them all. "If there's a God," he thought, "it's not in religion."

He heard Diane shouting "Get off, go away. Help!"

He turned to see Diane standing on the wall and below her were three dogs. They were jumping up at her in a friendly way, thought Al. "It's OK, they're just trying to be friendly, just get down and pet them!"

"No they're trying to bite me, they won't leave me alone. They might have rabies!"

"But they're only little," said Al.

"No they're not, they're massive. They're not dogs – they're wolves. Help! Please!" She was really freaked.

Al just shooed the dogs away. They went off down the street, stopped and looked back. Al shouted "Go!" Off they went, hunting for food probably.

He helped Diane climb down. She hugged him.

"Well obviously, cos she took three, she's right out of it", thought Al.

He grabbed her by the arm and they went back to Sigis where they could relax in a good friendly atmosphere and listen to some good rock music.

"Kabul streets at night", he said, "Not good on acid!"

That was a good decision. Diane calmed down and they both enjoyed the rest of the trip, going back to the Peace Hotel with a nice piece of hash to smoke, until they dozed off as dawn was breaking and the Mullahs were calling the so-called faithful to prayer, from their minaret towers.

The following day, Al went back to Sigis and, sure enough, Pete Roscoe was there. It was the real Pete and they chatted a while about what they had been through and, of course, the devastating news about John and Mike. Pete said everyone was really worried about Al as news had reached Norwich that he had been ill.

Diane gave Al a book, called the "I Ching". He had in fact seen it before. Keith had shown him the book in Norwich before they had left. It was the "Book of Changes", an oracle, not so much a fortune teller, more of a clarifier. Al learned from Diane that by throwing three coins six times and recording the results, one could "ask" the book a question, for advice, and the coins would reveal a set of lines that led to readings.

And so the days passed, pretty much day to day, up and down Chicken Street, getting high, meeting people, eating western foods and waiting. No more acid though!

Then came the day that Diane was given her replacement passport – now she just needed the entry visa.

That same day in the morning there was a message at

reception for Al to go back to the embassy.

Off he went. Things are working out," he thought. He took a taxi to the embassy, just to be positive.

Al arrived at the embassy and was shown in to the office he had been in previously and met the same embassy official.

The guy told Al that the authorities had been in touch with Al's parents and they had sent some money, £170, enough for a flight back to London and some change.

"Well," thought Al, "that's about six weeks wages for Dad."

Then he thought: "Well God, if you are there, please let them be able to afford that, not let them get into debt." (I can tell you now as it seems the best time, but Al did not know for weeks afterwards, that round about that time they had had a small win on the "football pools" whatever that is – it as in fact as if his prayer had been answered.)

Al told the embassy chap that he did not want to spend all that money getting home and agreed to take seventy pounds in cash, English money, and leave the rest at the embassy.

"That way," he said, "I can get home and get my friend Diane home too."

He took the money and arranged that he could get the rest transferred to any country on route or get it refunded to his parents.

He already had his visa, Diane had her passport, all that was needed was to make the return bus ride to the border.

He went back to meet Diane at Sigis restaurant, that had become their regular haunt. They would go for a "slap-up" meal.

After a milk shake and a smoke, Al found the name of a

good restaurant and took Diane for a big meal. Well, it ended up that the only vegetarian food available in this top restaurant in a big hotel, was Kabuli rice with vegetables on the side, yoghurt, bread and fruit. They could have eaten exactly the same in a local cheap restaurant for a fifth of the price and in a better atmosphere.

LEAVING DIANE

Al said to Diane, "So tomorrow morning we can get the bus to the border and back and sort out your visa, then we can get tickets and head back across Iran. It'll be fun."

"I've told you loads of times, don't you listen," she said, "I'm not going, it's stupid, they know I am here. If they say I can't get out of the country without a stamp to say I came in, that's just daft! So what I can't even fly out. What about if they wanted to kick me out, they'd soon do that. End of!"

The following morning, Al got himself up and when he woke Diane, told her if she wanted to go to the border today, get up and go with him.

Diane refused. They had a noisy row.

Al realised that she was not going to cooperate.

Al turned to his "I Ching" and, throwing three Afghani coins, asked "what should I do? Stay with Diane or make the journey home alone?"

It seemed very sound and clear advice from the book -hat he had to make the journey home; the alternative suggested led to disaster.

Later that day he told Diane "Tomorrow I am getting up and

going to the bus station. If you want to come, we will go to the border. If not, I'm going to catch a bus to Herat

"Look, here is half my money that's left, thirty pounds" handing her the English notes and a few Afghani notes.

"So it's up to you. Fifty pounds should get us both back to London if we share."

"Thanks," she said, "Maybe I'll see you in England one day. I'm not going to the Pakistan border and if they aren't going to let me out to Iran, I'll have to stay here."

Al struggled but he could not understand why she was being so stubborn, it was only a bus ride.

"If I stay here I am going to die," he said.

After that they did not talk about it and drifted back to a day at Sigis getting high.

KABUL TO TEHRAN AND HOSPITAL AGAIN

The following morning, fighting with his conscience, finding that Diane was not going to join him, Al left. He went straight to the bus station and caught a bus to Herat, via Kandahar. It was normal for the bus to stop one night at Kandahar and he would sleep on the bus.

In that way he arrived in Herat the following day, spent one night there, bought a ticket to the border and from there a ticket all the way to Tehran.

Al crossed the border at Islam Qala and on to the Iranian side at Tayebad on September 3, 1972. He had been in Afghanistan this time for forty days and forty nights.

Heads, Hats and Tall Tales

It was about fifteen hundred miles from Kabul to Tehran, Mashhad being about half way.

That five hundred miles to Tehran from the border took a day and a half, overnight Al slept on the moving bus.

By the time he reached Tehran, he felt filthy dirty not having washed properly for four or five days. He was very tired and very hungry and thirsty. He found a small hotel near the bus station, booked a room for one and before long was asleep.

The next morning, Al awoke and had a good breakfast at a small café. He decided to head off to the American Express offices to see if they could get any money that was waiting for him in Delhi sent to him that day in Tehran. Then, he planned, he would organise transport somehow to Istanbul. From there he would seek a lift closer to the UK at the Pudding Shop.

He thought a lot about Diane, hoping she was OK, but that was her choice. Al believed in freedom of choice. "Well," he thought, "She was penniless when he had first met her in Delhi, now at least she had money and a passport again and if she hangs about at Sigis she'll probably get a lift. She'll be OK, she's a survivor and it wasn't her that was dying from dysentery and Infectious Hepatitis.

He was given directions to the American Express Offices, left his bag in the room and with me upon his head, started to walk the busy streets.

But it was getting hotter and hotter. Al was feeling weaker and weaker. He had to sit down.

The only place to sit was on the dirty pavement.

He must have looked terrible. His long hair and his clothing was dirty. He was very thin. It turned out that he had lost about a third of his body weight, now being a little over ninety pounds.

He sat there a while. The street was crowded, the road full of traffic, as usual a great honking of horns as cars, taxis, buses and trucks fought to some space to drive into. The traffic was very slow.

Nobody seemed to care about Al – he thought about the "Good Samaritan" story in the New Testament. Would there be one here?

He tried to stand up and almost fainted. He tried getting the attention of a passer-by for ages, to no avail. Then, when he had stopped trying to get help, it came in the form of a young guy, probably Iranian, in jeans and shirt.

The chap asked Al if he was OK.

"No, I am not and thanks for stopping. I think I have to go to the British Embassy, do you know where it is please?", said Al.

"Sorry my friend, I do not know, but the American Embassy is around the next corner and you will see it, not far my friend, I will show you," said the guy and with that helped Al stand up and took him to the street and pointed.

"There is U S Embassy," he said, pointing.

But what Al saw was the Union Jack, the British flag! It was the UK Embassy building after all.

Al said thanks and goodbye and headed down the street, crossing over and going in through what looked like an entrance. At the gate stood a large security guard in some sort of ceremonial costume.

As Al approached the guard said "Embassy closed today!"

"I'm British," aid Al, "I am ill, you cannot stop me coming on to British soil can you? I want to see somebody for help."

"You can go inside but there is nobody here to see you today – come back tomorrow, Sir," stressed the guard.

So Al walked in, the guard following saying again to come back tomorrow.

Al saw a wooden door and it opened so he went in. Inside was a large room with wooden tables and chairs, some wooden benches by the wall, and at the far end what looked like a reception office with a closed shutter.

He headed for a bench and lay on it.

"I will wait here until somebody comes and please bring me some good water to drink."

The guard went off and a few minutes later he came back with two sealed glass bottles full of water.

Al drank almost a whole bottle, lay down again on the wooden bench and fell asleep.

Some time later, probably several hours, an embassy official arrived.

He seemed a pleasant and sympathetic chap and Al explained his situation.

"Well, you can't stay here. I think we should get you to the hospital so they can do some tests!"

Al agreed and the official led him out to a car and took him a few miles to the outskirts of Tehran where the hospital was.

Once inside the hospital, the embassy official stayed until an English-speaking doctor came and Al had explained his problems. Then he left saying that he would stay in touch.

The doctor said Al should stay at least one night and they would do tests. He took Al's pulse and blood pressure, listened through his stethoscope at Al's chest, pressed on his abdomen and took a sample of blood.

Al was then told to lay on a bed trolley and with me in his hand, was taken to a small ward and led to a bed. Of course he did not have clothing to change into, but they brought him some over-sized pyjamas. They also brought Al a hot meal but it had meat in it. Al explained that he did not eat flesh and, although he felt that the nurse really did not understand either what he was saying or why he did not eat meat, the meal was soon replaced with rice and vegetables and no meat. It was delicious and felt wholesome.

Al was shown where the wash room with shower and quickly stripped off, washed his body and hair and washed his clothes, all at the same time. He did not wash me though. I think I needed it to rain, I was dirty too.

He went back to his bed. He was feeling a lot better now. He fell asleep. I was on a small cabinet next to his bed, next to some bottles of water and a small vase with flowers in!

Some time later, a male nurse woke Al up and handed his some tablets, which he swallowed. He went back to sleep.

It was the following morning that he awoke. They served him a breakfast of some sort of porridge, eggs and bread, yoghurt and a rice pudding.

The doctor came and explained to Al that they had the results of the tests and that he should stay a few nights and take the tablets.

"When you go it is very important. You must not drink alcohol and you must not eat fried food or fresh fruit or salad."

Later that day the embassy official came to visit Al.

He told Al that the best action for him was to take a flight home.

Al explained his lack of money but that he had money in Kabul and maybe some at the American Express if he could get it sent from Delhi offices.

The guy left and came back about an hour later.

He said that if Al signed a paper giving authority, the embassy could arrange with the embassy in Kabul and the American Express in Delhi. Al could stay at the hospital another four nights and then the Embassy would arrange for a car to pick him up and he would be able to fly to London.

Al told him yes but his bag was at the hotel and he had to pay the extra bill.

So the official said "OK, we will pick you up by car and take you to your hotel, you stay only for one night, OK? Then we take you to the airport."

Al agreed. That was the last he saw of the official. But for four more days and nights he felt warm and clean and was well fed and medicated.

BACK TO THE UK

On the final morning, sure enough, a car from the embassy arrived and took Al first to the American Express where he picked up just twenty pounds that had been sent to Delhi and then he headed back to the hotel. He paid his bill.

After a small outing to a nearby restaurant where he ate vegetables and rice again, he went back to his hotel feeling very tired as if it had been a hard day, and soon again he was asleep.

The following morning after breakfast, Al went out and bought some limes as he had been told they were good to fight Infectious Hepatitis.

Soon enough, the car arrived again and Al was taken to Tehran airport and given his ticket for a flight to London Heathrow airport. He asked the driver to ask the embassy to phone his parents to tell them he was due to arrive, writing down the phone number.

Al put me into his rucksack and that was all I knew until we landed.

Al had to go through customs at Heathrow.

They opened his rucksack and there I was, soon to be back on Al's head and back in communication.

Next to come out was Al's worn and dirty sleeping bag – but as it was being pulled out, about half a dozen limes came with it, falling to the ground and rolling down the slightly inclined floor. The customs officer quickly caught them and put them back into the rucksack saying "Thank you, you can go!"

Al found a phone box and phoned his parents in Wales, telling them he would catch a train to Cardiff and then a bus.

Al's mother said "We'll pick you up in Cardiff. We have a little car now and your Dad is driving. We had a little win on the pools just after we heard you were ill and that was how we got the money so quick."

"Prayers do get answered," thought Al to himself.

When his parents met Al on Cardiff General railway station, his Dad said "You look like Gandhi – you are so thin."

Back in Wales, the following day, the family doctor visited and said that Al would have to go to hospital and stay in for a while and have tests to see what was wrong. Al explained that he was on tablets from the hospital in Iran and that he was diagnosed with Infectious Hepatitis and dysentery. The doctor asked to see the pills.

"I'll keep them, you don't need them and we don't know what they are. They may not be good for you if they are from Iran! We'll get the tests done and find out the problem."

So Al was taken to a hospital near Cardiff. He had written some letters to friends in Norwich, such as Pam and also to Australian Paul, as well as John's parents saying how sorry he was to hear the sad news about his death. Al asked his Mum to post them. As he was leaving his parents house, he picked me off the hook I had been on, saying "Mustn't forget my hat, my old travelling buddy."

Al explained to the doctors that he was vegetarian and had been told not to eat fried food, fruit or salads. The doctor said "We'll see when we've done the tests"

They fed him on salad and chips!

GURU MAHARAJI

Al's Mum visited every day, and one day she came again, with some letters from Norwich and a newspaper.

One letter was from two good friends, Pam and Steve, saying that he could stay with them when Al got back to Norwich and saying how sad they had been to hear that John was dead.

John had been a very much loved man and admired man by so many. Everyone that knew his was devastated at the news, they wrote.

But "stay away from Paul, he's taken up some sort of Guru called Maharaji", they wrote.

The second letter was from Paul, saying how he had given up drugs and was meditating on something called "Knowledge" that he had been shown by a boy just of fifteen years of age called Guru Maharaji.

There was another letter too, from John's parents, wishing Al well and saying "John died amongst the people he loved so much."

Al finished reading the letter and picked up the newspaper. He opened it randomly and there in front of him was an article about the "Boy wonder Guru Maharaji" that had come from Haridwar in India, an ashram called Prem Nagar, to bring his "Knowledge" to the West. There was a small picture with a caption that read "Lord of the Universe".

"How strange," thought Al - "that must be the place opposite where I nearly drowned in the Ganges. I wonder if that is some sort of child prodigy for that Maharishi Yogi guru guy that the Beatles had seen – but that was called Transcendental Meditation and now this is called Knowledge".

A couple of days later, the test results were through and sure enough he had Infectious Hepatitis and dysentery – they gave Al pills and a strict diet of no alcohol, no fried food and no fresh fruit or salad.

He went home and stayed with his parents for several weeks, putting on weight and rebuilding his strength. I stayed on a hook by the front door.

Later Al put me into a special box.

The next thing I knew, I was in Norwich.

Al was staying with his two good friends, Pam and Steve, and visiting Australian Paul and his wife. There were no more chillums and joints with Paul. Instead, Paul told Al much about his boy teacher, the Guru Maharaji, and the techniques that the boy gave to enable people to experience the "Knowledge" within inside themselves.

Al was now actively seeking some sort of answer to an uncertain question about life and the universe. He started asking the 'I Ching', the book that Diane had given him in Kabul, for guidance.

One day whilst Al was about to consult the "I Ching" again, having thrown the coins and drawn the lines that would reveal the "hexagram" and reading, there was a knock on the door.

It was Australian Paul and his wife and another follower of

the Guru Maharaji.

Al did not want to be unsociable, so made tea, and then whilst the three guests chatted away, telling him once again about this "Knowledge", Al could not resist picking up the book again.

The "lines" pointed him to read Hexagram 5:"The Waiting": as he wished that Paul would stop talking so that he could focus on the reading, Al reached the lines that read:

"Six at the top means:

"One falls into the pit.

"Three uninvited guests arrive.

"Honour them, and in the end there will be good fortune."

It did not take Al long to realise that the three uninvited guests may well have been sitting in his living room.

So he started listening and began to understand that Paul was talking about some sort of experience within a person, an experience that he called peace.

Al started going to public meetings about this Knowledge. The meetings were called "Satsang". He learnt that it was free for the asking but took commitment, "to yourself," the Guru said.

One day Al picked up his "I Ching" again and asked "Who is Guru Maharaji?"

The result was the revelation of Hexagram 1 "The Creative" changing to Hexagram 50: "The Cauldron" with changing lines in positions first and fifth.

Al was determined to find out – but that is another story.

I can tell you now, that Al never saw Mike, Miriam, Hellmut

or Diane again and never went back to Turkey, Syria, Iraq, Iran or Pakistan. He wonders to this day where those people that he met were today and whether they were still alive.

I have since travelled with Al on many occasions and I have more adventurous tales to tell you about. Until then,

Peace be upon you.   Myhat.

Heads, Hats and Tall Tales

BACK TO THE EAST
INDIA, NEPAL AND KASHMIR

INTRODUCTION

I had not been to India since 1972, a strange trip with no previous foreign travel experience, very little money and not a lot of common sense. So after several months of travelling overland by various means of transport, including coaches, cars, trucks, on the back of a motorbike, a horse and cart, a tractor, a train and even a boat, we had reached Lahore in Pakistan and took a plane to the land of rickshaws. A few weeks there and I became sick. I spent time in hospital in Delhi, Kabul and Tehran, eventually flying back to the UK from there. But I survived. Not everyone did in those days. But it was an unforgettable experience that cannot be repeated today. That story is told in my book which is also on Amazon and Kindle: 'All About My Hat The Hippy Trail 1972'.

I had wanted to go back the India, such a mixture of good and bad places and experiences, ever since.

My next trip there was to be a holiday on the houseboats of Kashmir, with a pony trek along the way, with a friend called Lizzie, in 1981.

In 1985 I made a two month journey around Northern India, Nepal and Kashmir with Lesley.

This book was written up from my notebooks from those times. I have included some scanned photos and poems.

Many of the descriptions of places, temples and such, have been copied from entries in my journals of the times which themselves were copied from pamphlets. However, I have also added in more up-to-date information from on-line, to make them more complete.

Appreciation

Thanks to the Baktoo family in Srinagar.
Thanks to Simon King and Steve Land for proof reading.
Thanks to ABeFree Publishing for formatting the soft-back edition.

1981 KASHMIR WITH Lizzie.

5th October: Delhi

We left Heathrow on Kuwait Airways flight KU380 22.00, Boing 747. The flight was great with some excellent views over the Alps and later of the coastlines of Yugoslavia (as it was then) and Greece. We arrived at Kuwait airport in darkness. It was noticeably new and clean; we did not have a long wait before we were on the 747 again, to Delhi.

We took a dusty taxi ride to the Hotel Asia where we had a double room booked. Apparently, we were told, all the taxi fares had gone up 50%, presumably specially for us.

Heads, Hats and Tall Tales

The smell of Delhi was so familiar to me; it hadn't changed in 9 years. It was already very hot and dusty so the first thing was a few hours rest before we go to the Air India office.

After going to the office and confirming our stay on a houseboat in Kashmir, we went to a good looking and clean looking restaurant near Connaught Circus for dinner.

The food was actually quite good, the service friendly and the décor pleasant.

Yet after we had finished, I saw a look of horror on Lizzie's face, as she sat opposite me. She pointed at the window. I turned to see a rat on the window sill. I called the waiter. He calmly walked towards it shaking a tea towel. The rat ran out of the open window.

We slept well, however, that night. I did not dream of rats!

6th October

We spent the day riding round Old Delhi and New Delhi on a tuk-tuk, a three wheeler scooter.

Our first stop was the Lal Qila or Red Fort, with its huge gardens and many red stone buildings which were constructed in 1639 by the fifth Mughal Emperor Shah Jahan (of Taj Mahal fame) as the palace of his fortified capital Shahjahanabad when he decided to move his capital from Agra to Delhi. Lai means red and Quila means fortress.

The Red Fort is named after its massive enclosing walls of red sandstone. The imperial apartments consist of a row of pavilions, connected by a water channel known as the Stream of Paradise. Many of the buildings are now used by Government administration.

We spent the afternoon trying to get flights for tomorrow to Srinagar, but they are all booked, so we went to the train station instead. After queueing some time, an Indian lady approached us and said we did not have to queue, as ladies could just go straight to the front. So we went to the front and Lizzie bought first class tickets one way, which cost 400 rupees, about £25.

Fortunately the room was air conditioned as my head was spinning from all the politeness, ramblings and bargaining.

It's strange, as I always think of India as being Holy, slow and dreamy, whereas Delhi was fast and dusty and the main religion seems to be money, everybody wanting it but few having it. There are a lot of luxury hotels and offices and guys dressed in

suits but far more poor people and beggars in rags. The roads are crowded with buses, trucks, cars, motorised tuk-tuks, bicycles and bicycle rickshaws, donkey carts and even an elephant. People drive on their horns. The rule on the road was Might Is Right.

8th October: **SRINAGAR AND DAL LAKE**

It was Thursday. A lot seemed to have happened since Tuesday. It was a long train ride. Yesterday, we caught the 16.00 train from Delhi to Jammu. The first class compartment with two tier sleepers was not even up to third class in the UK but we did get tea and a meal and at least we could stretch out, if not sleep. We met an

Indian family that had lived in Zambia but moved to London.

We arrived in Jammu about 8 AM (two hours late) and met up with Mary, an English girl who was planning to marry Farook Baktoo, the son of a houseboat owner. Also there was Abdullah, a Kashmiri chap, who worked at the Himalayan Holidays company offices. We took a taxi with them to Srinagar, which took nine hours, stopping for tea and meals.

Mary was a very pleasant, red-haired young lady who seemed to be very much in love with India, especially Kashmir although she did not tell us much about here previous experiences.

On the road we saw where rockfalls and landslides had partially blocked the road and disrupted the heavy flow of trucks and buses. It seemed too remote for rapid

repairs; remembering this was India, it could take years. We passed many hundreds of people, some driving goats or sheep, and some camels and some monkeys watching to see what they could grab. The road passes through, or rather up and down, two valleys in Jammu, before entering the Kashmir Valley. The views, as much as we could see out of the taxi windows, were incredible. There was no stopping for photos but I did get one or two.There were road signs reading 'Better Late Than Never', 'Avoid a Crash and Don't be Rash' and 'No Hurry, No Worry'.

Not that it deterred all drivers – we saw three overturned trucks. 'Keep Your Nerves on the Curves!', 'Alcohol in for Refreshment, not for Intoxication', 'Life is short, Don't Make it Shorter'.

Other signs read 'Spray your house with DDT' and

'This is not a Rally, Drive Slow in Kashmir Valley'.

Also a sign suggesting a stop for one's first view of the Kashmir Valley.

I have forgotten so much I was going to write about. Lizzie asking "Why have those men driven their trucks into the river?" Me: "You can drive a truck to the river but you can't make it drink."

The road there included a tunnel built by Germany in 1958 and over 1.5 miles long, guarded at each end, with photography prohibited. One way was closed that day, so we had to wait for traffic coming towards us to clear. The other tunnel was full of donkeys and goats. After a section of treacherous road, it descends into the valley. Beautiful! Then what was after quite a long way, but suddenly, we arrived in Srinagar.

DAL LAKE

Upon safe arrival in Srinagar, we transferred by shikara boat to the beautiful Kashmir Paradise houseboat. All meals provided, and now, need a rest.

Srinagar was the largest city and the summer capital of the Indian union territory of Jammu and Kashmir. It lies on the banks of the Jhelum river, which was called Vyath in Kashmir, a tributary of the Indus and on the Dal, Nageen and Anchar lakes. The river passes through the city and meanders through the valley, moving onward and deepening in the Wular Lake. The city was known for its nine old bridges, connecting the two parts of the city. The city was also known for its natural environment, its gardens, waterfronts and houseboats. It was also known for traditional Kashmiri handicrafts, walnut carvings, carpets, shawls and dried fruits. Srinagar was often called 'The Venice of the East'.

On the houseboat we met an English guy, John, who works on the Daily Mail and an American couple who work in Saudi Arabia, but they are leaving tomorrow.

The other guy that we met and became fond of was Habib. He was not one of the Baktoo brothers but brought us our meals, cleaned up and looked after us well. They called him "the servant" but I did not like to call him that.

Habib

The dinner was good, the evening was cool and I look forward to seeing our surroundings in daylight the next day.

Not being able to swim and not being over keen on boats, I must say that I found this houseboat safe and forgot that we were actually afloat all the time.

9th October.

I slept for eleven hours. Much needed.

Toast and marmalade for breakfast. The room was quite luxurious especially by Indian standards, with wooden walls and carpets on the floor. The mesh at the windows and the wooden ceiling was decorated with interlocking twelve-sided shapes.

Apparently, like most things I guess, the weather in India had been strange for the last few years; the summers were getting longer and this year there was no monsoon in the North.

THE BAKTOO FAMILY

We went for a ride to see the Perfume Garden houseboat, the pride and joy of the Baktoos and to meet the head of the family, Mr Baktoo, whom Mary said was a devoted Moslem who had been to Mecca.

The journey by shikara took an hour each way; it was

superb, slow and peaceful and relaxing, surrounded by still unspoilt beauty. The water in lake Nageen was so still, the reflections of the mountains and houseboats doubling the beauty. They allowed swimming and had water-skiing there.

There were all sorts of houseboats, large deluxe for rental and smaller ones that people live in. By the side of the lake were hotels, shops and stalls, with the beautiful mountains behind them. A treasure to hold in the heart.

Apparently some of the buildings on the lakeside were three hundred years old.

Sharing a Shikara ride with Mary

When the British were here, the local Government was

able to ban foreigners from buying land. Nowadays, the large houseboats cost tens and even hundreds of thousands of pounds, so many local businessmen had made partnerships with foreign investors. Kashmir Paradise, for instance, was part owned by Mr Baktoo and part owned by a German. Mr Baktoo had several sons, Ali, Farook, and Jimmy (Mohammed); there was no mention of daughters. The father talked to us about the possibility of us selling Kashmir holidays back in the UK. I told him about the Norfolk Broads,

The return journey was just as good but it was getting cool. We passed several groups of children singing their equivalent of Christmas carols and there were firecrackers and rockets.

There were lotus plants and reeds on the lake and lots of ducks and other birds.

Heads, Hats and Tall Tales

I took a photo of the shikara man (above) and promised to send him a print.

The dinner that evening was excellent, vegetarian for me and lamb for Lizzie and Mary, but they both wanted to eat some of mine: curry vegetables, spinach aloo, spicy cabbage, pilau rice, chapati, bean bhaji, apple stew, apple juice and chai.

Lizzie was a small and thin English girl from Sheffield, slightly younger than me. She could be short-tempered and sharp-spoken, but generally meant well. She was very much an environmentalist. I had know her for about ten years before this journey.

10th October

We took a shikara to the landing spot and waked into

town. We went to the Post Office and also to pre-book our tickets back to Delhi for the 23rd. Lizzie went off to buy a swimming costume.

The town itself was like most towns, full of people, hustle and bustle, yet somehow still slow. At one point Lizzie ran across the road to buy tobacco. As I watched I saw almost everyone else stop to watch her! People did not run in the streets of Srinagar unless it was an emergency!

Many of the shops were selling paper maché boxes, carpets and such, for tourists, but there were few beggars and those that were there had apparently come from Delhi, so we were told.

I wondered whether the Kashmir craftsmen would make Welsh dressers.

There are seventeen languages in India. Religions include Islam, Hinduism, Christianity, Buddhism, Sikhism, Jainism, Judaism. In Kashmir they are mostly Islam. Pakistan wanted Kashmir, coincidentally India's richest state. Personally I hoped it either became independent or stays in India, as I think Pakistan would industrialise it too much.

Unlike much of India, there was a lot of meat eaten there in Kashmir but not pig, although vegetarian food was also easy to get. Three of the four sheep that were outside the houseboat on a clump of grass had disappeared. We were told that they had been slaughtered, one for the family, one for the relations and friends and one for the poor.

Some had appeared on our dinner table for Lizzie and Mary. Lizzie would not eat it even though she normally ate meat.

11th October

Awoke for a hot shower and breakfast of porridge, fried eggs, toast and tea. I bought some nice papier-maché boxes and egg cups; good quality.

The Charas here was quite strong. Just a one-skinner (tobacco joint) was enough to share. We could not finish a three-skinner between us that evening.

Kashmir green tea was delicious. It made a change from sweet milky chai.

The Sikh couple, Ravi and Rami, that were staying here had gone to stay in a hut in Gulmarg to do some walking. They were planning to stay on the houseboat for a few days and they suggested we go to visit them. Of course, if we had, they may have been out walking. Ravi was a captain in the Indian army and also a part-time farmer. His father was a judge in Delhi, he said

The afternoon was spent on a shikara ride to Lake Nageen to the other houseboat and Lizzie took a swim. I thought that I would not be surprised if she became ill later. We passed the floating gardens on the way, where they grow vegetables during the summer.

Again it was quiet and dreamy on the lake and on the

houseboat with the occasional smoke.

12th October

We went to see the Forewest Wood Emporium

The quality of the craftsmanship was excellent and impressive. I thought that I could sell some back in the UK. Statues, Buddhas, tables and chairs, boxes and lamp stands, chests and nests of tables, a writing bureau, chess tables, sewing boxes and wine cabinets.

We crossed the Golden Lake where houseboats were joined together for large groups of guests. Sometimes there were just planks of wood between them, so guests literally had to walk the plank.

I spent the afternoon sitting on the sun deck relaxing and smoking, Lizzie was sick.

She would not accept that it was connected to her having swam in the lake. She was fasting for the day. Mary also had diarrhoea, so maybe it was the meat. Apparently she had suffered with jaundice and typhoid in Delhi a few weeks previously.

13th October

I was almost forgetting which day of the week it was, not that it mattered. We went back to the town and I bought a Kashmir sweater for about £5.

Cashing a travellers cheque took ten minutes as people

pass around their forms while we waited. Then off to the post office to get letters and postcards franked so nobody can steam off the stamps, which was apparently common in India.

The previous night, Mr Baktoo had spent an hour telling Lizzie that in India she could become a guru! I couldn't imagine why he would think that.

Mr Baktoo had said that he had been to Mecca. In his younger days, he said, he used to drink alcohol and smoke, but stopped. In fact he still smoked joints. He smoked joints with us, as did his sons, but as soon as one of the others appeared, they put down the joint. They each asked us not to tell the others. Yussef did not smoke. He secretly drank whiskey though. By the time

Mr Baktoo stopped talking, Lizzie was very stoned, so she went to crash out.

We stayed on the Kashmir Paradise houseboat that night.

At 8.30 PM was the only one still up.

The room was lovely, with its own bathroom and WC, but the massive double bed was not at all comfortable. Once the light was turned off it was pitch dark.

MR SULTAN BAKTOO

KASHMIR LAKES

Mogul sounds, ring round
The glorious snow-capped mounds.
Sheep and cows, outside now,
The friendly servant humbly bows.
The air is cold, the valley bold,
The view, the peace the beauty sold,
For rupees, pounds or marks,
Or items brought from Marks and Sparks.
The atmosphere here is safe for sure.
The beggars try to ask for more.
The market places always full,
Of paper maché, carpets of wool.
The walnut carvings are the best,
In all the world, east or west!
The peace that finds itself so near,
Is peace that travels everywhere.

Heads, Hats and Tall Tales

Heads, Hats and Tall Tales

14th October

We went to a carpet factory with Mr Baktoo; also it's a sales room, of course. The carpets, silk and wool in various size, were beautiful. I bought a woollen one, five by three feet, for £220, probably paying too much, but I was stoned. It had 440 knots per square metre and supposed to be top quality. I paid just 200 rupees deposit and had to send the rest from the UK.

The following day, we had planned to go for three days camping and pony trekking.

We knew little about where we are going or how hard the walking will be, but we are assured that everything will be provided and Mary, Farook's wife-to-be, was coming along with us.

We were told it will be just six miles moving each day over three hours.

The French couple that had been staying here warned us about cobras; they said that the army tents that they had seen all had anti-cobra precautions. Mr Baktoo said there are no cobras in the mountains.

Lizzie bought a sweater and some plimsolls for walking, but I thought they would not much good, she needed good boots. I told her but she would not listen.

Whilst we were strolling around, we passed a park. I spotted some weed growing near the wall, so pulled off some heads and dried it in the sun back on the deck of the houseboat. It was a nice smoke. Apparently, as we were told, the family was a strong unit here and when a man took a wife she lived with her parents and did not see much of her own family. Divorces were rare and considered shameful, so much so that the wives of the brothers of the divorcees brothers may even divorce their own husbands. Men were the bosses of the families. Mr Baktoo said women should serve; not Lizzie apparently as he had said she should be a guru!

15th October:

PAHALGAM

We left Srinagar to Pahalgam by taxi. We passed a wedding precession on the way.

The groom was being carried and covered with money and flowers and surrounded by people. We didn't see the bride. She was probably washing dishes already.

The taxi journey took a few hours. We stopped on the way so they could buy some chicken.

By the time we arrived, our tents were pitched in the 'Familiarisation Camp'. We were set behind a half-dried up river, called Aru, I thought, with three tents and some donkeys. All the equipment was here, for cooking etc and so were our cook and guide.

It turned out the chickens were alive and one had disappeared already. Lizzie seemed very philosophical, asking questions such as "Why does God allow suffering? Why did he create evil?"

Then Lizzie and Mary went off for a short pony ride whilst I stayed and contemplated the river; but wherever I sat, on the cushions, there seemed to already be a chicken hiding there. Silly things, if they had known their destiny they would have run off, but no, they just hung about the camp.

Heads, Hats and Tall Tales

RIVER ALIVE

Whether we laugh, or whether we cry,
The river of life goes rushing by,
Down the hills and mountain sides,
Into valleys, long and wide,
Towards the ocean that is its goal,
Its journey travelled by our soul.
When I was but little boy,
The river rippled and dashed with joy,
And as I grew and longed to learn,
The river for the ocean yearned.
As young man travelled round the world,
The river twisted, turned and twirled,
Eager to find its resting place,
Eager to travel in time and space.

And as the seeking man grew older,
The river found the bigger boulders,
But on it travelled without care,
It knew its destiny's not there.

> The rushing water's now quite slow,
> The river old has nothing to show,
> Its happiness is calm and deep,
> As old man takes his final sleep.
>
> The ocean that is never ending,
> Is to the sky its waters lending,
> To rain again on mountain top,
> To make sure life's rivers never stop.
> The rivers message lies in this
> Ocean of Mercy, Peace and Bliss

It was getting dark and cold. It would be a cold night but the sleeping bags that they had provided looked and felt warm. The girls came back and dinner was about to be served as the mountain peaks disappear into the night.

Guess what they served the girls for dinner? Chicken of course! That's what had happened to the missing chicken. The girls would not eat it but they were too embarrassed to say anything, so they threw it away and ate some of my vegetarian food. I realised as I started to doze off that I don't even know the names of our guide or cook.

16ᵗʰ October

ARU

It was quite cold and it rained during the night, but we were up at 7 AM for breakfast and ready to go.

I had been fell walking when I was at University 1969 to 1972; I had walked up Ben Nevis, Snowdon and several mountains in the Lake district including Skafell, Coniston and Helvellyn but I had not walked up many hills since then. I used to go caving and rock-climbing too. Used to, I stress..

We set out to walk to the tiny village of Aru, sometimes spelt Arru. It was lovely walk and fantastic scenery. I had thought it would be more difficult but mostly we walked on a road. We passed lots of small ganja plants, too small to harvest.

It rained again so we sheltered a while under trees and eventually reached Aru by 11.30. On the road we met a guy that Mary knew and when we got to Aru all his children were waiting for us. His house was the first house on the left! He invited us in for chai and a chance to dry off a bit.

He had about seven children of various ages, all beautiful. Well I assumed they were all his. We never saw the mother but granny was there, nodding and smiling at us.

We had to wait quite a time for Habib and our pony man.

WAITING FOR HABIB

The folk in the village of Aru,
Had eyes fixed on us both like glue,
Their eyes shining, open wide,
As they're sitting side by side.

The granny's there, old, toothless and bent.
Her happy life is almost spent,
But still, just now and once a while,
She looked at us and gave a smile.

Whatever it was they were trying to say,
We never knew before on our way.
Their hospitality was ever so warm,
Amidst those mountains tall and calm.

We waited for three hours and more
Before Habib's donkey man we saw,
Then off we strode with just a wave,
To walk, eat and sleep midst memories saved.

For Roxana, Musaka a place called home.
For us it was a stepping stone.

After three and a half hours the ponies had still not arrived, so we walked back to the camp where the tents were already pitched again.

It was raining again, slightly, so we sat around the campfire and all was well.

The river was rushing now, the valley was luxurious, the mountain peaks were white with snow.

17th October.

We were up early and Habib was ready for us with breakfast; cornflakes, eggs, bread and chai.

The sun was shining on the mountain tops and creeping down the valley but neither Lizzie nor Mary ate breakfast, even though there was no chicken. Another chicken had disappeared.

We walked back to Aru where we mounted our ponies and rode most of the way to Lidderwat.

When I got on my pony it seemed to stumble on the

stones;

I dismounted, thinking I was too heavy for it, being about ten stone. Habib said no, get back up. He said the ponies play games and if I did not ride it, it would always try to pretend I was too heavy and stumble. After that, it was no problem even on the hilly rocky bits.

I expected Lidderwat to be a small village but in fact it was just two small wooden huts, one for us. The scenery around us was simply amazing. Snowy mountains and pine trees. The sun was shining and the sky a deep cloudless blue. It was autumn here, so there were green pines and golden and brown trees.

Lidderwat was about six miles from Aru. One could carry on to Kolahoi which is the highest glacier in Kashmir, but we were already about 9,000 feet above sea level so we decided not to go any further. We were not equipped to walk in the snow and the ponies, as we were told, did not like it.

The girls were not eating the chicken in the packed lunches. It's a shame that the birds died for nothing.

Riding the pony was fine. It seemed like they know where to go and compete to lead the way. Occasionally they started trotting to get in front and we collided.

As we arrived, three or four children rushed up from nowhere, asking for cigarettes. The pony trek man said they were charas and gave one to the oldest girl who broke it up and looked. Then they all ran off shouting in unison, I know not what. Then they were back again, whispering to each other, watching me write and Lizzie laying in the sunshine.

The wooden hut was named 'The Paradise Hotel'.

18th October

We were up at 6.30 and the sun was shining and sweeping down the hill.

Lizzie had constipation. We stayed there until after lunch then headed back to Pahalgam. From there we took a taxi back to Srinagar. I pledge to come here again.

Pahalgam was a small town, just a few streets with cars, coaches and ponies, almost like the wild west but without cowboys.

We were in a different room on the houseboat. Lizzie said she had ant bites all up her legs

19th October: **HOUSEBOAT**

I woke up feeling fed up. Not sure why. Suddenly I started to wish I was back in Norwich. I thought it was because I knew we only had a few days left here. I felt like I had been too long in Srinagar and not seen anywhere else except Delhi. It makes sense to stay somewhere a while to get to know it but even two weeks was not long enough and I loved to roam new places.

Lizzie was now coughing a lot, like she had bronchitis. But she would not listen to advice or take help.

The she told me that she had lost her bank card and rupees. Stupidly she had put them on her back pocket when riding the pony. So we were short of money to pay the bills. Mary said we could send the money later.

20th October

Last night the electricity was off all night and still off when we got up, but it was sunny again, which improved the mood.

Mary talked with Mr Baktoo about her marrying Farook. He told her his wife would want her to sign a statement in court to say that she would stay in Kashmir and only go away if given permission and that she would never ask for a divorce. Then she would talk with Ahmed and ask him what to do. Also she would have to wear Moslem clothes in the presence of the family and friends. Under modern law also Farook could take up to another six wives! Mr Baktoo said he would pay for them to go anywhere for two or three months but after that she had to stay in Kashmir or Delhi.

Lizzie asked Mr Baktoo to read her palm, which he said

Heads, Hats and Tall Tales

he would. He held her hand and said to think of a flower. Then he said "rose". He was correct. Now he was calling her his guru!

He said he was very rich and owns many houseboats but his peace comes from keeping his family happy. He said he went to bed at 8 PM and got up at 4 AM. That evening, after he had been talking to us, we could hear his wife calling him. He said he only had one wife as he was happy with her. I wondered if he had intended proposing to Lizzie.

I gave Habib a gift of my telescopic umbrella. He was very happy with that. He said "I hope it will rain soon".

Habib gave Lizzie a red coral necklace which Mr Baktoo said was good but "only cost two rupees". The bastard! He may be rich but he may be mean too. Maybe he will give her a gold one, after all, she was his guru!

21st October

It was getting cold at night so we had hot water bottles. The electricity went off again at 11 o'clock last night. We had spent most of the evening talking with Yussef about trekking, whilst he was drinking whiskey and moaning about people smoking hash. He drank a whole bottle. He said he had travelled to the UK overland, but the law was that after getting back to India one must stay for at least eighteen months. One way out, he said, was through Nepal..

Mr Baktoo said that he thought that the Ayatollah was a number one fool and that he and Iran were very bad because they fight fellow Moslem and the Koran says not to fight. Personally, I am never keen on talking religion or politics as it so often offends.

We heard that crowds had gathered in town because somebody had seen a cobra. So we went into town to take a look at what all the excitement was about. We found the place quite easily and saw about two dozen people staring at a patch of ground; cars were stopping to take a look; apparently that had been going on for about a week; we saw no sign of any snakes. People were saying that there are four snakes underground but nobody there had actually seen any,

There had been a government order that the houseboats had to be moved about. Lake Nageen was to be for deluxe houseboats only, Lake Dal for class A and class B and some of the houseboats at the smelly Dal gate were actually on dry land and would have to be moved. The river below the Dal Gate bridge was not a pleasant sight or smell.

Nageen was cleaner than Dal. They were lucky there were few motor boats.

22nd October

We spent last night at the Perfume Garden houseboat on Lake Nageen. The bathrooms had sunken baths.

Back on our "own boat" playing scrabble, then off to town to try to buy rolling tobacco and skins for Lizzie.

23rd October

We heard that we were going to be flying to Delhi tomorrow.

Lizzie insisted that I bought some condoms so she could swallow some hash to take back to Norwich. I knew that would not be easy. We went into town and it was so hot, I just wanted to sit down and have a drink before going shopping. She started screaming at me to go now. I went into a cafe and she stormed off.

I went to several chemists to ask; I tried calling them condoms, Durex, French letters to no avail. Then a boy of about thirteen approached me and asked if he could help.

How could I explain what I wanted. So I asked for a pharmacy where they spoke English and he took me to one. I asked and the guy at the counter said "Ah, you want rubber Johnnies?". He went to the back of the shop and came back with quite large plain cardboard box which was full of condoms. He asked me "How many". I said "four" and the business was done.

I went back to the houseboat. Lizzie was asleep; I put the condoms in the bedroom cabinet drawer.

Later, when she woke and we were served dinner, she would not speak to me. Mary asked what her problem was and she said because I refused to help her. I said "Your condoms are in the drawer." That seemed to work, but she was still quiet all evening.

24th October

So after a long wait at Srinagar airport, followed by a short flight and taxi ride, we were back in Delhi and at the Himalayan Holidays Office with Farook. He phoned Kuwait Airlines to confirm our flight back to the UK without problems. He then booked us a room for the night.

At 4 AM we took a taxi to Delhi airport.

To be honest I am glad to be home although it was a great holiday and I am already thinking of returning to Kashmir with somebody else. Lizzie was not the ideal travelling companion.

=====================

Heads, Hats and Tall Tales

1985 INDIA, KASHMIR AND NEPAL WITH LESLEY

13 March 1985: Delhi

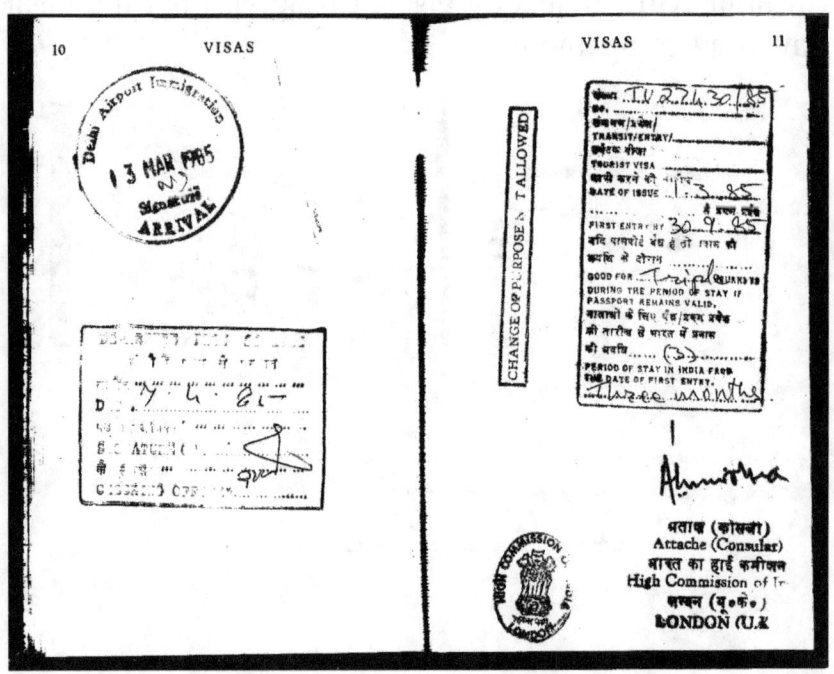

I had only known Lesley for a few months but we got on well. We had already been to London for a couple of days in order to buy our visas from the Indian Embassy, which was remarkably simple but involved staying overnight and going back to the Embassy the following day

DELHI

Lesley and I arrived at Delhi airport just after midnight, after a reasonably comfortable eight-and-three-quarter hour flight from Heathrow with quite good food, free drinks and videos. Naturally we were tired.

A soon as we left the plane the heat hit us like a hair drier, even at midnight. The first thought was to get to the hotel that had been booked for us by Himalayan Holidays rep Ali Baktoo, whom I had met in Kashmir a few years earlier.

But as soon as we left the airport, spotting no taxi available, we were approached by a three-wheeler motor rickshaw, that they called a tuk-tuk and invited to board, "at cheap money", as he said, he had brought somebody to the airport from Delhi and needed a return fare. So in we jumped.

We gave the driver the address of the hotel.

"I am sorry Sir, but last night there was fire at that hotel so it is closed, so I take you to good cheap hotel."

I'd forgotten that tuk-tuk drivers were not bound by any oath to tell the truth. Rather so many were devoted to money, but we already on board so we stayed and said OK.

It took ages to get to Delhi. It was hot and the two of us with and our cases and bags but were pleased to arrive safely. It was Old Delhi and the hotel was called Natraj.

Of course, I would say, they were full so the only room left was in the attic, a small room with one bed, costing just 90 rupees, not a lot; it was clean but stuffy and we struggled to sleep.

In the morning we realised there was no breakfast here so we strolled down the dusty and dirty crowded street to find an eating place which turned out to be right next door, on Chitragupta Road. That sufficed so we quickly went back to Natraj which really should have been called Ratbag, freshened up and took a taxi into New Delhi to meet Ali Baktoo at the Himalayan Holidays office.

Ali asked where we had been as our hotel had phoned him to say that we had not arrived. It had not had a fire after all. I should have known.

So he quickly booked us a room in a much better hotel

and a taxi to Ratbag and back to get our luggage, then he said he would take us to our hotel and talk about our holiday, as we had not arranged anything at all. We had planned on eight to twelve weeks but had no confirmed flight home. So off we went, no problem at all.

After arriving at our hotel near Connaught Circus, we spent a few hours wandering about and eventually back to the office, where Ali said he could book us trips to Agra to see the Taj Mahal, the Fort and Fatepur Sikri. We would go by train and stay a few days. Then we would fly to Khajuraho to see the temples, fly on to Varanassi also called Benares, and back to Delhi. We would also travel to Jaiselmer in Rajasthan and go into the desert on camels, Nepal and Kashmir to stay on a luxury houseboat and go pony trekking. The price would include all transport, hotels and meals.

It was far more than we wanted to pay though, so thus started some hours of bartering, with changes to hotels and we would have to buy our own food except breakfast and on the houseboat and camel and pony trekking trips. We would also have to pay for our hotels in Nepal when we got there.

We settled on £1675 for the two of, not cheap but not bad as it covered eight weeks at least and included several stays in Delhi, plus we would have a few days in Delhi before taking the train to Agra.

That evening we felt honoured to eat dinner near the office, at the Baktoo home with Ali and his brother Yussef; spicy potatoes, rice, dahl, yogurt and Kashmir tea, eaten with our hands. The rice was put on our plates by hand and we took our own dahl and subji (vegetables) which we mixed with the rice with our fingers as did our hosts (right hands only – the left hand is used for unmentionable tasks like washing ones bum). It was quite delicious. We never met the women of the family. This was a Moslem house.

Our new hotel was the Ashok Yatri Niwas, Ashok Road, room 1027. This one we had to pay for, but that had to be in foreign currency or travellers cheques. Of course not as simple as it should have been as they said Lesley's signature did not match the one on the cheque, so next day we had to go to American Express to get cash in pounds.

14th March

We hardly left the hotel as we both felt exhausted. We ate just toast and lassi, the Indian Yoghurt drink for breakfast in the snack cafe downstairs, masala dosa for lunch. The tea was horrible. We strolled up and down Connaught circus, spotted a small restaurant where we would eat that evening, planned the next day and slept soundly.

15th March: **LAL QILA: THE RED FORT**

In the morning we got out before it became unbearably

hot again and took a ride to see The Red Fort, Lal Qila, constructed by the workers of Shah Jahan between 1638 and 1648. It was meant to be the centre of his new capital city but he never completely moved there from Agra because his son, Aurangzeb, deposed him and imprisoned him in Agra Fort. That was said to have been due to Shah Jahan having "wasted" too much money building the Taj Mahal as a mausoleum to his deceased wife and then planning to build a mirror image on the other side of the river.

The Emperor used to ride out of the Red Fort, on elephants, into the streets of Old Delhi (there was no New Delhi then), in a display of pomp and power.

It was beautiful place with incredible architecture, very

peaceful and quiet, especially after the busy, noisy streets of Chandi Chowk.

The Jani Masjid mosque was huge, very crowded and surrounded by stalls, food houses and beggars. It was built 1644 to 1658. Huge wide steps rise to the mosque with four angled towers and two minarets, forty metres high, built from alternating red sandstone and white marble. The Mosque can hold up to 25,000 people. We did not go inside, something to do with Lesley's socks not being allowed!

Then we went to the Mahatma Gandhi museum, filled with newspaper clippings and items from his personal life. That also included one of the three bullets which had killed him and the blood-stained dhoti that he was wearing that day. The "Room of Violence" was quite disturbing, filled with pictures of suffering people. The Museum itself was dedicated to peace and entrance was free.

The Mahatmas ashes are nearby along with those of Nehru and of Indira Gandhi.

We took lunch at a dilapidated restaurant called Nirulas, opposite the museum and then went to the air conditioned underground bazaar just off Janpath, to buy some zips that Lesley wanted and ended up also buying her an outfit ready for Rajasthan.

Heads, Hats and Tall Tales

It was nearby, I think, where we were approached by a group of young women and teenage women, probably about eight of them, all smiling and asking for baksheesh. Sometimes we gave beggars a few small coins but this time not as there were so many. They crowded around us, especially Lesley. I gripped my shoulder bag tightly as we had to push our way through them. Later, Lesley realised that at least one hand had been inside her bag and stolen a small tin of Nivea hand cream and some make-up.

We took a tuk-tuk back to the hotel. On the roads I noticed so many forms of transport in one place: there were tuk-tuks, coaches and larger tuk-tuks, horses with traps, donkeys and men pulling carts, trucks, cars and even an elephant.

That evening we met up with Ali Baktoo again and he gave us our itinerary for the next two months, which we were well satisfied with, except there was not enough time, we felt, in Nepal. So he agreed to extend it to two weeks there and go to Kashmir later.

I ate a decent vegetable Thali downstairs at Hotel Ashok Yatri Newas for fifteen rupees – getting used to the food now. Lesley had Sheesh Kebabs. Slept early that night so we could explore Delhi by ourselves the next day.

16th March

For breakfast I had an India pancake called a Dosa, filled with spicy vegetables and served with dips. Delicious!

That day we ended up spending most of the day inside the hotel as it was so hot outside, going out at 5 PM for a meal at Pot Pourri, Nimla's. I ate pizza and Lesley ate Mutton Tikka, with soda water drinks and banana split. That came to 80 rupees, just over three UK pounds. Afterwards we went to see Ali, drank some rum and played backgammon. I played against Ali and his brother Mohammed called Jimmy, who said he was unbeaten. I beat both of them several times. Ha!

18th March: **AGRA**

We arose at 5 AM to catch the 7.05 AM train, the Taj Express, to Agra, arriving at Agra Cantonment at 10.00 AM. Both stations were, of course, crowded.

As we left Agra Station we were approached by a smiling taxi driver who introduced himself as Maxi and offered to show us around at a "very good price" whilst we were there.

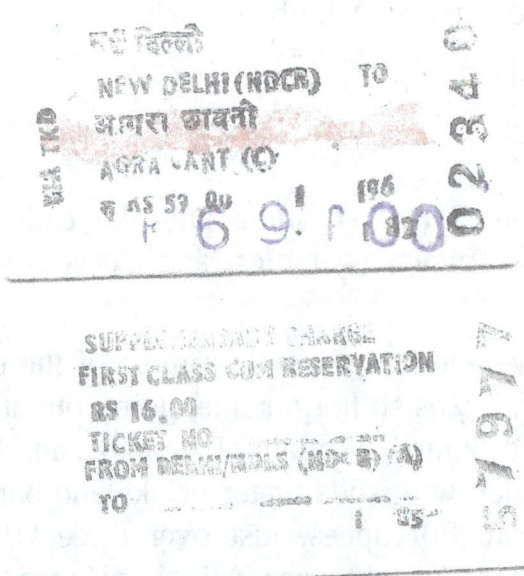

AGRAMAXI

We arrived in Agra and were led to a taxi,
By a smiling Moslem, name of Maxi,
Who took us all the sites to see,
Simple charges, a few rupees
You have to spend in every shop
Within which he took us to stop.

"Come in, sit down, don't walk past

"Look at my stones and see my brass,
"Quality friend you cannot be missing
"Excuse me Sir, I must do some wishing.
"You like some chai, cold drink, coffee?
"No don't talk now of your money!"

"Only to look and not to buy,
"See here it's cheap, and here is why -
"See the craftsmanship is fine,
"And it can be yours if you'll just sign
"The cheque or bill or pay in cash,
But first my friend, just smoke more hash!"

Maxi asked us for just 80 rupees for the whole day visiting the Taj Mahal, Agra Fort, the Mogul Palace. Our itinerary from the Baktoos included a one night stay at Hotel Amir, which looked clean, with a restaurant downstairs, free tea, a carpeted room with a shower and bath. Breakfast included cornflakes, already a treat!

Of course as well as site seeing, Maxi took us to shops, where of course he always earned a good commission despite our haggling. We bought rings, semi-precious gem stones including aquamarine, a marble inlaid table top (which, in 2021, I still have) some silk paintings and soapstone pieces.

I thought that it I could sell them back in the UK it would go some way to paying for the holiday.

Heads, Hats and Tall Tales

AGRA RED FORT was a massive red fort, one third of which was open to the public; the rest was used by the Indian Army. Emperor Akbar started the building in 1565 and it was continued by his grandson, Shah Jahan. The one that built the Taj Mahal and was later overthrown by his own son Aurangzeb (Muhi-ud-Din Muhammad).

Inside the fort there were several palaces and also a beautiful and fine view of the Taj Mahal. The extensive walls were surrounded by two moats, one of which previously had been filled with water and the other with wild animals. One entered through the Amar Singh gate. The other gate, the Delhi gate, was used by the army.

The Moti Masjid, or Pearl Mosque, looked beautiful from the outside but was closed off.

The Hall of Public Audiences had amazing acoustics so

that people even a hundred yards away (modern measurements of course) could hear the Emperor, even if he whispered.

The Hall of Private Audiences had two thrones, one for the Emperor and opposite that, one for his chief councillor. It was here that secret meetings were held under canvas. The Peacock Throne was kept here before it was later carried off to Tehran.

Jahangiri's Palace may be the most noteworthy building inside the Agra Fort. The Mahal was the principal zenana (palace for women belonging to the royal household), and was used mainly by the Rajput wives of Akbar. It was a form of Islamic architecture. The palace was built by Akbar. It was one of the earliest surviving buildings of Akbar's reign. Jahangir in his memoirs stated that the buildings were erected by his father Akbar but did not take any credit for the construction of Jahangiri palace. Mahal Mughal Empress Nur Jahan used this magnificent palace as her residence until her death on 17 December 1645. There was a huge bowl called Hauz-i-Jahangiri that was carved out of a single piece of stone. This was used as a container for fragrant rose water.

The Shish Mahal or Mirror Palace was once full of tiny mirrors and used by concubines.

The beautiful Grape Gardens (Anguri Bagh) probably never had grapes! Built by Shah Jehan in 1637, with Khas Mahal to its east and red sandstone arcades on the other three sides, it was the principal square of the zenana apartments or the living area of the royal ladies. There was a marble paved platform with a fountain in its centre and the garden itself was divided into compartments in intricate geometrical pattern.

In front of the Jahangiri's Palace, there was a huge bath, about 5 feet deep, carved out of a single piece of stone. Underneath was a cool room used in summertime, and above it was a white marble palace. When the Emperor Jahan's wife died and she was buried at the Taj Mahal, it was closed up so nobody could see the detail and care taken in building this masterpiece.

Inlaid marble table top

One entered the grounds through a sandstone arch inscribed from the Koran. A watercourse runs from there through the gardens to the Taj Mahal.

Heads, Hats and Tall Tales

The shops of Agra offered a variety of fine crafted goods. The marble shop had table tops of marble inlaid with slivers of semi precious stones, boxes, table mats, lamp stands, chess boards and much more. Some of the work was very detailed. The patterns were drawn on the marble and the shapes cut out and filled. Much of the work was done by children. The gem shop contained many precious and semi precious stones, with Star of India, Black Stars, Lapis Lazuli, Aquamarine and Tigers Eye, of fine, medium and poor quality, sold at rupees per carat. They would place a stone in a ring or almost anywhere else you want it. For a price! They also sold silk paintings, inlaid bags and belts and small items. There was also a sitar shop with beer, charas and music. Small sitars were from £35 to £50, larger single drum £100 to £200, and a beautiful double drum for £400. They said sitar was easy to learn how to play. The bulbous part was made from pumpkin.

The beautiful copper and white brass pot is 21 inches tall

The brass shop was piled high with lots of shelves with many brass items. The most impressive were the copper and white brass coffee pots in various sizes, many inlaid with semi precious stones. I bought one lovely piece about fifteen inches tall, with a decorated handle and dragon-like headed spout. I still have it to this day. It was to be shipped back to the UK along with the many other items that I bought with the intention of selling. These included many wind chimes of small brass bells with shapes of animals or birds or letters spelling out words such as LOVE and PEACE. They were sold by the weight. Also several beautiful enamelled brass vases and lamp stands, a wine set consisting of a tray, decanter and goblets, various ashtrays shaped like playing cards, hearts, diamonds, clubs and spades, brass lighter covers and several coloured enamelled brass bowls of different sizes.

Heads, Hats and Tall Tales

That evening we ate at Zorba the Buddha: clean with a good selection of vegetarian food. It was run by Sanyasi. The Sanyassen were dressed in orange it was an unusual modern cult of devotees that had relinquished their possessions but did not seem limited to any particular lifestyle or ritual either. Still, they seemed happy so good luck to them. I had met some back in Norwich. Most of them smoked chillums of hash..

19th March: **THE TAJ MAHAL**

I had been in Agra in 1972 and visited the Taj Mahal and Fatepur Sikri, both wonderful. At that time, I had stayed in Government Rest House on the outskirts of Agra and got around by bicycle rickshaw and buses. Fatepur Sikri was where we were heading, by taxi with Maxi.

There were four obvious differences between 1972 and now, 1985. The streets were more crowded with local people, rickshaws and much more motorised traffic and correspondingly noisier and dustier. There were far more tourists and hasslers. There was more electricity and more telephones. Everyone seemed much more in a rush.

We made quite an early start. Maxi was waiting for us outside our hotel. I was beginning to wonder whether he was simply a profiteering but friendly taxi driver or some sort of Government employee to keep a watchful and caring eye over us. We soon arrived at the Taj.

Heads, Hats and Tall Tales

This was from a guide book:

"The Taj Mahal or Crown of the Palace was built from white marble and was on the southern bank of the river Yamuna. It was considered to be one of the most beautiful buildings in the world. It was commissioned in 1632 by the Mughal emperor Shah Jahan (reigned from 1628 to 1658) to house the tomb of his favourite wife, Mumtaz Mahal who died on 17 June 1631 while giving birth to their 14th child, Gauhara Begum; it also houses the tomb of Shah Jahan himself. The tomb was the centrepiece of a 17-hectare (42-acre) complex, which includes a mosque and a guest house, and was set in formal gardens bounded on three sides by a defensive battlement.

"The tomb was the central focus of the entire complex of the Taj Mahal. It was a large, white marble structure standing on a square plinth and consists of a symmetrical building with an iwan (an arch-shaped doorway) topped by a large dome. Like most Mughal tombs, the basic elements are Persian in origin. The base structure was a large multi-chambered cube with bevelled corners forming an unequal eight-sided structure that was approximately 180 feet on each of the four long sides.

"The most spectacular feature was the marble dome that surmounts the tomb. The dome was nearly 115 feet high which was close in measurement to the length of the base, and accentuated by the cylindrical "drum" it sits on, which was approximately 23 feet high. Because of its shape, the dome was often called an onion dome or amrud (guava dome). The top was decorated with a

lotus design which also serves to accentuate its height. The shape of the dome was emphasised by four smaller domed kiosks placed at its corners, which replicate the onion shape of the main dome. The dome was slightly asymmetrical. It's columned bases open through the roof of the tomb and provide light to the interior. Tall decorative spires extend from edges of base walls, and provide visual emphasis to the height of the dome.

"*The main finial section of the roof was originally made of gold but was replaced by a copy made of gilded bronze in the early 19th century. This feature was a clear example of integration of traditional Persian and Hindu decorative elements. The finial was topped by a moon, a typical Islamic motif whose horns point heavenward.*

"*The minarets, which are each more than 130 feet tall, display the designer's penchant for symmetry. They were designed as working minarets, a traditional element of mosques, used by the muezzin to call the Islamic faithful to prayer. Each minaret was effectively divided into three equal parts by two working balconies that ring the tower. At the top of the tower was a final balcony surmounted by a chattri that mirrors the design of those on the tomb. The chattris all share the same decorative elements of a lotus design topped by a gilded finial. The minarets were constructed slightly outside of the plinth so that in the event of collapse, a typical occurrence with many tall constructions of the period, the material from the towers would tend to fall away from the tomb.*

"The exterior decorations of the Taj Mahal are among the finest in Mughal architecture. As the surface area changes, the decorations are refined proportionally. The decorative elements were created by applying paint, stucco, stone inlays or carvings. In line with the Islamic prohibition against the use of anthropomorphic forms, the decorative elements can be grouped into either calligraphy, abstract forms or vegetative motifs. Throughout the complex are passages from the Koran that comprise some of the decorative elements.

"The calligraphy on the Great Gate reads "O Soul, thou art at rest. Return to the Lord at peace with Him, and He at peace with you." The calligraphy was created in 1609 by a calligrapher named Abdul Haq. Shah Jahan conferred the title of "Amanat Khan" upon him as a reward for his "dazzling virtuosity." Near the lines from the Qur'an at the base of the interior dome was the inscription, "Written by the insignificant being, Amanat Khan Shirazi." Higher panels are written in slightly larger script to reduce the skewing effect when viewed from below.

"The interior chamber of the Taj Mahal reaches far beyond traditional decorative elements. The inlay work was a lapidary of precious and semiprecious gemstones. The inner chamber was an octagon with the design allowing for entry from each face, although only the door facing the garden to the south was used. The interior walls are about 82 feet high and are topped by a "false" interior dome decorated with a sun motif. The four central upper arches form balconies or viewing areas, and each balcony's exterior window had an intricate screen cut from marble. In addition to the light from the balcony screens, light enters through roof openings covered by chattris at the corners. The octagonal marble screen bordering the cenotaphs was made from eight marble panels carved through with intricate pierce work. The remaining surfaces are inlaid in delicate detail with semi-precious stones forming twining vines, fruits and flowers. Each chamber wall was highly decorated with dado bas-relief, intricate lapidary inlay and refined calligraphy panels which reflect, in little detail, the design elements seen throughout the exterior of the complex.

"Muslim tradition forbids elaborate decoration of graves. Hence, the bodies of Mumtaz and Shah Jahan were put in a relatively plain crypt beneath the inner chamber with their faces turned right, towards Mecca. Mumtaz Mahal's cenotaph was placed at the precise centre of the inner chamber on a rectangular marble base.

"The complex is set around a large square garden that uses raised pathways that divide each of the four-quarters of the garden into 16 sunken flowerbeds. Halfway between the tomb and gateway in the centre of the garden was a raised marble water tank with a reflecting pool positioned on a north-south axis to reflect the image of the mausoleum. The elevated marble water tank was called al Hawd al-Kawthar in reference to the "Tank of Abundance" promised to Mohammed."

That reflection was really beautiful. From the far end there were always people taking photographs.

When we left the Taj, Maxi was waiting for us with two cups of tea, some small cakes and a bottle of water. He seemed anxious to take us to our next stop, Fatepur Sikri, about 20 miles and over an hour away.

FATEPUR SIKRI

Fatepur Sikri, which as I said I had also visited in 1972, this time had other tourists strolling around on the various levels. It may not have been as immediately visually impressive as the Taj but was a fascinating place to see.

"The city itself was founded as the capital of Mughal Empire in 1571 by Akbar, serving this role from 1571 to 1585, when Akbar abandoned it due to a campaign in

the Punjab and was later completely abandoned in 1610 due partly to a shortage of good water.

"It's a massive complex on several levels surrounded by a five mile wall on three sides and a lake on the other. Entrance was through a series of gates, namely, Delhi Gate, the Lal Gate, the Agra Gate and Birbal's Gate, Chandanpal Gate, The Gwalior Gate, the Tehran Gate, the Chor Gate, and the Ajmeri Gate."

It was quite confusing inside, up and down the various levels, so we did not get to see it all, with no guide.

Heads, Hats and Tall Tales

"The emperor Akbar tried to start a new religion here, called Deen Illahi, a synthesis of several religions of that time.

"Inside the walled area, are palaces such as Jodh Bai, used by Akbar. The court ladies used to sit here watching the goings on below Bhirbal Bhavan.

Some of the important buildings in this city, both religious and secular are: "Buland Daewaz: Set into the south wall of congregational mosque, the Buland Darwaza at Fatehpur Sikri was 180 feet high, from the ground, gradually making a transition to a human scale in the inside. The gate was added around five years after the completion of the mosque to commemorate Akbar's successful Gujarat campaign.

Fatepur Sikri, India

It carries two inscriptions in the archway, one of which reads: "Isa, Son of Mariam said: The world is a bridge, pass over it, but build no houses on it. He who hopes for an hour may hope for eternity. The world endures but an hour. Spend it in prayer, for the rest is unseen".

"The central portico comprises three arched entrances, with the largest one, in the centre, was known locally as the Horseshoe Gate, after the custom of nailing horseshoes to its large wooden doors for luck. Outside the giant steps of the Buland Darwaza to the left was a deep well.

"Jama Masjod was a Jama Mosque meaning the congregational mosque and was perhaps one of the first buildings to be constructed in the complex, with a massive entrance to the courtyard, the Buland-Darwaza added some five years later. It was built in the manner of Indian mosques around a central courtyard.

"A distinguishing feature was the row of chhari over the sanctuary. Chhatri are elevated, dome-shaped pavilions *used as an element in Indian architecture. The word literally means "canopy" or "umbrella." There were three mihrabs, raised platforms, in each of the seven bays, while the large central mihrab was covered by a dome and it was decorated with white marble inlay of geometric patterns.*

"The Tomb of Salim Chishti was a white marble encased tomb of the Sufi<u>i</u> (1478–1572), within the Jama Masjid's courtyard. The single-storey structure was built around a central square chamber, within which was the grave of the saint, under an ornate wooden canopy encrusted with mother-of-pearl mosaic. Surrounding it was a covered passageway for walking round in a circle with carved stone pierced screens all around with intricate geometric design and an entrance to the south.

"On the left of the tomb, to the east, stands a red sandstone tomb of Islam Khan, son of Shaikh Badruddin Chisti and grandson of Shaikh Salim Chishti, who became a general in the Mughal army in the reign of Jahangir. The tomb was topped by a dome and thirty-six small domed Chattris and contained a number of graves, some unnamed, that were all male descendants of Shaikh Salim Chishti.

"Diwan-i-Aam or Hall of Public Audience, was a building typology found in many cities where the ruler meets the general public. In this case, it was a pavilion-like multi-bayed rectangular structure fronting a large open space. South west of the Diwan-i-Am and next to the Turkic Sultana's House stand Turkic Baths.

"Diwan-i-Khas or Hall of Private Audience, was a plain square building with four chattris on the roof. However it was famous for its central pillar, which had a square base and an octagonal shaft, both carved with bands of geometric and floral designs, further its thirty-six serpentine brackets support a circular platform for Akbar, which was connected to each corner of the building on the first floor, by four stone walkways. It was here that Akbar had representatives of different religions discuss their faiths and gave private audience.

"Ilbadaht Khana or House of Worship was a meeting house built in 1575 CE by the Mughal Emperor Akbar.

"Anup Talao: Anup Talao was built by Raja Anup Singh Sikarwar, an ornamental pool with a central platform and four bridges leading up to it. Some of the important *buildings of the royal enclave are surround by it including, Khwabgah (House of Dreams) Akbar's residence, Panch Mahal, a five-storey palace, Diwan-i-Khas (Hall of Private Audience), Ankh Michauli and the Astrologer's Seat, in the south-west corner of the Pachisi Court.*

"Hujra-i-Anup Talao: It was said to be the residence of Akbar's Muslim wife, although this was disputed due to its small size.

"Mariam-uz-Zamani's Palace was the building of Akbar's Rajput wives, was built around a courtyard, with special care being taken to ensure privacy.

"Naubat Khana, also known as Naggar Khana, meaning a drum house, where musician used drums to announce the arrival of the Emperor. It was situated ahead of the Hathi Pol Gate or the Elephant Gate, the south entrance to the complex, suggesting that it was the imperial entrance.

"The Pachisi Court was a square marked out as a large board game, the precursor to modern day Ludo game where people served as the playing pieces.

"Panch Mahal was a five-storied palatial structure, with the tiers gradually diminishing in size, till the final one, which was a single large-domed Chattri. Originally pierced stone screens faced the facade and probably sub-divided the interior as well, suggesting it was built for the ladies of the court. The floors are supported by intricately carved columns on each level, totalling to 176 columns in all.

"Birbal's House, the house of Akbar's favourite minister, who was a Hindu. Notable features of the building are the horizontal sloping sunshades and the brackets which support them.

"The impressive Hiran Minar, or Elephant Tower, was a circular tower covered with stone projections in the form of elephant tusks. Traditionally it was thought to have been erected as a memorial to the Emperor Akbar's favourite elephant. However, it was probably a used as a starting point for subsequent mileposts.

"Other buildings included Taksal (mint), Daftar Khana (Records Office), Karkhana (Royal Workshop), Khazana Treasury), Hammam (Turkic Baths), Darogha's quarters, stables, caravanserai and such."

Whilst we were there we were approached by a family of about 15 who insisted on having a photograph with me, which Lesley took. Not all of them wanted to be in it, but it's a great pic that I still have and I promised to send a copy which I did when we got back to Norwich and had the films developed. There were no digital cameras in 1985.

Well that was a whole lot to remember so I copied the information from the pamphlets.

Heads, Hats and Tall Tales

Heads, Hats and Tall Tales

20th March: **KHAJURAHO**

After a whole day of sightseeing, we were of course well worn out, but nevertheless we were up and on our way to Agra airport and there by 7 AM. After about an hour of hassling, our seats were finally confirmed and we boarded the 737 for Khajuraho, a flight of just 40 minutes. We took a taxi to our five star hotel, which had a large double room with hot and cold water. We rested a while then had lunch of vegetable curry, dahl, rice and chapati with lassi drink and chai, for me and mutton biriani for Lesley. Then we walked across the road to see the Western group of temples.

Those temples were built in the tenth century and mostly in good condition with thousands of small statues. Some were damaged with bits that were missing because they had been cut off and sold. Most were built between the tenth and twelfth centuries. Exactly why they were built here, nobody knows. The remoteness and isolation of Khajuraho probably helped preserve them.

The site seemed remarkably quiet and peaceful after the hustles and bustles of Delhi and Agra. We both loved it there and there were no hustlers at all.

Each temple had a three or five part plan. One enters a temple through a porch behind which was a hall which leads to the main hall. It was supported by columns. A vestibule leads to the inner sanctum or garbhagriha.

Outside each temple was layered with statues of people

in various poses, many explicitly sexual, fighting, hunting, processions, an orgy scene and more, even a man having sex with a horse, going up to higher towers that top the inner sanctums.

The entrances face east so they catch the light inside.

The blocks were carved together with no use of mortar and made from sandstone carried from about 20 miles away.

"The Lakshmana Temple, built 930 to 950 AD, was dedicated to Vaikuntha Vishnu, an aspect of the god Vishnu. It is the best preserved of the temples in this complex. "The wall portion was studded with balconied windows with ornate balustrades. It had two rows of sculptures (refer images of temple's outer wall) including divine figures, couples and erotic scenes. The sanctum doorway is of seven sakhas (vertical panels). The central one being decorated with the ten incarnations of Vishnu. The Lintel depicts goddess Lakshmi in the centre flanked by the gods Brahma and Vishnu. The sanctum contains four-armed sculpture of Vishnu. One of the niches had the image of the sculptor and his disciples at work. The Main image is of tri-headed and four-armed sculpture of Vaikuntha Vishnu, The central head represented a human and two sides of boar.

"Behind the temples is a beautiful flowered garden, quiet and serene with the temples built on one base. The largest and most ornate is the Kandariya Mahadeu, built 1025 to 1050 AD, 100 feet high with 226 statues inside and 646 statues outside, mostly about three feet in height."

An incredible amount of work and admirable skills. They are in three bands, goddesses, women and erotic scenes. Some of the positions depicted would surely win prizes in the sex Olympics.

"In the interior space from the entrance there are three mandapas or halls, which successively rise in height and width, which was inclusive of a small chamber

dedicated to Shiva, a chamber where the Shiva linga, the phallic emblem of Shiva was deified. The sanctum was surrounded by interlinked passages which also have side and front balconies. Due to inadequate natural light in the balconies the sanctum had very little light thus creating a "cave like atmosphere" which was in total contrast to the external parts of the temple. Women walk round that and sit on it and say a prayer for pregnancy. In the interior halls of the temple and on its exterior faces there are elaborately carved sculptures of gods and goddesses, musicians and nymphs. The huge pillars of the halls have architectural features of the "vine or scroll motif". In the corners of the halls there are insets which are carved on the surface with incised patterns. There was a main tower above the sanctum and there are two other towers above the other mantapas also in the shape of "semi-rounded, stepped, pyramidal form with progressively greater height".

Heads, Hats and Tall Tales

The main tower was encircled by a series of interlinked towers and spires of smaller size. These are in the form of a repeated subset of miniature spires that abut a central core which gives the temple an unevenly cut contour similar to the shape of a mountain range of mount Kailasa where the god Shiva resides, which was appropriate to the theme of the temples here.

"The exterior surfaces of the temples are entirely covered with sculptures in three vertical layers. Here, there are horizontal ribbons carved with images, which shine bright in the sun light, providing rhythmic architectural features. Among the images of gods and heavenly beings, Agri, the god of fire was prominent. They are niches where erotic sculptures are fitted all round which are a major attraction among visitors. Some of these erotic sculptures are very finely carved and are in mithuna (coitus) postures with maidens flanking the couple, which was a frequently noted motif. There was also a "male figure suspended upside" in coitus posture, a kind of yogic pose, down on his head. The seven fearful protector goddesses include: Brahmi seated on a swan of Brahma ; Maheshwari with three eyes seated on Shiva's bull, Nandi; Kumari; Vaishnavi mounted on Garuda, the boar-headed Varahi, Narasimhi; the lion-headed and Chamunda, the slayer of demons Chanda and Munda. The image of Sardula, a mythical creature with lion face and human limbs in lower panel was a unique figure seen in the temple.

"Next to this temple is Mahadeva temple which was largely defaced, and the smaller Jagadamba. They were

originally dedicated to Vishnu, but now to Kali or Parvati. Inside was the blackened female goddess.

"Nearby is the Chitagupta temple, lighter in colour, dedicated to Surya, the Sun God. Here we saw statues of dancing girls, processions and elephant fighting. In the southern wall was a statue of the eleven-headed Vishnu. Inside was Surya with his seven-headed horse.

"The Parvati Temple is in front of the others and mainly ruined. It was dedicated to Vishnu and had sculptures of Ganga, the river god, riding a crocodile, and Yamuna, a river god, riding a turtle.

"The Vishnu and Nandi Temple was built about 1000 AD. A five part design with a statue of Shiva's bull, Nandi facing it outside. There are high steps flanked by lions and elephant statues. Also we see sculptures of a woman holding a baby, another combing her hair, another putting on makeup with a mirror and some in Playboy-like poses."

We visited the nearby museum which contains fine images of gods, Vishnu, Buddha and an elephant god with six arms.

That was enough for us. There are two other groups of temples which we did not see,

21st March

That day we were supposed to take a flight to Varanasi.

We got up at 7 AM and took a taxi to the airport.

Guess what! The plane was full! So back we went to the Indian Airways office at the Hotel Temple and plan to give it another try tomorrow after being promised seats, that we had paid for. We were on a waiting list. "No problem Sir, see you later! God wants you to stay!"

We were a bit pissed off but will get to see more sites.

This was when we met Rameshwar, supposedly an official government guide, who wanted to stick to us like glue as if keeping an eye on us. We spent most of the day with him.

22nd March

Again no seats on the plane, so we had to stay another night, this time at the house of Rameshwar and his family: wife and children, mother and elder brother.

First we went going with him to see the Jain Temples.

"Two of the large temples still stand in a good state of preservation in the original form. The portico of the Adinath temple was a later addition. The enclosed Shantinath temple, just 100 years old. It houses a massive monolithic Shantinath image. It also incorporates at least one other Chandella period temple."

I smoked a chillum with a monk at one of the Jain temples, very little tobacco, from a roasted cigarette then moistened with dew from a plant nearby and rubbed in his hand. It was a hot, dry smoke but very effective. Nice!

It was an extremely and uncomfortably hot day. Rameshwar kept wanting to take us one at time on the back of his scooter, trying to split us up. Obviously I was not at all happy about this.

He persuaded Lesley to go first to see a waterfall, despite my warnings. He was supposed to come back to get me within 30 minutes but time was passing and it was well over an hour and no sign of them. I was glad I got him to write his name and address in my notebook. It's worrying but what could I do? I couldn't really call police or anybody at this stage, it would end out being a problem either way. I was sure that I would have to pay. So it was a matter of lazing around, waiting.

The creep brought Lesley back a few hours later. She said the waterfall was dried up so had taken her to a lake. She had no idea where she was. Later she told me he tried to kiss her and threatened to throw himself into the lake. Shame he didn't, but no harm done.

That evening Rameshwar wanted us to go to another lake. He said would we go for a walk with his children but when I said OK he said I would walk with them and he would take Lesley and unbelievably she said yes. I said no, we all go together, so he promised to take her and come back in ten minutes. He said he would take us to see his "other Babu", whatever that means. Then we were all going together. The journey took about fifteen minutes, so there was no way he could have come back in ten.

We went to a small cinema that was packed, showing a film in Hindi, just local people. Before I even knew it, Lesley was gone again. So I went outside to look for her. I did not find her at that time though. Rameshwar had said that he would take her first and come back in ten minutes. I said "no chance", so we all went together, walking; it was not very far. It was just dimly lit back streets in a village. Actually it was a waste of time, just a house with young women and a few guys. I wonder if it was a brothel.

We were soon back at Rameshwar's house where we met his family.

There was a strange vibe from the elderly mother. I found out that she was upset because Lesley had not touched her feet. Lesley said she would not do that but I persuaded her that it was a custom and sign of respect, so she did. Remeshwar's brother went to change his shirt, so we could take photos; "but no touching", he said.

Rameshwar offered us a separate bedroom with a small bed; I slept on the floor. I put a chair up against the door in case anyone tries to come in during the night. Lesley said not to do that as they will feel insulted. I said that they would not know unless they tried the door.

Sure enough, early morning, somebody tried to come in.

23rd March:

VARANASI / BENARES AND SARNATH

A while later when we were up and dressed, Rameshwar said his wife asked did we fuck on the bed!

So back to the airport again, hoping for a flight – third time lucky?

Varanasi was 88 degree Fahrenheit, that's 31 degree centigrade but it felt even hotter as we left the airport just before noon. We took a taxi into town to our hotel and ended up booking some tours to see temples.

Sanarth, about six miles away, was lovely, calm and peaceful. It was said that the actual Buddha came here to preach, in what was now a deer park. It was close to where the river Ganges and the river Varuna meet.

"Sarnath had been variously known as Mrigadava, Migadāya, Rishipattana and Isipatana throughout its long history. Mrigadava means "deer-park". "Isipatana" was the name used in the Pali Canon, collection of scriptures in the Theraveda Buddhist tradition and means the place where holy men landed.

"The legend says that when the Buddha-to-be was born, some devas (heavenly beings) came down to announce it to 500 rishis. Another explanation for the name was that Isipatana was so-called because, sages, on their way through the air (from the Himalayas), alight here or start from here on their aerial flight.

"Before Gautama (the Buddha-to-be) attained enlightenment, he gave up his austere penances and his friends, the Pañcavaggiya monks. Seven weeks after his enlightenment under the Bodhi tree in Bodhi Gaya, Buddha left Umvela and travelled to Isipatana to rejoin them because, using his spiritual powers, he had seen that his five former companions would be able to understand Dharma quickly. While travelling to Sarnath, Gautama Buddha had no money to pay the ferryman to cross the Ganges, so he crossed it through the air.

"Ashok, a Buddhist emperor, erected monuments and stupas there.

"Sarnath was once populated by 1500 priests and monks and the main stupa was 328 feet high. A stupa ("stupa" was Sanskrit for heap) was an important form of Buddhist architecture, though it predates Buddhism. It was generally considered to be a place of burial or a receptacle for religious objects. At its simplest, a stupa was a dirt burial mound faced with stone."

"The Dhamekh Stupa was about 500 AD, said to be on top of a previous construction. It had geometrical floral patterns.

"In front of the main shrine stands the Ashoki Pillar which once stood about 60 feet high and had four faces of lions. It was a museum. There are four creatures: the lion representing bravery, an elephant symbolising Buddha's mother's dream, a horse representing Buddha's journey from home on horseback and a bull.

"The Dhamek Stupa is an impressive structure, 128 feet high and 93 feet in diameter.

"The Chaukhandi Stupa commemorates the spot where the Buddha met his first disciples, dating back to the fifth century or earlier and later enhanced by the addition of an octagonal tower of Islamic origin."

There was also a Bodhi tree planted by said to have been grown from a cutting of the Bodhi Tree at Bodh Gaya.

Also there was the Maha Bodhi Society Temple containing Japanese frescoes of Buddha's life.

It was certainly tranquil on the site and we spent some time just sitting in the shade of a tree.

Now we were back in town with its crowded streets of dustiness and noise, and off to see the Durga Temple and the Monkey Temple where monkeys hang out. Durga is the goddess of power and a terrifying form of Shiva's consort Parvati. "You can look inside but you cannot go in", we were told. So we took a peep. Outside was a pool of very smelly water where pilgrims wash! Also goats were sacrificed here at festivals. We were told that years ago children were also sacrificed here. Hinduism is not at all like Buddhism. I much prefer Buddhism, devoid of gods and bloody sacrificial rituals.

The new Vishwaneth Temple was however open to visitors. It was a replica of the original temple. Inside was a Shiva lingam. Women wanting pregnancy were supposed to strip and sit astride the lingam several times, praying for a baby. I don't know if that worked but pretty sure they would also need a man.

"The Bharat Mata Mandir, or Mother India Temple, was erected by Mahatma Gandi. Anyone can enter and inside was a map of India and the Himalayas, Bay of Bengal and Shri Lnka (also known as Ceylon). You can go down some steps and view it from there."

To be honest, we were both getting fed up being led around by guides or government spies or whatever they are, even though it helped to have somebody explain things to us. That day we were thankful that the guide just said goodbye but often we ended up drinking chai or lemonade in a shop. The shop staff were very good at getting sales when we had no intention or buying anything to start with. They were very polite and jolly, taking time to carefully show each piece as if it were a treasure, then asking which we like best. Then the inevitable bartering. One had to be careful not to buy stuff that we would not have room in our luggage to take home. But the quality of the goods was also excellent and prices cheap.

On the way back to the hotel we spotted several Naga (naked Sadhu) strolling down the street. Meanwhile, even being clothed, we were both suffering from mosquito bites. Lesley had reacted badly to them and was scratching.

24th March.

TRYING TO FLY AND WONDERING WHY

Varanasi airport is quite a dump.
It's run by a man who is quite a chump.
Now we cannot board the plane.
Later we will miss our train.
Money flowing down the drain,
India Airways fucked my brain.
Seems the way here is to cheat,
So the system you can beat,
Just don't let them squash your feet,
Push for schedules try to keep.
"Baksheesh - don't say that word here sir,
We're all paid well by Indian Air "
And "you don't know the system here."

Well I think it fucking weird!

In India, it's different, so we're told,

Totally corrupt since times of old.

No problem sir, your seats we've sold,

Paid in Karma but now with gold.

We were supposed to be flying back to Delhi this day, to catch a train. That didn't happen. So we flew back another day late

25th March:

BACK TO DELHI, VISITING THE ZOO

Back in Delhi a day late so we had missed our train to Rajasthan. Ali Baktoo tried to get us a flight, to no avail, so we would go by train later.

In the meantime, we made a visit to Delhi Zoo.

The zoo contained a wide variety of birds, buffalo, deer and donkeys. There was also an elephant house where we had a private visit. Lesley was pleased to pat and befriend an elephant. He probably remembers Lesley until this day.

Then we went to Connaught Circus where Lesley had her shoes re-heeled, and then a nearby park where I reluctantly surrendered to a massage.

All of a sudden that evening, we found ourselves rushing to Old Delhi railway station where we picked up tickets and squashed into a second class department.

The carriage compartment was meant for eight but there were twelve of us trying to sit down.

As this was an overnight train, we wondered how we would ever sleep. But later a guard came along and got some people to leave and we climbed up the three tiers to our uncomfortable beds.

Heads, Hats and Tall Tales

We arrived in Jodhpur at 11.30 AM and catch another train to Jaiselmer.

26th March **JODHPUR**

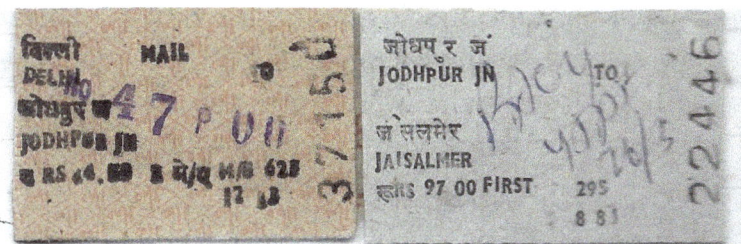

Breakfast on the train consisted of two vegetable cutlets, toast and tea or coffee. It was jerky ride, constantly stopping and starting, probably due to cows on the line. Cows are considered very Holy in India and a train killing or harming one would be regarded very seriously.

Outside the window we could see the countryside was becoming more and more parched, with just a few trees and camels, a few goats and chickens here and there near small settlements and villages.

Lesley was now covered with mosquito bites which she had scratched raw, so her arms were covered with red blotches and people were noticeably keeping their distance!

When we arrived in Jodhpur it was incredibly hot, far too hot to go site seeing to the famous fort.

First we had to get a new ticket to Jaiselmer as the other one was for yesterday and then discovered we could only get a refund back in Delhi (thanks Ali) We managed to get first class.

We spent some time that afternoon wandering the streets and Lesley went off to buy me some Indian white cotton pyjamas. I had a delicious thick lime lassi drink in the Agra Sweet Home opposite the Sojati Gate. Inside the gate there were long, winding streets full of small shops, rows selling cloths and clothes, rows selling clocks.

Jodpur Station, India

27th March: **JAISELMER**

The night train to Jaiselmer arrived at 7.30 AM. It was already quite hot but bearable. However by the time we had taken chai, all the taxis were gone, so we had to phone the manager at out Hotel Fort View and he sent a taxi to pick us up.

The hotel was superb, with a very friendly and helpful manager and, best of all, an incredible view of the beautiful town and fort. Although the rooms were basic, with twin beds and shower downstairs, it feels good here. He explained the best times to see the sites and told us all about our three day camel trek in the desert. He confirmed our tickets back to Delhi on 2nd April.

By 10.30 it was much hotter so we decided to hang out in and near the hotel and take a stroll later. So far Jaiselmer looked like a dream or something from Arabian Nights. The fort was quite magnificent, built in 1156 by Rawal Jaisal on top the 260 feet Trikuta Hill. About a quarter of the population lived within it. Also within was a seven storey palace.

Jaiselmer was once an important stopping place for rich

merchants travelling from Karachi and then here by camel and on to Delhi and all over India until the port of Bombay opened up. The population at that time was 20,000. Jodhpur had 400,000 people living there.

There were many shops selling, amongst other things, silk paintings and dresses which I knew I could sell easily back home, so a visit to some was on the itinerary, but not that day. I did buy a long piece of bright yellow cotton to wrap round my head for when we did our safari. We also bought light clothing for the days, warmer for the evenings, water bottles and plenty of purification pills and my camera. When we left we would be travelling with a camel riding boy, a guide and a cook. They will provide our meals and comforts and we would sleep under the stars.

WE PROVIDE

SIGHT SEEING & SAND DUNES
TAXI-TOURS

1. 9 am to 2 pm : All Important Places, Sand Dunes & Big Villages
   Rs. 30/- per person
2. 3 pm to 7-30 pm : 5 Places Including big Sand Dunes return after Sunset
   Rs. 20/- per person
3. Special : Wood Fossil Park & 3 Important places
   Rs. 30/- per person
   (Subject to minimum number)
Visit us; See map & other informations

TO MAKE YOUR VISIT FULLY ENJOYABLE

HAVE ALL SORTS OF

TOURIST INFORMATION

AT

HOTEL FORT—VIEW

OR

 214

Central Market, Square
JAISALMER

28th March: **CAMEL RIDES**

Up and ready to go at 6AM, whilst it was still comparatively cool. My breakfast was cornflakes Indian style, toast and chai. There were lots of pigeons and other birds about.

Sitting on the camel was a lot more comfortable than I thought, on straw-filled cushions. The camels are strange, the way they tuck their hind legs under, which does not look at all comfortable. Then we climbed a short ladder and perched ourselves on the bags, one camel for me and one for Lesley. As they stand up we were jostled back and forth, as they had two knees on their front legs and go up one at a time. They moaned and groaned but off we went.

We saw some succulent bushes, some flowering cacti and lots of sand and stones.

Our "camel boy" was named Salima, a jolly teenager.

We soon stopped at a place that, from a distance, looked like a palace, but close up we could see it was mausoleum, tombs of the family of a Maharaja.

Soon we stopped again at a water hole for lunch, chapati, vegetable subji, oranges and coffee in the shade of a tree, with those ultra-cheap tiny bidi cigarettes to smoke. Bidis are small hand-rolled tobacco in tendu or temburni leaf, an Indian plant. This place was called Barabagh.

Later as we continued into the desert, we came upon the ancient capital of Lodhruva, with a Jain Temple and a black-faced god with wings and large eyes, that had been rebuilt in the 1970's. There was a lot of camel and cow shit in the desert.

RAJASTHAN DESERT SONG

Lesley and I went down to Rajasthan
Desert, with Salima, a camel riding man.
Through a morning trotting on,
Just the sound of Salima's songs.
Peahens, crows and tinkle bells,
Crowds of men at water wells,
Telling tales of who-knows-what
While we're wishing it not so hot.
Stop for lunch, a shady tree,
Eat some vegetable chapati,
Drinking some chai, hot and sweet
Try to avoid the deadly heat.
All around us golden sand,
Shrubs and cacti about this land.
"Be careful please, where you sit,
"Cos desert's full of camel shit."

At about 6.30, we stopped for the evening for dinner at another water hole. Suddenly a wind came up, with moisture in it so we thought it was going to rain. But it didn't rain at all. We slept under a tree. I awoke during the night and wow, what a clear starry sky!

29th March

Up, breakfast and ready to go at some unearthly hour but it was overcast and cooler until about 10.30. We passed several small villages but saw no activity. There were wild camels in the distance. Our camels seemed to fart a lot.

When it became hotter, we stopped at the Sam sand dunes at a water hole for lunch. Salima invited me to follow him for a "very good site". I imagined a fantastic view over a valley with the walled city of Jaiselmer or somewhere equally exotic in the distance, as we winded in and out between the dunes. Suddenly, he stopped.

"Look," he smiled and smirked.

As I looked around, all I could see was sand. Not even my own footprints. I realised quickly that I was at his mercy. If he ran off I would maybe not find my way back. All I would be able to do was shout and hope that the others came and rescued me. I didn't even have my water bottle. I thought I would last long if he ran off.

Thankfully he didn't and just took me back. We weren't actually a long way from the others, maybe just the other side of a dune. The sand was very hot and rippled, and ran into my footprint as soon as I took another step. I should have spotted where the sun was, but so trusting

I was.

We spent about 4 hours there before continuing for another hour before stopping for lime and soda in a small village; better than the warm, treated water we had in our bottles that was keeping us alive. The village had a small shop that sold a few vegetables, Coca Cola and Fanta and cigarettes, what everyone seemed to want even right out here in the desert.

The guide gave me a small lump of opium which I ate. That helped me relax. Another surprise. Who would have thought, eating opium with a camel in the desert!

Another beautifully clear starry night at another water hole.

30th March

That morning we started out at 7.30; it was already hot. We stopped at a deserted desert village called Culdrah which had quite a large temple. There were few images here, just some mutilated statues and a few poor ones of monkeys. Salima said, or rather agreed to what I had said, that people left due to lack of water. But later a Canadian guy we met on his own Safari trek said it was because there had been a lot of conflict driven by Moslem invaders from Pakistan against the Hindus about eleven years earlier (1974) .

By 10.30, it was so hot that I was falling asleep on the camel.

We spotted another couple of camels coming towards us and they waved us closer. One had a Japanese girl on top, red faced looking exhausted. Her camel-driver guide said she would not drink the water. I gave her some purifying tablets and told he she must drink – it was even sometimes better to drink dirty water than not to drink at all, but the water from the well was OK, which was why they call it well water. She left happier. Now I thought, maybe I saved her life.

Almost suddenly we were on our way back to Jaiselmer. We stopped at a small village called Amar Sagar where a Jain Temple was being restored.

Suddenly we spotted Jaiselmer in the distance.

JAISELMER

(Rajasthan, 1985)

Jaiselmer, oh Jaiselmer
Not a lot of hassle here.
Just cows walking in the streets,
Adding smells to earthly heat,
Makes us want to drink more chai,
But "No milk!" the people cry.
All those cows yet still no milk,
All those shops that just sell silk,

Desert life's just not the same,
Camels struggling, what a shame,
To let us climb upon their backs
And if they moan they know the crack.
Driver up there perched on top
Passing songs until we stop
At water hole or shady tree
To eat a precious chapati
Made by the men, full of pride,
Over fires with veggies fried,
In spices which do not have names,
But we don't care 'cos we have pains,
In legs and arms and even feet
From riding camels in this heat.
Three days the desert journeyed on,
We listened to the Rajput's songs,
Passing temples, villages
Passed to us through ages.
Suddenly, the words we hear:
"See over there, sweet Jaiselmer!"

Heads, Hats and Tall Tales

Back in the Hotel Fort View. All in all it was sometimes a bit too hot but it was an incredible experience although Lesley said that her coccyx was struggling and she still says she never recovered (now in 2021). She was also upset because she'd lost a bead from her hair.

The hotel manager asked me to write a comment in his guest book, which I did. I read through some of the other comments which were all positive. One read: "The best thing about riding the camels is that one could fart loudly and blame it on the camels."

3ʳ1st March

Jaiselmer was built in 1156 on Trikuta Hillby Rawal Jaisal – did I already write that?

There are 99 bastions around the circumference. It was very impressive. Just inside was a seven story palace and Jain temples from the twelfth to fifteenth centuries, dedicated to Rikhabdeuti and Sambhavantiji. The temples are only open until 11 AM. Also there was a Shiva Temple and Ganesh Temple. Ganesh is the elephant-headed god.

We spent most of the rest of the day in the hotel, just wandering out for a delicious lemon lassi drink and a 'special' cheese toast sandwich with garlic, onion and tomato. We tried to buy some henna for Lesley, without success. We saw a monkey sitting on a wall, eating a tomato, and lots of cows wandering about the streets.

> Wherever we go in India, once we stop, we see people looking at us with no sense of embarrassment.

EYES

> In India, no matter where,
> The people seem to stand and stare,
> Looking mostly at Lesley,
> Her wondrous form just there to see.
> As if she's wondering around topless,
> Ignoring all the smelly mess.
> But then it's India here we're told,
> Their staring seems to be quite bold.
> They don't realise she gets upset

> She's not quite used to it quite yet.
> Women, men and children look,
> As if we're out of some special book,
> But maybe she'd take it more pleasantly,
> If they had used some subtlety.

1ˢᵗ April.

They had April Fools Day here, but no tricks.

We visited some mansions built by the rich traders that passed through on the trade route before Bombay was opened up as a major port. Patwon Ki was the best; outside was intricate stone carvings and lattices; inside paintings. Another was Salim Singh, about 300 years old. That one had been lived in by a prime minister called Salim Singh, who built two storeys of wood on top, but that was later torn down by Maharaja.

Our next stop was a shop where I bought beautiful silk paintings and more cotton dresses. Whilst we were inside the shop, all of a sudden there was a downpour of very heavy rain, apparently the first time in years, with rushing water washing down the streets for about an hour.

This was our last night here; we are both sad to have to leave.

2ⁿᵈ April

We arrived in Jodhpur at 6,30 AM. We soon met a guy who said he was a doctor and a young guy Ramesh who collected stamps. The doctor said he could change our ticket to a second class on a super-fast train back to Delhi. It seemed like a good idea but Ramesh warned us against it. We went to the ticket office where another chap warned us, saying we would not get a refund until back in Delhi and maybe not even then. So we kept our tickets for the train at 15.10.

When we took breakfast it was already 10.30. We ordered cornflakes, toast and jam with coffee. But when it arrived it was tea, so we asked for coffee. It came back in the same teapot. We were sure they had just added coffee to the tea! Soon we were back down Agra Street for spicy samosa and superb thick lemon lassi. Then we had poached eggs and chips.

It was soon time to board the train and the doctor turned up to say goodbye and for some reason gave us his son's address in Delhi.

3ʳᵈ April: **DELHI AGAIN**

We arrived back in Delhi early morning. The train was very slow for a good few miles before pulling into the station. From the carriage window it was a real sight for sore eyes. We were moving alongside a shanty town and the large number of people there clearly had few facilities and were using the railway track as a public convenience; there was a long line of bare arses facing us. I could only imagine the excrement dried up every day or maybe was eaten by rats. Not a pleasant sight or thought but then again, quite funny.

Also on the journey some of our fellow passengers somehow got the idea that I could read palms. One guy gave me a piece of paper to write on; I saw it was an invitation for a job interview so told him he was about to get a new job. He seemed very pleased and I hope it encouraged him so he got the job. But that only encouraged others. I just made some positive stuff up telling them all good news or good changes were coming. Indians are a very superstitious nation.

That day, as it turned out, was the holiday day for Lord Mahavir Jayanti, although most shops were open. So after getting back to the Ashok Yatri Newas hotel and checking in, we planned to get some passport photos done in preparation for our applications for visas to Nepal.

Two people were arguing at reception because they were told they had to pay in foreign currency like pounds or dollars. For us this was to be a nuisance too, as previously they had taken rupees with an exchange chit. So now Lesley had to change a travellers check into rupees, then change enough for the hotel bills back into pounds. In India there were ever changing rules and regulations, a bureaucratic system that wanted everything in triplicate.

By now all my white shirts were either stained and dirty, so we had to get them cleaned too. It would have been cheaper to buy new shirts.

We went back to the office to see Ali Baktoo and get details for our trip to Nepal and find out about visas. There was another guy there. He said "Ah, I see you have been in the desert, because you have a red nose! I have been too, you see I have a white nose!" He explained that though my nose was burned red, his was bleached white!

4th April

The visa for Nepal cost 120 rupees each, about six pounds. That was no problem for us. Ali sent somebody to get our passports stamped.

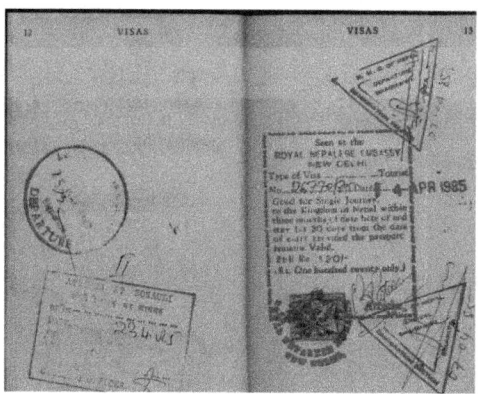

Apparently, Delhi had 50,000 rickshaws, one million bicycles, 3000 animal-drawn carts and 80.000 motor vehicles including cars, buses, trucks and rickshaws, resulting in 5000 road accidents every year.

That day we strolled along Parliament Street and Janpath area trying to find Jantar Mantar astronomical gardens and observatory, which was supposed to be just a short walk from Connaught Circus. After quite a long walk up the wrong street, we came across a Sikh Temple. Suddenly we were back on Ashok Road at our hotel.

We had missed Jantar Mantar altogether!

Then we learned that Parliament Street was actually called Sansad Marg, which we had passed several times whilst walking back and forth. By then we had learned that Jantar Mantar was just behind our hotel, on the "backside" as they say here. So off we went again.

Jantar Mantar was a collection of stone astronomical instruments built by Maharaja Jai Singh The Second about 1725. There was a large salmon-coloured odd shaped structure with steps everywhere, a huge sun dial supposed to be accurate to half a second and another triangular shape and semicircles meant for plotting the courses of the stars and predicting eclipses and predict the times and movements of the sun, moon and planets.

It was difficult to see how they were used but it included the use of shadows cast upon graduated concave plates. It was all set in a green garden patch. The word Jantar was derived from yantra, meaning instrument, while the suffix Mantar was derived from mantrana meaning consult or calculate.

6th April

So we booked out of the Ashok Yatri Newas hotel. We had to get a special slip from reception to present to the security guard on the door. This took ten minutes. When we got to the door, the guard wasn't there.

Next we took a rickshaw down to the Tourist Camp to board the "Deluxe India super coach" which looks like a wreck, to Kathmandu. The 4 PM departure time became 4.45, not too bad for India. At about 11 PM that night, the coach broke down.

After very little sleep it was 8 AM and the coach had not moved.

PRAYING FOR A BUS

We left Delhi 4 P.M. today
To Kathmandu by bus
But midnight whilst still on the way
We stopped without a fuss.

It had been quite a bumpy ride
Through places without names
The seating wasn't very wide
No sleep, it was a shame.

Half day upon this bus we are
Frying in the heat,
This is no deluxe bus by far
It is a lying cheat.

Another bus soon coming here,
Well that is what we're told,
Exactly when is not made clear,
No Indian is that bold.

Then still we're waiting on the bus,
Later on that day,
A Foreign girl invited us
To come along and pray.

"We'll do some prayers and puja chants
And maybe sing a song,
If that don't work we'll maybe dance
And bus will come along."

The bus to Kathmandu we think
Will much improve our mood,
And on the way, perhaps a drink,
And then a plate of food.
"Oh bus! Oh bus! Show us your magic!
Come and save this day,
For this trip we're on is become quite tragic..."
Oh! Now we're on our way!

7th April

I felt as if we'd worked out some bad Karma after such a bumpy ride, being at the back of the bus and constantly being tossed into the air, often hitting my head on the inside bus roof and hardly sleeping at all.

We reached the border with Nepal about 10 AM. We were still here at 5.30.

The Nepalese customs officers seemed to be looking through every Nepalese and Indians cases and bags, but not ours.

This place was called Sunauli. It was very dry and dusty. We had a good Thali meal for lunch; that's a metal plate with small amounts of vegetable, rice, potatoes, yoghurt, chapati. It cost next to nothing.

We had now been approached by a group of boys and young teenagers; they were very friendly and seemed to think that Lesley was a film star. They provided us with information and directed us to a bank. One boy, named Sankara, just wanted his photo taken with Lesley. I did not want to get the camera out.

There were a number of younger kids about, trying get us to change money or to sell us cold drinks or spicy cucumber slices; cucumber was one of the few fruits or vegetables that I detest.

The journey from the border was again very bumpy. In the future I will offer baksheesh if necessary for a seat up front. We stopped along the road at a couple of nameless places for chai. In one place there were jugs of water on the tables. They had bits floating in. I saw an old guy remove his scarf and use it as a filter.

8th April:

KATHMANDU

Eventually we arrived in Kathmandu and were taken by bicycle rickshaw to our hotel. It's about £5 a night for a double.

The hotel and room are clean and we had a hot shower and room service. At 7 AM the view from the window facing westerly was magic, with several pagodas and stretching over the city to the distant mountains, with a very magical palace-looking building on the hill. The light was perfect.

At dawn the city wakes to the sounds of chanting and singing, bells and musical instruments, car horns and beeps.

Later though, it became hazy.

WAKING IN NEPAL

Outside

Is a cloudy sky, bright sun between, a slight breeze,

The sound of one man chanting.

And all elsewhere a few notes on some type of magic flute -

A strange cacophony of bells and horns and clattering.

No two horns seem to sound the same.

Another engine? Sounds like a tractor - probably a bus!

Beep, beep, beep.

If I look out of the window I see tin rooftops,

Blimsen Tower, a glorious white standing before the blue;

And there - a temple, a pagoda, a woman sitting with washing lay out to dry,

Pigeons coo-ing, crows a-crowing, gardens growing,

Potted plants that people tend,

A bicycle rickshaw, a cow, a man with a bundle of wood on his head!

A cockerel crows as another motorbike passes 3 men trying to move a fridge,

Young girl, proud, staring into space,

Three boys rolling rubber wheels of glee amidst the

rubble,

Whilst more look on admiringly.

Yet another dog - a tempo (three-wheeler) barking as two boys, hand-in-hand,

Laugh at a goat.

Cock crows, horns, far away mountainous silences

Surround the Monkey Temple,

Like a golden palace on the hill.

Behind - another hill.

Shame about the dusty haze.

We spent most of the day resting up, sitting on a hotel balcony recovering from that dreadful journey, but it's feeling very good here. I reckoned we'd try to get some Nepalese hash tomorrow. We had spaghetti, rice pudding and a sad looking scone for dinner followed by an early night.

9th April

I slept to the sound of barking dogs and awoke feeling exhausted and not too well.

Again we heard devotional songs, chanting and bells. We had to sort out tickets back to Delhi for a couple of weeks time and get a city map, then go exploring.

It was not at all like I had imagined it, not really like India at all. There was a lot of British stuff in the shops; cigarettes and rolling tobacco and skins, chocolates and sweets and alcohol, all cheap.

Nepal was a religiously tolerant country, with Buddhists, Hindus, Muslims, Christians and other all living together seemingly in mutual respect and tolerance. Restaurants sell meat and fish meals as well as plenty of vegetarian.

We strolled about the Square and found Freak Street, where all the westerners, Americans and Australians go, famous for its hash shops. Ganga Road and the Post Office.

I bought some cheap headphones, then we went back to Durbar Square.

There was a collection of many temples there. As we walked, we saw the Shiva-Pavati Temple and from a window there people watching the street below. Some temples had erotic carvings of Tantric yoga, in particular the Jagnarth Temple. Some people believe that the carvings were done in praise of the goddess of lightning, whom, being a chaste virgin, would not strike a temple with such shocking carvings.

Behind that temple we saw the Kalo Bhairab, a massive stone image of the said-to-be terrifying Black Bharab. This was once used as a lie detector; suspected wrongdoers were forced to touch the feet of the god and swear innocence and anyone that told untruths would die.

The Palace was near here. Along the outside there are inscriptions in eighteen languages including English and French. It was established by King Malla in the seventeenth century. Legend says that milk will flow from the spout in the middle if anyone can read all the languages.

At the gate to the palace was a statue of Hanuman, the monkey-headed devotee of Rama. His face was obscured by red paint put on it by the faithful.

There was a police station on one side of the square and near here there are giant drums built in the eighteenth century.

Also near here lies the Kumari Devi Temple. This was three storeys high.

There was also another temple here, the Taleju Temple, dedicated to a family deity and built in the sixteenth century. At 115 feet in height, it was Durbar Square's most magnificent temple stands at its north-eastern extremity but was not open to the public. Even for Hindus, admission was restricted; they can only visit it briefly during the annual Dasain festival. The 35m-high temple was built in 1564 by Mahendra Malla. Taleju Bhawani was originally a goddess from the south of India, but she became the titular deity, or royal goddess, of the Malla kings in the 14th century. The temple stands on a 12-stage plinth, dominating the Durbar Sq area. The eighth stage of the plinth forms a wall around the temple, in front of which are 12 miniature temples. Four more miniature temples stand inside the wall, which had four beautifully carved wide gates.

When we left the Square, we bought some reasonable but not excellent quality hash near the Swiss Travellers Restaurant and ate an excellent fish tandoori just down the road in the Other Room and Bar. Lesley had paratha and salad and we washed it down with brandy coffee – all for about six UK pounds.

It seemed like there are a few interesting places worth seeing not far from Kathmandu. A bus ride to Bhaktapur and a short trek to be considered.

10th April

It rained during the night. That had freshened the air.

We walked to the Post Office again and then went to Bhimsem Tower also called Dharahara. This was a nine-storey, 203 foot tower at the centre of Sundhara. It was built in 1832 by Mukhtiyar, equivalent to a prime minister, under the commission of Gueen Lalit Tripurasundari. The tower had a spiral staircase containing 213 steps. The eighth floor had a circular balcony for observers that provided a panoramic view of the valley.

Then we went to near the park to see where the buses to Patan leave from.

So then we went to Tina Travel to confirm the bus back to Delhi on the 23rd. Nothing being as simple as we thought, we were told that he would need to contact Ali to change the dates for our trip to Kashmir, so we had a few more days here. We also booked bus tickets to Pokhara. The money we have was going fast but that could not be helped. I decide to write back to Norwich for more money and get it sent to Delhi or Kashmir.

KATMANDONEIN

Now we've been in Kathmandu a while.
Is it just the highness makes us smile?
Is it the atmosphere makes us light?
Or the mountains within our sight?

Lesley reckons people here take bigger steps!
Maybe they are all secret tantric cult adepts?
Anyway you look at it, they're happy
Even if their ways are sometimes crappy!

How come everything here seems so cheap?
Yet money seems so hard to keep?
Don't seem to spend a lot in any place
Just drifting round the city in a space.

Decided to stay here a few more days,
Smoking trying not to get out-hazed.
In the morning here if there is no sun,
Read a local Tantric yoga book, it could be fun.

1th April

We went to bed early last night, before 10, and woke up at 6.30 feeling tired. I didn't think I had fully recovered from the bus ride from Delhi and maybe a bit dehydrated. Also I was becoming more irritated by flies.

But there was plenty of lovely bird song to lift the mood. As we looked down from our window we saw a small courtyard with what looks like a shrine with a small lingam, opposite the hotel. I had not noticed that before. But it was no big surprise as there were shrines everywhere, many seemingly abandoned and uncared for.

The eyes we saw that are painted on some temples and other places were the all-seeing eyes of Lord Buddha, often incorporated into statues of Hindu gods in Nepal and seen as an incarnation of Vishnu, as were Rama and Krishna. There are quite a few temples and statues of Ganeesh, the elephant-headed god.

Ganeesh was not actually an elephant, but an elephant-headed humanoid, also known as Ganesha Ganapati and Vinayaka, and was one of the best-known and most worshipped deities in the Hindu Pantheon. He was widely revered as the remover of obstacles; the patron of arts and sciences; and the diva of intellect and wisdom. As the god of beginnings, he was honoured at the start of rites and ceremonies. Ganesha was also invoked as patron of letters and learning during writing sessions.

Ganesha was the son of Shiva and Parvati and he was the brother of Karthikeya (or Subrahmanya), the god of war. He was created by his mother using earth which she moulded into the shape of a boy. As Shiva was away on his meditative wanderings, Parvati set her new son as guard while she bathed. Unexpectedly, Shiva returned home and, on finding the boy, and outraged at his impudence in claiming he was Parvati's son, Shiva called for his gang of demons, the bhutaganas, who fought ferociously with the boy. However, the youngster easily held his own against such fearsome adversaries and Vishnu was forced to intervene in the form of Maya and, whilst the boy was distracted by her beauty, the demons, or Shiva himself, lopped off his head. At the commotion, Parvati ran from her bath and remonstrated with Shiva for so summarily killing their son. Repentant, Shiva ordered a new head to be found for the boy and, as the first animal available was an elephant, so Ganesha gained a new head and became the most distinctive of the Hindu gods.

That day we took a three-wheeler tempo to Patan, which cost us about 50 pence.

Patan, sometimes called Lalitpur, was on the other side of the Bagmati river; the name means City of Beauty. It was the second city in the Kathmandu valley, but nowadays it's really just part of Kathmandu itself. It's a Buddhist place. We get out of the tempo just outside the city gate, where we find the Royal cafe and stop for a samosa. Then we walk down some very smelly streets with open sewage and rubbish, to reach another square.

On the way we visit a Buddhist monastery called Hiranya Varna Mahabihar, built in the twelfth century with its gold-plated roofs. Inside we see many prayer wheels and paintings of Buddha. It was a three-storey structure with Buddha images in the courtyard.

PATAN

Nearby was the five-storey Shiva Temple called Kumbeshwar; the water in the courtyard was supposed to come from Gosain Kunda, a lake in Nepal's national park at over 14,000 feet. It was considered as the abode of the Hindu deities Shiva and Gauri.

Patan's Durbar Square was crowded with temples. The first seen in Bhimsen Temple with a pillar at the front and a lion on top. Bhimsen was a character from the scripture called the Mahabharata and one of the strongest people that ever lived.

Next to the shiva temple are two stone elephants that guard the door.

Also in the Square are two statues, one of King Malla on the other of Narasimha, and another Shiva temple.

Down one side of the square was the Sundari Chow or beautiful yard.

There we saw the royal bath and a small replica of the Krishna Temple. Inside the courtyard there were three

Heads, Hats and Tall Tales

statues of the gods Ganga and Jumna, standing or dancing on a crocodile and turtle.

Back outside in the street, we saw statues of Ganeesh, Narsimha and Hanuman.

12th April

We were told that it was now Nepalese New Years Eve. We did not walk far, feeling a bit queasy, maybe due to altitude.

LOOKING FOR NEW YEAR

Kathmandu: morning mist, disappears, mountain view...
Clouds spreading, sun shines, sky turns seamless blue.
Magic palace on the hill, silver morning light,
As the haze clears away, giving city sights.

Street below slowly wakes, dogs with horns and bells
All the homeless people there, washing at the wells.
Today is Nepalese New Year, should be celebrations,
Where they are is not too clear, to our mild frustration.

Maybe dancing in the street, or are there parades?
No-one here seems able to tell, where New Year's Day is made.
Life goes on as usual, everywhere you glance,
New Year doesn't seem like here, the spirit to enhance.

> Where would we go in England,
>
> If New Year we were there?
>
> Down a pub or round a house
>
> Or down Trafalgar Square?
>
> I guess that from outside, it'd look all much the same,
>
> Like we don't celebrate New Year, they'd think it was a shame.
>
> So maybe here in Nepal, because I cannot see,
>
> There's celebrations all around, invisible to me.

13th April

It was New Years Day in Nepal.

The Sikh guy, Navneet Singh, who we met at the hotel roof last night, let us use his taxi for free, so we visited Daxinkali, about a 45 minute drive away.

The drive there had some great views through the Chobar Gorge. Legend says that the valley was once a lake and once the god Manjushree, the god of wisdom, struck a rock with his sword and water came out, sweeping away all the snakes. But the snake king, Karkotak, who lived here was now in a nearby pond called Taudaha Balaju, in a small park with flowers and ponds with black fish and water spouts.

Inside was also the small image of a Sleeping Vishnu

which the King of Nepal was allowed to see whenever he wants, and a small temple flanked by Hindu temples dedicated to Ganeesh and Buddha, with a Shiva lingam

Here was the temple to the goddess Kali and every Saturday, like this day, there was a scene of the devotional slaughter of goats and chickens, with pools of blood; they are killed in the temple and washed in the dirty water outside, then taken for a feast. There was a long line of people queuing to kill.

There was a larger Sleeping Vishnu at Budhanilkantha, where he was laying on a bed of snakes. It was said he sleeps for four months each year, separating the monsoon season. Legend said that a farmer, whilst tilling his land, struck the stone below and blood came out. Every morning there was prayer and devotional rituals involving rice, vegetables and money and even a bottle of sauce. The King of Nepal himself was said to be an incarnation of Shiva and not allowed to see this place. Strangely it felt like Holy ground, more than any of the other temples.

By 1 PM we were back in Kathmandu eating egg and chips.

We found out that the palace on the hill was actually a Buddhist temple at Swayambhunath; it was also called the Monkey Temple.

14th April

We lazed in bed until midday, chatting and smoking. By the time we reached Eat at Joe's for banana and honey pancakes with lassi drink and lemon tea, it was already very hot. It's more humid here than Delhi. I am not happy with the quality of the hash we bought yesterday so I took it back. I managed to swap it but that was no good either. The guy said they only sell weak stuff because otherwise "hippies sit in the street and that is bad". So I asked for my money back and he gave it to me.

Late afternoon, we walked round Durbar Square, down the streets and bazaars called Indrachowk and Kel Tole. On the way back we found Pig Alley or Pie Alley and a nice cafe with excellent lemon meringue pie and walnut custard pie. That evening I had Prawn with peas and cashew nuts at Ani Anis restaurant with beer. I must say there was a much greater variety of food here than in India where we had been. There were extensive India, Chinese, Italian and other menus as well as Nepalese food.

15th April: **POKHARA**

We got up at 5 AM to catch the 6.30 bus to Pokhara. It was a pleasant journey with beautiful scenery and often children on the side of the road. We passed four rivers, the Trishuli, the Marshyangdi and the Seti Gandaki, then a bridge over the Madi.

We passed many paddy fields. At Mugling, a small town, we saw the longest suspension bridge in Nepal over the Trishuli river. It looked like a lovely little town.

Pokhara itself seemed a quiet peaceful place. We stayed at the Ashok Guest House, with a great small garden, restaurant and beautiful view of the mountains. It cost us £2 a night for a double

Heads, Hats and Tall Tales

Heads, Hats and Tall Tales

The lake was called Phewa.

In the afternoon we walked to the end of the village, along several roads, both tarmac and rubble, to rows of supply shops for trekkers, restaurants, cheap lodges and souvenir shops. We passed the Royal Palace but it did not look like there was much to see. We passed a small temple with a walled garden full of marijuana plants, more rows of stalls, passed the Guru Restaurant and the Anand Restaurant, then sat by the lake under a tree.

The only unpleasant things here were the flies and the young hasslers; the latter, at least, seemed to be doing well out of tourists, all shouting Namaste and trying to put a distance between us and what little money we had to spare.

17ᵗʰ April

We decided to going to laze around that day. When we went into the garden we saw that the cloudy haze had cleared and behind the mountains we had seen were massive snow- packed peaks, the Fishtail Mountain, Machapuchare.

But we were both feeling short of energy and did not want to do much but we had some good grass to help us relax.

AS THE MIND FLIES SO THE BIRD WALKS TO THE MOUNTAIN,
OR ZEN AND THE ART OF BEING LAZY

Today, outside, the weather is hazy.
Stayed in all day, feeling quite lazy.
Where to go now, we often talk,
Then decide it's too far to walk.
Two hours there and two hours back,
"Let's stay here, and have a snack".
Just fifteen minutes up to Baba's.
And we know that there, food's better by far,
But here we eat, for our stomachs sake,

Whatever's available as it's no effort to make.
"Well", I say, "I guess that's what
A holiday's for on a day that's hot."
"We're free, we don't have to do anything.
We can fly like a bird with a broken wing."
"How can that be, such a bird can't fly?"
"We can't do much either and here is why-
Cos - cor it's hot outside today,
And wherever we go we have to pay",
Or "My leg's aching, stiff and weak,
And there's nothing in the bazaar we seek."
"Stomach queasy, or head aching?
Let's be another chillum a-making."
Then, "Let's go in a boat!"
"No, don't want to row!"
Or, "Let's climb that mountain, look at the snow!"
Oh, if only we could get up there and back,
Without having to walk on that mountain track.
If you close your eyes and lay on your bed,
You can go anywhere inside your head.
If you know how to master the Traveller's Trick,
You'll be there in an instant and come back so quick.

But later we did go to see the "Cultural After Sunset Dancing" at the Hotel Fishtail Lodge near the lake, original Nepalese dancing troupe. We went across the lake on a wooden raft pulled by a yellow rope. An hour of dancing plus transport cost us £6 each but beers were £8. It was fun anyway and afterwards we went to Baba's eating house for grilled fish and chips.

ANNAPURNA FOR SALE

The calm serenity of Annapurna
Sweeps lazily over the town Pokhara;
People here have more time to smile,
Occasionally to come chat a while.
"Namaste, hello, good morning" they say
Then to business or change money.
Still, at least themselves they try to keep,
Yet their starting price is steep
"American, French, where you from?"
Like the opening line of a Nepalese song,
Which they teach in their local schools,
To say to tourists who like fools,
Are parted from their cash to soon,
As "Better prices before afternoon,
Or "First business I make today with you,
"So if you like one, why not buy two?"
Whether beggars or hasslers or honest men,
Want dollars, pounds or even yen.
As much as mountains beautiful

We all need a living our stomachs to fill.
"Here we are, no problem way of life,
"Is she your friend or is she wife?
"You want charas or marid-u-are-na,
"Opium, mushroom or brown sugar?"
"What you want buy?", so often heard,
As if just looking is absurd.
It would be good to walk one day,
Without these offers filling our way,
To absorb life's energy so obviously close,
But then that's part of it, I suppose.

18th April

We did nothing that day but eat, smoke and relax.

19th April

This day we took a shaky meccano-like bus to another Post Office near Mahandra Pool and started to walk to the bazaar but it was of no interest to us so we took the bus back to the lakeside and had lunch, vegetable dopiaza for me and buffalo cutlet for Lesley, at the Hotel Snowland. We scored some weed on the way back to our hotel. Thunder just as we arrived. There was no clear view of the Annapurna mountain range or the Fishtail. There were no bicycle rickshaws in Pokhara.

20th April

HOTEL EDEN, KATHMANDU

That day we took the bus back to Kathmandu; we both enjoyed Pokhara and would like to come back here one day, but that happens to many places that I visit, especially after leaving!

The bus seemed quite cramped at times but we had some great views again.

So we arrived back at the Hotel Eden, where we stayed before. We had a problem with the taps that were hard to turn and the toilet would not flush so we had to pour down water from a bucket from the bath. The bath had no plug. The radio had only one station.

We were in a different room, now with a view of Bhimsen Tower in all its glory.

21st April

A horrible day, we both felt dreadful and just wanted to sleep all day. Maybe it was the altitude. It was 4600 feet above sea level, about the same as Ben Nevis. We did manage to get down to Freak Street to the Magic Apple, for dinner of sweet and sour chicken.

Lesley dropped the lid off the cistern trying to get it to flush and it broke on the floor. This room was not as good as the other one. It had holes in the windows! Opposite us was a room with some noisy and dodgy-looking guys, so all in all, we were both feeling irritated.

We were also fed up with street hasslers trying to change money or sell drugs including heroin.

The national newspaper here in English was The Rising Nepal. It was six sides of news from around the world including news of dawn raids by the Indian Army at he Golden Temple in Amritsar, a very beautiful place that I visited and stayed at in 1972. Also explosions in Brussels and other pieces about Ronald Regan, lepers in Nepal and quotes from King Birenda (Benda) telling people to do well. Also people had been arrested for drugs in Pokhara. There was also a shortage of drinking water in Pokhara, a facelift had been ordered for the Krishna Temple in Durbar Square. A Dutchman at the airport had been arrested with two kilos of hashish. The world went on while we were away, far from most of it but then still close.

22nd April

Still felt weak. We had breakfast at a place called Mom's, muesli, mango juice and tea. Then we wandered up to the nearby supermarket which was in reality a row of shops and a three-storey building with more shops. So back in the hotel still feeling bad but a cup of chai and a chillum helped.

The Sikh guy Mavneet Singh reappeared at the hotel. He said he was back to continue his gambling investments at a casino, this time for a week. He never seemed to smile, even though he was quite pleasant and friendly.

We were offered some good quality jump suits made from cotton and Lesley asked if they could be altered to include a zip and a pocket. We ordered about a dozen, they were very cheap, so Lesley went off to collect them and she was well pleased. I will sell them back in Norwich.

I had been reading Paul Scott's book, 'Staying On', which I had just finished.

It was a good read. He builds up Tusker to a character we feel we know and then we lose him when he dies and his wife suffers with sadness and fright at being alone in India, until the end which comes as a shock, but hammers home the common situations people can fall into. All after a lifetime togetherness even with all the personal differences and likes and dislikes, fondness and hatred, fears and passions for one's partner; suddenly one must be terribly alone. Alone, we seem to me to be constantly trying to build bridges, to dream that we can reach a common knowledge and awareness of each other so we are not alone like the islands that they say we may be. We so often want to be a part of somebody else, intermingled, so our differences can be overlooked, whether that was good or bad, each to see oneself in the other. That can be and usually was hard work but if tackled bravely and with passion, can be rewarding, for a while. Be alone but be not afraid to be with others. Til death us do part.

23rd April

BUS BACK TO DELHI

We were up at 5 AM ready for the bus back to Delhi, but a problem getting breakfast or a taxi from the Hotel Eden after we ordered both last night. Eventually we got to the Hotel Withies to board the bus.

This time we had good front seats.

The journey down the valley was smooth with some good scenery, although the driver seemed to think he was on a race track. Nobody on the road seemed to want to get out of anyone else's way. The rule here was simple: "Might is Right".

It now seemed that many Nepalese and Indians like playing head games, so when when we said chai, char, tea, we were met with blank stares. Then, if you shouted, like barking an order, they suddenly understood. Maybe they were all just stoned.

We reached the border with no problem and the customs came and took all our passports to inspect whilst we sat on the bus outside the customs shed. They did not inspect any luggage.

But whilst we sat there a young boy outside spotted Lesley through the window. He obviously recognised her from when we passed through before. He was knocking on and waving through the window. Lesley waved back. He ran off and soon returned with some other boys and motioned us to open the window. They started throwing newspaper packages through the window. I opened one. It was weed. We are right outside the customs office. I through it back out shaking my head. More came in. I through them back shouting no. A couple of minutes later a guy came from further back on the bus and gave me two wraps, saying that the boys had asked him to give them to me. I threw them out too.

After a while the boys waved goodbye and left and soon we were on our way. The last thing I wanted was to get busted for weed at the border.

Across from us were two guys, one looked like David Soul from the Miami Vice TV series. They were smoking small joints and passed one to me. There was just enough for Lesley and I to have two puffs each. It was wonderful and strong Nepalese hash. They said they had trekked into the mountains to a village to get it.

They made another small joint and we had another puff.

The bus took off and we were flying several feet high.

Into the darkness we went.

A few hours down the road, the bus suddenly stopped. It was the Indian customs officers.

They came on the bus and immediately told me to get off the bus. Strangely, as I was holding my shoulder bag on my lap, I passed it to Lesley. They ignored that. They also ignored Starksy and Hutch. They got some people from the back of the bus too, Nepalese I think.

It was dark outside so they all had torches, about six cops. They took me to the back boot and got me to show them my rucksack, which I opened and they emptied. They took my camera, a torch (the bulb no longer worked) and a tin a sardines. I told them the camera was cheap and so I did not need to declare it, the torch bulb was no good and the tin was fish. One guy said that if the fish were inside, they would be dead. Then another guy, presumably their boss, came and said "OK, mister, what you have?" I told him camera, torch and fish. He said "Is that all?" I said yes and he said "OK, get back on bus."

That was the end of that. They searched some other bags and off we went again, to Delhi.

24th April

By 9 AM it was very very hot on the bus. We were both

aching, queasy and probably dehydrated.

We passed through a place called Bareilly. There was a modern looking place with some nice architecture. Suddenly, a little further on, we realised this was the dump of place where our other bus had broken down, on our way to Kathmandu. So that time we had sat there for many hours in the heat with just a tiny chai shack and our prayers and mosquitoes, whilst five minutes walk away was that lovely looking new place that probably had a restaurant.

Later we passed though Rampur, which was mentioned in the book 'Staying On'.

When we reached Delhi at about 6.30 PM. As we were getting off the coach, I looked under the seat to make sure we had not dropped anything. I found two newspaper wraps of weed, about ten grams or so. A nice surprise.

We took a rickshaw back to our regular hotel, Ashok Yatri Newas.

25th April

After breakfast we went to see Ali Baktoo at his office. There was no money from the UK for us. I felt let down by my lodger, "Fat Stan". He owed me money and should have sent it by now.

It was 96 degrees Fahrenheit, 35.5 degrees Centigrade. We checked for mail at the post office and American

Express, nothing.

There was a scooter strike that day. We walked to The Indian Coffeehouse in Connaught Circus area, which I had often visited in 1972.

Then we went back in the hotel to eat Masala Dosa and ice cream and felt better.

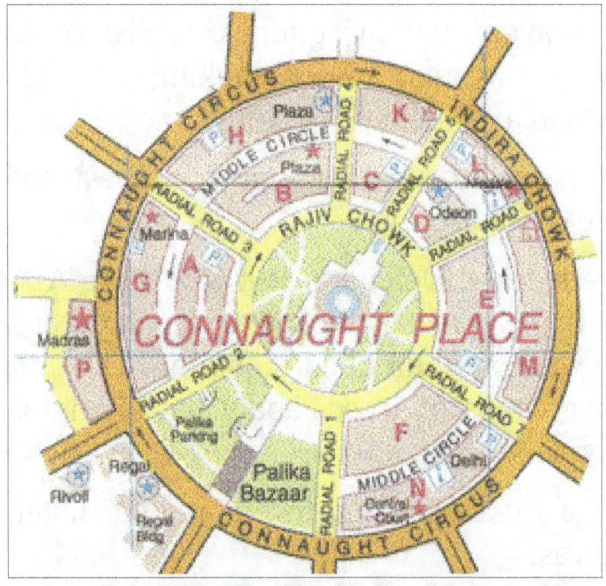

29[h] April: Kashmir by bus.

RAM RAM BUSES

From Delhi on an Indian Tourist bus,
We left thinking they'd take care of us.
An Indian video humbly plays and we're
Told in 24 hours we'll reach Kashmir.
The journey goes into the darkest night,
As jungle and hills slowly dodge our sight,
The road now is just long and straight,
No bumps and bends or jerks to hate.
We're speeding along, ever so fast,
As if this journey is our last,
The road the driver's trying to keep,
Me - I'm just trying to fall asleep.
Suddenly, we swerve, a crash, a jolt,
Us thrown around, bus comes to a halt,
We look through windows only to see,
We hit a small tractor and just missed a tree!
Spite driver's brave efforts to curve and sway,
One side of the bus has been torn right away!

Amidst cries of Oh God!" - in Hindi "Ram Ram",
And in my own mind "Oh shit, oh damn!"
No one here seems able to tell,
Whether we're earthly or in heaven or hell.
But nobody's hurt, so we all get out,
A policeman a sweeper's given a clout.
For without thought he's just learned that he'd officially signed
A statement unread because he was blind.
There's nothing to do now but sit and wait,
Arriving Kashmir we know we'll be late.
Then mosquitoes surround us and all rush in,
"There's three dozen humans in a half open tin!"
They must have shouted and told their friends,
"We can buzz all about them and insanity send!"
Well I know it's our blood they are trying to drink,
And "Kill the bastards" is what I think,
And now the sun has gotten bright,
People are gathering to smile at our site.
Apparently the tractor driver was drunk,
The cop wanted baksheesh or he'd be sunk.
Ah, now they're trying the bus to fix
With hammers, wires and broken sticks!

It'll be midnight tomorrow before we arrive,

If just 36 hours more we can somehow survive.

But surprise, surprise we weren't there all day,

For two hours later we were on our way.

30th April: **JAMMU**

We stayed the night at the Hotel Palace in Jammu, although not exactly a palace. We had to share a room with a Canadian guy. We were up at 6 AM to continue our journey on the bus.

Of course we were going to be many hours later so whoever was going to meet us at the bus depot will probably not be there.

It seemed to be that every long bus ride in India comes with a little adventure.

It was a nerve-wrecking drive through excellent scenery with sights such as monkeys and herds of goats along the way; sometimes we had to stop for the goats on the road. The herds and goats were driven along by what looks like whole families.

There was a 5200 foot long tunnel and signs reading "This is not a race or rally, this is Kashmir Valley". I was not sure that our driver could read though.

Heads, Hats and Tall Tales

One surprise was seeing stalls along the way, selling cricket bats, made from local walnut.

SRINAGAR

When we finally arrived in Srinagar at about 6.30 PM, we were met by a group of young hasslers each claiming that they had been sent to meet us, not one seem to know of the name of the person that sent them, so we went to the office to phone Kashmir Himalayan Holidays. Before we got an answer, a guy arrived with all our details and off we go by Rickshaw and Shikara to our houseboat, the New Wild Rose.

Shikaras are of various sizes and are used for multiple purposes, including transportation.

The usual shikara seats six people, with the driver paddling at the rear. Like the Venetian gondolas. They are a cultural symbol of Kashmir. Some shikaras are still used for fishing, harvesting aquatic vegetation (usually for fodder), and transport, while most are covered with tarpaulins and are used by tourists.

We met Ibram and Bashir who were there supposedly to do our will. Omelette and chips served, we were shown to our room which was OK, but not as good as the Kashmir Paradise where I stayed in 1981.

1st May

It rained all last night and most of the day, which I spent playing backgammon. It was almost chilly after Delhi. I was glad I had my sweater. Outside were some salesmen on their shikaras, touting for business. One was selling furs. Lesley had ordered one and given her red leather jacket so they can measure it. In the distance we heard children probably at school, horns and the whistling and squawking of geese and other birds. A simple meal of rice, vegetables and dahl, cooked was served to us on the houseboat.

2nd May

It had stopped raining so we took a shikara to the land and walked to the poste restante at the main post office. There was letter from my friend Stan, back in Norwich, short with no mention of money.

The two Australians, Brad and Kelly, who were staying on our houseboat were both sick, which made me wonder abut the hygiene here, or lack of it. Although the water looked clean here, we were downstream from many other houseboats. Down by the bridge where the poorer families live on far less luxurious boats, it was stinking. And it seemed like the toilet empties direct into the lake, where they also seemed to wash dishes and clothes.

3rd May

After breakfast we went on a shikara ride round Dal

lake. We were able to stretch out and relax on a mattress with cushions under a canopy. Very relaxing.

The view of the mountains was beautiful and tranquil. Nehru Park was in the middle of the lake, then Rup Lank (gold island) with its four chiner trees. The

houseboats were less crowded here. The view was even better with the reflections in the clear waters. We could hear the sound of chanting and musical instruments from the shore.

Nighat Gardens were between the lake and the mountains. We decide to pay them a visit. They had been there since 1833, splendid gardens of grass, flowers and trees, with its own canal and cascades running down the middle and a series of terraces takes one up to the fine lake views.

To our left we saw Hari Parbat Fort on top of Sharika Hill. It was built 1592 to 1598, during the reign of Akbar. Visits were only possible with written permission from the Director of Tourism. Outside was a shrine to the 6th Sikh Guru.

On our way back, we passed the Hazratbal Mosque. New and shining white, supposed to house hair from the Prophet.

When we got back to the New Wild Rose, I read in a book that a trip on Dal Lake was a sybaritic experience. None of us actually knew the word but we instinctively knew what it meant - fond of sensuous luxury or pleasure; self-indulgent.

4th May

A warm day, much spent just enjoying the sun on the houseboat.. Lesley, Brad and Kerry were all feeling better. Now I was slowing down! I felt fine.

We called in to see Yussef Baktoo in his office. He said that in Kashmir Lesley was "Puxley" and Alun was "Ali".

The guy who met us from the bus, Gulab Khar, told us a tale. When he was a baby of four years old, a vulture swept down and carried him off; his father quickly threw a stone and it hit the bird which dropped little Gulab ten feet and the father caught him. Lucky Gulab!

5th May

We spent most of the day lazing around on the deck of the houseboat, watching the clouds and shikara boats. We had a splendid view of snow-capped mountains. I bought a silver box, also earrings with coral.

The local Islamic people were fasting that day.

It rained heavily during the night.

6th May

Suddenly at 7 Am we were awoken by loud voices and knocking on the door.

"Quick, quick, come quick, water is coming into boat".

So with pounding heart I jumped out of bed and put on some clothes, making sure Lesley was doing the same. I am not sure she believed what was happening.

We rushed outside then Bashir says "No, it is OK, go to sleep, as they are bailing out the water with buckets."

Apparently one end of the boat was lower in the water and caused a panic.

By noon it was too hot to sit on the sun deck.

It was either a holiday or a strike.

7th May

Trying to find the Thomas Cook office was not easy despite the offers of help from the holiday company. Mr Kahr said it was at the Oberai Hotel.

Lesley bought some medicine called Amelast that contains dioxamide and tridazole, an intestinal anti-parasitic drug.

In the afternoon we went on a shikara ride to the beautiful lake Nageen to see the new Butterfly Houseboat, which looked palatial with beautiful paintings in the Mogul and Indian rooms, carvings in the Kashmir room, and in the Shikara room a bed shaped like a shikara.

On the way back we called at a carpet shop. I bought a woollen carpet on my previous visit to Kashmir in 1981 for £200, so did not want one this time, but Lesley bought a beautiful silk one for a deposit and then monthly payments when back in the UK. They will send it to her by air mail. Of course there will be duty on it so it will cost her over £400.

8th May

So far we had seen shikaras selling jewellery, now it was saffron. It's cheap though.

Lesley had developed a habit of saying "Maybe later" and inevitably they come back.

I wrote a letter to the Sitar shop to arrange a later date to meet the guy back in Delhi with the Sitar I bought as we would be there later than expected. I gave it to Jimmy to post.

VALLEY OF THE SHEPHERDS, PAHALGAM

9th May:

We went by taxi to Pahalgam and a few miles more to the toll gate. It was raining hard. By the time we walked to Aru we were soaked.

The previous year we had camped by the river but now it was too wet so we are staying in the Rest House in the little town of Aru, before we start our pony trekking tomorrow. Our guide was another Ali.

The village lies on the left bank of the Aru river, which was a tributary of the Lidder river.

The village was a base camp for trekkers to the Kolahoi Glacier, the Tarsar-Marsar lakes and the Katrinag valley. It was also a base for the treks to Lidderwat, the Vishan-Kishansar lakes and Kangan.

Aru was situated at 9,000 feet. The population was less than 50.

10th May:

PONY TREK

We set off walking and sometimes on the ponies. The rain had eased off and the scenery was absolutely incredible. We walked for about two hours and when we got there, a place with no name, the tents were already pitched.

With the snow capped mountains and rushing stream, it was lovely. It rained again in the afternoon after we were served omelette and chips, but the tent with fly sheet and ground sheet was quite adequate.

11th May

We walked and rode towards Kolahai, crossing the snow line. Kolahoi Peak was the highest mountain in Kashmir with a peak elevation of 17,799 feet. Obviously we had no intention of going to the top!

But, as was typical here, they did not tell us what was happening and suddenly we were walking into the snow, with the ponies behind us along with my rucksack and shades which I would certainly need to avoid snow blindness at that height. "Ponies wait for us to come back," said Ali, "they not like snow."

We stopped a little way past some empty huts. Ali and Martin, the Canadian guy that had joined us, were to walk on to see the glacier. We would go back. Fine with us.

The air was so thin that even cigarettes went out when one stopped puffing on them.

They returned after two hours. Martin was almost blind. The snow had become too deep and dangerous for them to continue. Ali should have known that. We are not mountaineers, were not equipped for that. This was supposed to be a pony trek.

We returned to our camp, which we are told was called Lidderwatt, such a beautiful tranquil spot. Ali told us tales of who died here last year. Two fell off ponies crossing the river and one whilst rafting.

Heads, Hats and Tall Tales

At some point we met an old chap that asked if we had any aspirins because his wife had toothache and he was on his way to walk to Pahalgam to buy some. He was barefooted. I had some in my bag and gave them to him. He gave me a small piece of nice black hash. Hash is no good for toothache.

On the way down, we stopped at a small shack. There was a smiling woman there with what may have been

her daughter. She invited us to drink some chai. It was pink milky and salty, just what we needed. The girl was fascinated with Lesley and her hair.

As we moved along a track with low branches handing down that I had to duck under, my pony fell behind the others. As they disappeared behind some trees on bend, my pony panicked and started moving faster than it ever had before with me on its back. But as soon as it caught sight of the others, it slowed down again.

15th May

Back in Srinagar. Lazing about, floating about the lakes, getting high.

Another warm day. We tried go to pick up sweaters that we ordered but there was fighting in town so we couldn't go. Lesley had decided she did not want animal fur and ended up losing her red leather jacket as they had not returned it.

We were trying to get the "Numero Uno" hash that Ali Baktoo spoke of. He reckoned that we had was 50% cow shit, even though we found it strong. In the evening we visited the other brother, Jimmy, at his request, on a houseboat, called Jupiter. It was a bit boring; he just left after half an hour. Then it took us an hour to get a shikara home to the New Wild Rose.

Meanwhile I found the letter to the Sitar company that I gave to Jimmy to post, in the drawer in the living room. When I told him, he just said "no problem". Well not for you Jimmy, but I would not get my sitar now.

16th May:
SONAMARG

That day we took a taxi to Sonamarg or Sonmarg.

Heads, Hats and Tall Tales

Beautiful mountain peaks with snow all around. We walked off towards the glacier but after a while we just stopped. It was so beautiful.

Lesley bought a musk ball; it's a lovely smell but a deer's testicle!

17th May

There was a curfew on in town that day due to a visit from some politician. Lesley had an upset stomach and cramps so we stayed on the boat; a massage with mustard oil helped.

Jimmy popped in and promised "Numero Uno" tomorrow and I gave him some cash. It was hard to get a good signal on the radio and the tape machine didn't work properly so there was not a lot of music, which was a shame.

18th May

We had planned go to Gulmarg but had put it off until the next day.

19th May: **GULMARG**

The taxi to Gulmarg did not turn up.

Instead we went to a shop, by Shikara, that was selling some beautiful carved walnut items. I bought some carved candlesticks, some statuettes including a dancing

Buddha, a sewing box and several carved cigarette boxes that they would ship back to the UK. They also had a beautiful carved dining table with six matching chairs but that was out of my price range. The cigarette box was a novelty; one put about ten cigarettes in the lower compartment, then when one lifted and dropped the top section, one appeared on the groove in the lid.

20th May

We wasted much of the afternoon trying to get to Thomas Cook's, which turned out to be at Johanson

Travel not the Grindleys Hotel as we had been told that money was coming. This was after being told for ten days that money for us was at Grindleys. But there was still no money there. So we sent a message to Thomas Cooks in Delhi to tell them to keep the money there.

Jimmy, who did not turn up last night where we were supposed to meet him at the Tourist Office and waited, came to see us and said he had been waiting for us on Houseboat Jupiter. He said that he would bring the smoke to the New Wild Rose tonight.

We never did get Numero Uno from Jimmy but I did get my money back.

I had asked for tickets back to Delhi tomorrow, but so far there are none, so we will be here another day. I had arranged to pay our bill later, either in Delhi or back in the UK. They said that was no problem. Yeah, like my sitar!

I just wanted to get back to Delhi, pick up some money and confirm the flight home. If we needed to wait a week, we could go to Kulu and Manali and get stoned, I thought.

The people here were all friendly enough, but they never say they don't know and brush everything aside as if nothing mattered to them but of course it did. In fact everything mattered. There was a lot of ignorance and lack of experience. Many lived such limited lives. They didn't understand tourists and travellers, think we are all super rich; well compared to so many we are, after all, we are there on holiday often living like kings, miles from our home, and they had so little and life can be hard. They don't even realise the harm that can come from washing in the sewage of Dal lake; they don't know that it was getting worse because they are polluting it themselves.

Many people are fighting for freedom, freedom from India. They mistakenly, in my opinion, think they would be batter off as part of Pakistan because they are Moslem. It's not violent in Kashmir, completely different to Pakistan. They are too bound by superficial religious appearance and ritual.

The family structure was very strong but men could take multiple wives and, strangely enough, although they would all smoke hash with us, they hid it away from each other; and many were secret alcohol drinkers.

They often used smiles and pleasant offers of chai or small gifts to buy their way into our pockets.

But still, Kashmir was one of the safest and most beautiful parts of the world.

21st May

SAYING GOODBYE

Suddenly Yussef told us our money was at Grindleys, so off went go again. But of course it's not. "The money has not been sent", they told us.

Then, suddenly, our flight back to Heathrow was confirmed for the 25th, four days time, so we planned to get the bus back to Delhi tomorrow.

In some ways I thought I'll be glad to be back in Norwich. In other ways I felt I could travel on.

22nd May

The bus ride back to Delhi was almost 24 hours, but it's the best one yet, with no problems. We spend some time in the driver's cabin, up front, so some fantastic views.

23rd May

Back in Delhi at 7 AM at the Ringo Guest House with air conditioning and shower, opposite the Indian Oil Building.

We went to Thomas Cooks and picked up some money. It's been there all the time.

We bought some cheap chokers and beaded necklaces and some very cheap women's shirts from the underground market where they had a sale. Some were less than £1 each and I know I can sell them for at least £6 each.

Ali met us and had Lesley's lost jeans from Rajasthan. He took her to a night club in the evening.

24th May.

I went back to the market and bought more cotton blouses, now my rucksack was packed very full. It was far too hot and uncomfortable outside during the day.

In the evening we went to the Mandarin room at the Hotel Imperial.

Then we went to see Ali and on to the airport.

25th May

BACK IN THE UK

We arrived back in the UK at Heathrow Airport.

I walked through customs without a problem.

Lesley got pulled by the customs team. They found her little musk ball and, she told me later, she said "That's not what you think it is."

So they did a strip search and called in a doctor and she had to hand over her little stash from her personal space and was busted. Fat Stan had come to pick us up with another guy called Nigel and we were waiting in the arrivals hall for Lesley when there was an announcement for Stan. Nigel went in to learn that Lesley was being detained for a few hours and so he gave her enough money to get back to Norwich by bus or train, as we could not wait.

A couple of months later, we took her to Uxbridge Court where she as fined £100. Everyone else in court, while we were there, was charged for having suitcases full of drugs at the airport.

AFTERTHOUGHTS

I had made three trips to India. The first, pretty much out of the blue because when we left the UK we had intended to travel only as far a Turkey, in a van. There were four of us. None of us had very much money. I had left UK with just about £60, three weeks wages in those days. By the time we reached Antalya, in Turkey on the southern coast, I had just £20 left. We slept either in the van or in a tent until we reached Istanbul, where we rented cheap rooms. After that, we slept in Turkey in the open. From Turkey, Keith and I took a boat eastwards, intending to travel to Beirut then back to Istanbul to meet up again with the others. On the boat, however, we were advised not to go to Beirut, so instead hitch-hiked across Syria into Iraq and on the Baghdad, then on by bus to Tehran. Then we headed east across Iran, Afghanistan, Pakistan and into India. The main problem for me was lack of money, so not being able to eat the food I should have been eating and staying in cheap and often dirty hotels. I ran out of money in Kabul, a dirty city but cheap and friendly. I sold a few items such as shirts and a compass and met a wealthy German guy called Hellmut, who helped us get to India, by plane from Lahore to Amritsar, one of the first passenger planes after the end of the Pakistan-India war. In Amritsar, we stayed for free at The golden Temple and I hitched a truck ride to Delhi.

I struggled on very little money, receiving just a few pounds in mail from the UK. Keith went on alone to

Nepal. I became ill and spend a week in hospital (free) in Delhi, suffering from dysentery and hepatitis. I tried to travel back overland to the UK but became ill again and again, being hospitalised in Kabul and Tehran, from where I had to take a flight back to London, which my parents paid for. I was 22-years-old. Looking back, it's easy to say I should have had more sense.

Yet looking back, it was also a pretty dumb thing to do, although very educational and an experience that I valued. But it was hard work in the east, with such different people, customs, lifestyles, religions, languages, foodstuff, politics and the divisions of wealth and poverty.

That was a disastrous trip, not only did I and Keith became ill, but after we left Turkey my good friend John Sullivan was killed when the van crashed in Antalya; the other passenger, Mike, was seriously hurt, broken leg, broken ribs and bang on the head. I did not even find out what had happened until I was back in Kabul, months later, and by chance met somebody that I knew from Norwich, Pete Roscoe, who was on his way to India.

From the moment we had left the UK, everywhere we went, we managed to buy hash, in every country we passed through with the exceptions of Iraq and Iran. In Iran, we actually stayed on an opium farm run by a licensed farmer who also supplied it illegally. He was also the village policeman.

That tail is told in my book "All About My Hat The Hippy Trail, 1972"

What did I learn?

The variety of people in our world.

The generosity and care we received from people with so little.

That I had people that I could call on to help when all else failed.

To travel with enough money to get one through and get one home safely.

To take more care of health regarding hygiene and diet.

So my next trips to India, both by plane, recorded in this book, were 1981 and 1985.

By this time many places had already changed in respect of politics and freedom, and it was not so possible to travel overland.

1981 was a two week holiday. 1985 was a two month journey.

At both times I had more money, enough as I thought, being older and wiser, as I thought. Yet in both cases we spent our money faster than we had anticipated and had to write home for more.

Of course another problem that was easy to have forgotten, was that contact with family and friends back in the UK was not instant and easy. A phone call had to be booked a week in advance and one had to hope that the call would be answered. Otherwise, it meant booking another call. Also in those days not everyone in the UK had a phone in their house and nobody had a

Heads, Hats and Tall Tales

mobile (cell) phone.

We were lucky to have booked the holidays through travel companies that were able to help us out.

So I'd reiterate my advice, make sure one has enough funds and remember, cash and bankers cards can be lost or stolen (as can possessions and passports).

Delhi and Agra, had changed noticeably since 1972 since I had visited those cities.

They were more populated with more traffic, more noise, more dirt and more beggars and hasslers on the streets. Also more "richer" tourists. Kashmir was attracting people with money, staying on houseboats, often isolated and even protected from the people and poverty on the streets. Corruption, baksheesh, favouritism and bureaucracy were all more common – you will have read about our problems getting seated on planes that had been overbooked.

One of the favourite sayings of many people was "no problem". Either they did not see a problem, did not see it as important or simply did not care. Yet paying baksheesh in advance would often avoid those problems.

'Jimmy', on the houseboat in Kashmir in 1985 never did post the letter that he had promised to post; that cost me a sitar.

Many Indians won't say that they don't know; instead they tell one what they think. An example was when we were told that our funds were at a bank when they were not and had not even been sent.

I certainly would not advise anyone to drive a vehicle in India. The rule of the road everywhere was "Might is Right". Walkers and people with carts pulled by animals got out of the way of cars, which got out of the way of buses, which got out of the way of trucks. Everyone was listening out for the loudest horns approaching them. Everyone in the cities seemed to drive using their horns more than indicators. Of course walkers and those with animal-pulled carts had no horns.

At one point in this book, you will see a photo taken from a rickshaw on a road in Delhi; you can see pedestrians, bicycles, rickshaws, cars, buses, trucks and even an elephant.

Of course food is another problem: you may have heard of "Delhi belly".

The difference between western and India food and water, the way in which so much ghee is used, often the lack of hygiene, that does not cause serious problems for locals, almost inevitably causes some problems for westerners on short holidays. Often these problems are short-lived, being simply a matter of adjusting, but one does not want or need to spend a few days feeling ill especially on a short trip.

At all times, one needs to be aware of thieves and conmen on the streets. People, both men and women, that will simply want to take advantage of you.

There are those that will simply try to pick your pocket or steal your bag; there are those that ask for money and won't take no for an answer; there are those that will tell lies and try to mislead you for their own advantage; there are those that say they just want to practice their English and end up taking you to a shop where actually they are friendly and often the craftsmanship is fine. That tactic includes foreigners as well as locals.

Thankfully those people, the ones that want to get you to but something, are in the minority and, in my opinion, far better than thieves. People without jobs or sponsors have to make their money. Beg, steal or sell their wares. Of course, in the cities, like most big cities, there are also drug dealers about on the streets and many of whom are also dishonest or unscrupulous, selling anything from hard drugs to fake drugs.. The majority will be friendly and helpful or simply stand and stare. One certainly has to become used to people staring. Also some people don't want their photographs taken and will ask for money or become very angry, whilst others will ask you to take a photograph of them with or without you.

The gap between wealth and poverty is sometimes atrocious and sickening. One can do nothing about it. In Delhi we made a quick visit to a five star hotel. Inside was spotless and elegant and a cup of tea cost about £5. Right outside the guarded gates that led to the garden from the street, was a tiny chai stall where a cup cost pennies and the street was littered with rubbish and rubble. One sees street food stalls selling hot and cold dished whilst donkey-pulled carts trundle by in the dust, dropping their crap as they go. Many people are unaware of hygiene or unable to do anything about it. Certainly it is essential to ensure that even bottled water in restaurants is actually bottled water and not just from the tap, or to use purification tablets.

But all that is India. That is part of the experience. But just as it is wise to wear a safety helmet on a building site anywhere, one needs to take care and precautions..

ALI BAKTOO RIP (2017)

Heads, Hats and Tall Tales

MYHAT IN EGYPT
THROUGH THE EYES OF A GOD

It was on a sunny day in early 1972 that my life was to change drastically and mostly for the better, for on that day whilst Konstantinos was standing in his doorway, there being no customers, and with me on his head, we spotted a small group of young people walking down the dusty street. Konstantinos called over a young man and presented me to him, saying "You have no hat. Here, take Myhat."

That is how I come to know my name as Myhat as before that I was called Kapelomou. My new head was called "Al".

Al was travelling eastwards with his small group of friends and eastwards we went, through countries called Turkey, Syria, Iraq, Iran, Afghanistan, Pakistan and India. Before that all I knew as my world was the barber's shop and the street outside. Now I was travelling the world. That is my other story: 'All About Myhat: The Hippy Trail 1972'.

In 1989, I found myself upon the head of Ed, after Al left me behind one day, and I travelled with Ed for over twenty years until, one day, he gave me back to Al.

One day, in 1989, I met Ed. Al had left me at Ed's house and Ed started wearing me a lot.

Ed and Ana and myself visited Egypt in 1989, 1990 and again in 2010 and this is the incredible tale of those journeys and what happened to us, on our travels through space and time.

In ancient Egypt the name Ana name meant Goddess.

I spent time also on Ana's head too.

By 1989, Ana had studied many languages. By 2010 she could speak Arabic and read some Hieroglyphs.

It seems strange to me that almost every country we visited had its own languages and often its own religions, politics and lifestyles; people had their own individual dreams and fears and even their own ideas and beliefs about what would happen after their bodies died and were disposed of in their various ways. I often wonder what will happen to me too. For me, my life has meant being passed round various heads.

I have experienced much more than anyone, I think, could anticipate.

Now I know that I am a God, much more than a hat, for I have seen the world through the eyes of a God.

Let me tell you how that came to be.

OUT OF MY BOX

Ed was planning to visit a country called Egypt for the first time, with a girl called Ana, who was younger than him. Ed was twenty-nine years of age.

Ed had met a great number of interesting people with fascinating ideas and one of the issues raised in his mind was about the Great Pyramid just outside Cairo. It was said to have been built almost 5000 years earlier, during the reign of a Pharaoh called *Cheops* or *Khufu*.

Ed, however, was not entirely convinced that a structure of that size and accurate construction could have been built in the so-called Stone Age.

Ed had calculated that this one Great Pyramid alone contained millions of heavy stones, placed with great accuracy and aligned to the poles, and that placement of stones would have to be done at the rate of more than one per minute almost non-stop if the task was to be completed in 20 years as the books claimed.

They would need to cut the stones and transport and lift them, some to hundreds of feet in the air, to be placed accurately by a people that did not even know about wheels and pulleys.

Moreover, galleries, chambers and corridors had to be built-in.

Apparently, nobody actually knew how the building was done.

Even with modern technology, Ed had read, no construction company in the world would take on such a project.

Neither did anybody know why the pyramids had been built at all.

Some say that the pyramids had been used as tombs, yet no body had been found within, just a large but empty stone sarcophagus with a broken lid.

Others said the pyramid served as an initiation chamber. But, Ed thought, there were actually three massive pyramids on the same plain at Giza, just outside Cairo. Why would they need three initiation chambers?

Others believed they were built in a way that represented the appearance in the sky of the constellation of Orion, known in ancient Egypt as *Osiris*, or at least his "belt", possibly, they said, by an unknown race on earth who wanted to send us a message.

Ed had concluded, there was not even any proof of when they had been built.

Ed had also read books that claimed that even small pyramids had strange properties; even when made from cardboard or wood, the shape was said to be able to sharpen razor blades, purify water and even heal illnesses.

Ed was determined to find out more about the Great Pyramid and hence planned to visit Egypt in 1989 with Ana, to spend a week in Cairo and a week in Luxor.

This is where our adventure was to start, yet it was to last another twenty years before it came to an end.

1989 CAIRO, THE PYRAMIDS AT GIZA

I went to Egypt with Ed and Ana in February to coincide with Ed's birthday. We flew from London, going from the cold weather to delightfully warm. We landed at Cairo airport and, as Ed and Ana already had their visas, we passed quickly through immigration and customs formalities and went to the bank to change some money. We were changing UK Pounds to Egyptian pounds at the rate of about one to four. Ed smiled as he approached everyone as he had been told that was the key in Egypt and he certainly received smiles back.

"Do you like trips?" asked the teller at the bank kiosk, smiling broadly.

For a moment. Ed wondered if they were about to be offered LSD. Surely not at a bank in Cairo Airport, he thought. It was then that he spotted a couple of bottles of fizzy drink, called '*Tripps*'.

"Yes we do", Ed said and he and Ana were promptly passed two bottles that were opened by the desk teller. They drank the *Tripps*, changed their money, waved goodbye and set of to find the pre-arranged shuttle bus to the Hotel Sheraton, a Five Star, in the city centre.

Ana was an attractive and intelligent lady, a couple of years younger than Ed. Ana had studied and graduated in languages at the same university of East Anglia as Ed had attended studying chemistry. Ed was very fond of Ana.

Ed and Ana spent seven nights in Cairo, visiting the many sites, realising there was much more in Egypt than the

Pyramids to fascinate them.

They would be visiting the Giza plateau pyramids and Sphinx and the pyramids at Saqqara.

Their first visit to see The Great Pyramid was on their second day in Cairo and they went by taxi. As soon as they had arrived and descended from the Shuttle bus from the airport, they had been approached (almost accosted) by a taxi driver who promised to be there waiting at their convenience and, sure enough, he was there that morning to take them through the noisy heavy traffic to Giza, to show them where to go, give them advice, and wait there for them whenever they chose to move on.

Ed thought it was a good move to have a personal taxi available and the price was very cheap. As if it had been his idea!

Ed and Ana approached the Great Pyramid of Cheops. It was totally massive. They were amazed and pleased to see that today it was open to the public.

They had to buy tickets and them climb up to an entrance that had previously been blown open with dynamite; it was not the original entrance. Inside they had to climb up and down wooden ramps as they moved towards the Grand Gallery and then the Kings Chamber.

It was unbelievably large; I know Ed and Ana were somewhat mesmerized. I just concentrated on staying on Ed's head as he had to bow down as he moved inside the entrance and along the ramps. Those ancient Egyptians must have been small! I certainly did not want to fall down a shaft in here. It could be thousands of years again before I was found.

The King's Chamber, which Ed knew was not actually a king's chamber at all, being named as such in relatively modern times, was spacious. It was made of huge stone blocks, cut and placed to precision without mortar, so that even a small plastic credit card would not fit between. Above them was a massive stone roof; who knows how much weight ready to maybe fall on and squash us for ever. In the wall Ed could see a small square shaft entry that was once believed to have been for air circulating in ancient times although no exit shaft had been found outside. There was also the large granite sarcophagus with its broken lid on top, which again must have weighed tons. Ed had read that it was actually too big to get through the doorway so had been built in, presumably.

Heads, Hats and Tall Tales

Heads, Hats and Tall Tales

Ed and Ana stood alone in the Chamber (being unaware, as they were, that I was actually with them). They stood in silence. A great silence and stillness. It felt neither hot nor cold. Ed wondered again why this had been built and then sealed up. What had it been used for? How could anyone know the age when it was built, after all, dating stone is not the same as dating a building made of stone, for stones are many millions of years old and buildings only thousands. I wondered how anyone could even talk about millions of years.

Suddenly there was a great commotion from just outside the doorway. A crowd of tourists were filing into the Chamber. They were all chatting and laughing loudly; Ed recognised their language as French. One man stepped to the front and shouted "Ce n'est rien. Ce n'est rien. C'est vide".

I felt Ed react negatively to that, which he understood to mean "There's nothing, It's empty".

Ed did not said nothing aloud, but whispered in Ana's ear, "He's forgotten himself".

Ed and Ana left the Chamber and headed back outside, first visiting the Queens Chamber which was equally incredible to have been built.

Back outside, Ed and Ana sat for a while at the base of the pyramid enjoying the sun again. Ed was pondering out loud.

"I think it's really hard to comprehend the size of this pyramid, just that it's massive. When we come down from the road we couldn't even see anyone here, now we can't really see the real height because it slopes away from us. But this first level is almost as tall as us, each stone must weight tons. And how on earth did they build in those chambers and corridors?"

It was just then that an elderly Arabian-looking man in robes and sunglasses approached them with a beaming smile on his face and clutching a staff that looked like a wooden shepherd's crook with an animal head.

"My friends, my friends, welcome to Egypt. Welcome to pyramids. My name is Moses and I can tell you all information and show you good places."

Ed smiled and held out his hand, which Moses shook firmly. "Hello, my name is Ed."

"Greetings and welcome my good friend," said Moses, turning to Ana, "And this your Queen?"

"Yes," said Ed, knowing that it is so often better just to say that they were a couple or even married, in many countries and cultures. "This is Ana."

Ana held out her hand and Moses lowered his forehead to touch it, instead of shaking it.

"Moses"

"You like me to tell you about pyramid? Very big, yes. I tell you about it." Moses hardly paused before he delivered what must have been a well-practised speech.

"This is pyramid of Khufu and they say built by many men in twenty years. About 4500 years ago.

"Size is 420 feet and each side is 755 each long altogether over half mile to walk around, but not legal to climb up only OK for entrance and very dangerous to climb."

Ed felt as if Moses had read his mind as he had just been thinking of climbing. Ed had had done rock- climbing and walking up mountains in the UK whilst at University but then he had been twenty years old. Now he was less fit.

Moses carried on: "Inside pyramid Khufu is two and half million stones, my friends. Inside will fit big Cathedral St Paul in London, also the Cathedrals of Rome, Florence, Milan and Westminster Abbey. Base of pyramid here like seven blocks in New York.

"Big Grand Gallery is 28 feet high and slope is 26 degrees and long is 157 feet.

"King's Chamber is 34 feet and 17 feet and height is 19 feet and big sarcophagus inside

"Queen's Chamber is little smaller."

"You want to go inside?", asked Moses.

"No, we have already been thanks," said Ed.

"OK I show you around? You want to walk around? It will take maybe thirty minutes, take your time. You have water? You go that way and walk to boat museum and I will wait for you there, show you museum, explain all to you, and show you special tomb if you want to go, not public, only for you to because I know you are good people. You are guests of Moses now!"

Ed and Ana did indeed have bottles of water as it was like a desert here and very hot and they agreed to meet Moses at the boat museum. Ed told Ana he was wondering what sort of boat would be in the desert.

The walk, as we had been told, was about half a mile but it was hot and sandy and they took their time, arriving after about half an hour at a building where they met again with Moses. He greeted them like old friends and took them to the entrance to the building that he said was "big boat museum".

Once inside the structure, Ed and Ana approached the boat. It was rather disappointing. Ed thought it was much larger. This one was impressive but Ed realised it would not actually carry anyone, But then again, he thought, it is no doubt symbolic.

Moses was standing next to them.

"You like?" he asked.

"Now you see real boat!"

Moses pointed upwards above their heads, and as Ed looked up, he realised they were actually standing under just the front section of the actual wooden boat itself; they had been looking at a model.

"This one of two Khufu ships," he said.

"This one built over 4500 years ago and put in ground in pieces. Now they put together again. It is hundred forty-three feet long and almost twenty feet wide. discovered in your 1954 by Kamal el-Mallakh. But this boat no sails so people say it was never on the water. It is with much Cedar wood from Leban. Now you go upstairs for good seeing, my friends, I tell you well."

Ed and Ana climbed the stairs and were totally impressed, I knew, by the wooden boat, lit by natural light through the roof. They were able to walk around it.

Back outside, Moses still talking and leading the way, waving his staff in the air and greeting everyone they passed, we headed towards the second largest pyramid, said to have been built a few years later for the Pharaoh Khafre.

"This little smaller pyramid," explained Moses, pointing.

"This one sides 706 feet and height is 448 feet. Also there were boats in ground but no longer there my friends. Khafre was son of Pharaoh Khufu. But Pyramid closed now for tourists."

A quick look outside and Moses suggested they visit "Tomb of Doctor". He led them back round the pyramid and a little way from it where sat a man. Moses spoke briefly to the man and said "You give him little baksheesh and he let you go down inside very beautiful my friend."

Ed knew that *baksheesh* was basically a bribe or reward for services and was the custom in many Asian countries. I had realised that although the smile and eye contact was the key to the meeting with most people, baksheesh was the way to get what you wanted and to say thanks. He had already been told to give just a few coins often, such as to the room cleaners at the hotel; just a few coins every day.

Ed had experience with caving, so when he saw the ladder going down just inside the doorway opened by the keeper with his large key, he was not perturbed.

"It's OK," he said to Ana; "I'll go first and you come down after me so you can't fall."

But it was very dark. The Keeper gave them a small plastic

torch and Ed started descending into the black pit with Ana hesitantly above him, also descending.

They went down what must have been thirty steps on the ladder before Ed switched on the torch as the daylight from above was fading. The batteries were almost dead, they could see nothing. Ana wasn't happy even though Ed pointed the torch upwards for her.

"I don't like this," she said, "I can't see a thing. I want to go back up. It's too scary and anyway we won't be able to see what's down there if there's no lights."

Ed agreed. What was the point of climbing down who knew how far in darkness to see nothing and then have to climb up again? I knew too that he was concerned just in case they were locked in. Nobody other than the Keeper and Moses even knew they were there, and they hardly knew Moses anyway. What they were doing was probably illegal too. So he agreed and they both climbed up. Ed gave the torch back saying it was no good and needed new batteries, they could see nothing.

The Keeper just smiled. Moses said, "OK, now we have camel ride then see Great Sphinx.

Ana and Ed did climb aboard a camel. Ed had ridden a camel in Rajasthan years earlier, that time along with a camel driver to keep control, for three days in that Indian desert. That had been an escorted ride but this was just a tourist gimmick. Ana held onto Ed tightly, she did not seem comfortable, whilst the tradesman took a few photos. They soon descended, then the tradesman gave Ed his thick djellaba to put on and persuaded Ed to climb up again, for more photos. When they descended, they had to pay, an amount Ed thought far too much, but he remembered the golden rule that he had forgotten: to always ask the price first, before getting into a taxi or even on to a camel. So he just paid.

FATHER OF FEAR

They visited the **SPHINX** complex, with the great stone beast itself dominating the view of the Pyramids in the background, and it's temples.

Moses related some information about the Sphinx which I knew Ed hardly heeded, being overcome somewhat by the view. I listened and remembered though. That is, after all, something I was very good at.

"Father of Fear," said Moses.

"This one looking east. This one built for Pharaoh Khafre and there also Stele of Thutmosis Four between legs. Now it has head of man and body is like lion. Some people say that there are hidden passageways or rooms underneath the Great Sphinx, but nothing found. Stone Stele here says that young prince fell asleep next to the Sphinx, after hunting all day and very tired. In dream Great Sphinx promised prince can be powerful king of Upper and Lower Egypt after cleared the sand over up to neck. When Thutmosis older, he became great leader.

"This Sphinx is 240 feet long and 66 feet height and not built like pyramids; this one carved in rock."

Ed and Ana said goodbye to Moses and handed him some money. They went back to their taxi and told the driver to take them to Saqqara to see the Step Pyramids.

SAQQARA

The step pyramid of King *Djoser*, which Ed pronounced as Hoser, was said to have pre-dated those at Giza.

Ed said that he found it an impressive site and Ana agreed. It seemed very different to the Great Pyramid, somehow more feasible, she said. They chatted about how there was so much more to see in Egypt than they had thought and that the history itself was a longer period of time since the time of the Romans til now. In fact, Ana said, she knew that the ancient Romans had been in Egypt because of the tales of Caesar and Antony and Cleopatra. Ed wondered whether they had walked here. This place, he thought, would already have been ancient history for Cleopatra. In fact, prehistory.

The other pyramid close by was that of the Pharaoh Unas.

There was plenty of other stuff to see at Saqqara, but Ed and Ana were both tired and overwhelmed, so took their taxi back to the hotel.

THE NATIONAL MUSEUM IN TAHIR SQUARE

The following day, Ana and Ed spent hours in the Egyptian National Museum in Tahrir Square, within walking distance of the hotel. Ed took me off his head and put me into his bag whilst we were inside. I could still pick up on some of what he saw. Ana had undone the styling of her hair and was now happier about it.

Inside the museum, I felt that once again Ed and Ana were both amazed and overwhelmed by the amount to see on several floors. There were tall statues, large and small stone carvings, sarcophagi with and without mummies, mummified animals, scrolls, sections and furniture from tombs, temples and palaces.

"You know," Sid Ed, "there are plenty of books and pamphlets but there isn't one I've seen yet that makes any sense or order out of all this, they either skim over it or focus on just one or two bits."

"Well you ought to write one," said Ana.

The museum consisted of two floors. On the ground floor there were collections of papyrus and ancient coins, as well as a lot of artefacts from the New Kingdom, the time period between 1550 and 1069 BC.

On the first floor there were artefacts from the New Kingdom dynasties of Egypt, including items from the tombs of the Pharaohs Thutmosis the third and fourth. There were many artefacts from the Valley of the Kings and especially contents from the intact tombs of *Tutankhamun* and *Psuesennes* the first. Ed pronounced that one "Sues-Anna's". Two special rooms contained a number of mummies of kings and other royal family members of the New Kingdom.

Ed had never even heard of most of the Pharaohs named here. He was, he thought, lost in time and ignorant of it all.

The day came to leave Cairo on the next leg of their journey into the mystery of Egypt. Ed was saying a lot, "It may be his story but is it history?" aware that much of what they were seeing was actually prehistoric.

Heads, Hats and Tall Tales

History was said to have started when a Greek traveller called Herodotus first wrote down some of the stories told for generations around camp fires. Anything before that was called prehistoric and based on word-of-mouth.

1989 LUXOR

So, after a week in Cairo, we flew to Luxor, which in Arabic is called *al-Uqsur*. I was very glad that Ed wore me on his head most of the time, although by now we had such great affinity that I knew what was happening around Ed even when not on his head, I don't think Ed even knew that I was anything but a simple head-covering though. Yet!

We stayed in Luxor in a bungalow in the grounds of a big modern hotel called Sheraton, the same name as their hotel in Cairo. This one was next to the river Nile and very beautiful.

As they stepped off the tourist coach they had taken from Luxor airport, they were greeted by a small group of musicians playing "Happy Birthday to You" on a variety of stringed instruments and a hand drum. They were smiling broadly and all the tourists handed them baksheesh, so Ed did the same.

Heads, Hats and Tall Tales

The five-star hotel was very grand; the foyer was huge and busy with new arrivals and each person was offered a glass of a hibiscus soft drink which Ed enjoyed. They were quickly booked in and were led to their bungalow by a young man who carried their luggage easily.

They tipped him.

There was an artificial pool in the hotel grounds and they had to walk past it between the main building where the reception and the restaurants were situated and their bungalow. Six large pelicans lived in and around the pool and often stood on rocks as if posing as Ed and Ana walked passed. "Almost as if they're grinning, definitely showing off", Ed said to Ana.

The evening meals were part of their holiday deal and consisted of serve-yourself buffets with a range of food, washed down with local beer. Ed found the local wine to be undrinkable; it had a smell far worse than the river, certainly not what he called a bouquet.

The first evening, after dinner, Ed read as much as he could about what there was to see in and around Luxor and realised there would not be much time to relax. He made some lists so he could chat to Ana about what they would do the next morning. Ed fell asleep quite late.

Ed was awoken very early in the morning by the sounds from the nearby minaret from which a Muezzin was shouting through a megaphone about how great Allah was and calling the devotees to prayer. Then he heard Ana's voice: "Hello, is that reception? Well there's a lot of noise outside. Somebody is playing a radio or something very loud and it woke me up!"

Ed quickly explained to Ana that the noise was in fact part of the religion and happened more than once every day, to call the people for prayer, and dawn was the first time. We would get it every day. She was like somebody in the UK complaining about church bells. Ana laughed and said "Sorry, I thought it was a radio" to the phone and put it down. I knew now that many places had phones, even from one part of a hotel to another, not like back in 1972 when I had been taken on another head, called Al, whom I mentioned before, to India. In India there were hardly any phones. Human communication had become much more electronic. As a hat, I am not sure if that is all good or all bad or some of each, but that day I imagined that reception wished there were no phones.

I wondered also if there would ever be phones for hats.

Ed never even knew that I was a being and that I had such a good memory. It was all one-way in those days. On the other hand, or head, I had never communicated with another hat and I did not know if those many hats that I had seen even had any story to tell.

I am Myhat, and have many tales.

Now, in Luxor in Egypt on the river Nile, I knew that neither Ed nor Ana knew much about the place, even less than they knew about Cairo.

Ed knew that there was supposed to be a great tomb here, said to have been discovered about a hundred years ago by Howard Carter and to have been the burial place of a boy king called *Tutankhamun*.

He knew it was in a place called The Valley of the Kings on the other side of the Nile, on the West bank where the sun set. He wanted to go there. He also knew, though, that there was supposed to be an ancient curse on anyone who went inside. I wondered if hats would be cursed too.

Ed and Ana sat and made a list of what they wanted to see and do. Looking through the brochures and day trips on offer by taxi or coach, there was a lot to see.

First there were the great temples of Luxor and Karnak.

Those were on the east bank, the same side as the hotel. There was a small local museum.

Across the river there was not only the Valley of the Kings which in fact had many more tombs than just *Tutanhkamun's*. There was also the Valley of the Queens, the Valley of the Nobles, The Mortuary Temples of *Hatshepsut* and *Ramesses*, and his *Ramesseum*, *Medinet Habu*, the Colossi of *Memnon* and the workman's village at *Deir el Medina*. They were all within reach of each other but surely it would take more than one day.

Also, Ana, being fond of boating, persuaded Ed to include an afternoon ride in a *felucca* on the river in their itinerary.

Heads, Hats and Tall Tales

They also chatted about taking a day trip to Aswan to see the dam and some temples on the way.

Also they wanted to see the Souk market and maybe catch some local life.

By the time they finished, there would be little time to laze around the swimming pools as many tourists seemed to enjoy doing.

Of course I never had any say in those plans, not that I would have known what to say, had I the chance. As usual, I focussed on watching, listening and remembering. The name *Hatshepsut* had captured my imagination too.

It was a slow breakfast that first morning and as the day got hotter they decided to take a taxi to Luxor Temple, the smaller of the two big temples in Luxor town itself and then to carry on to the much larger temple complex at Karnak, which was a few miles away, after lunch.

The taxi ride was just a few minutes; they passed many kalesh (local horse and carriages), as well as numerous taxies, buses, cars and trucks. All the traffic movement seemed very random to Ed, just about keeping to the correct sides of the road. They pulled up at an open green area where the entrance to the Temple was situated and they bought their entrance tickets. The taxi driver told them he would wait as long as they wanted and then take them to Karnak.

LUXOR TEMPLE was impressive even from the taxi. The columns were clearly very tall and what had survived thousands of years was obviously built well and with great devotion.

Heads, Hats and Tall Tales

As soon as they alighted from their taxi and paid, they were approached by several street hawkers offering papyrus cards, papyrus paper, papyrus bookmarks and small trinkets; many of the hawkers were children that looked no older that ten. They each shouted "Hello mister, welcome to Egypt, you want to buy?" insisting that their goods were genuine. Not that he wanted the stuff, but it was so cheap that he felt he had to buy some. Ana bought some greeting cards made from papyrus and a city map.

They headed towards the entrance to Luxor Temple itself to what was once a very holy place but now just, in fact, a tourist attraction. The massive stone entrance had a gigantic statue either side and a tall obelisk on one side.

Ed and Ana wandered about inside, looking at the lofty columns and pylons and admiring the courtyard, taking a few photos along their way. Although it was a massive construction, nothing like the pyramids, it was very impressive. They stayed for just about half an hour. It was already hot and they went outside to get a drink at a small stall they had spotted and then took a look at the Avenue of Sphinxes. Although many of the stone statues were damaged, Ed thought they were beautiful.

Their taxi was waiting outside and the driver called to them as they reached the road, so they jumped in and headed to **KARNAK TEMPLE**.

There was a short walk from where the taxi dropped us off and, once again, the driver said he would wait. This time he would not take payment and simply said "later".

As they approached the main entrance after buying their tickets, Ed and Ana were again approached by many street hawkers offering papyrus scrolls with beautiful colourful paintings of scenes from stories of the ancient gods and the afterlife; others offered small statuettes of kings and gods, cotton shirts and djellabas, postcards and books whilst one man even offered a ride in a boat across the Nile.

Ed and Ana walked down to what Ed thought was the other end of that Avenue of Sphinxes from Luxor, towards the main entrance which had tall statues on either side of the main doorway portal.

"Ed, I read that the Avenue of Sphinxes is a mile and a half long," Ana said.

"Let's sit here on the wall and I'll read a bit before we go in, 'cos I reckon it's huge and we'll never know what's what."

As soon as they entered through the massive stone pylons, Ed forgot almost everything the pamphlet had explained and was simply in awe of the size of the place, not least the height, width and sheer numbers of stone columns that had presumably once held up some sort of roof.

Of course, I remembered, as I did.

Ed said to Ana: "Just think, Pharaohs and priests walked here. It never used to be open to the public in those days. This was the holiest of places and they had secret ceremonies."

Ed and Ana tried linking arms around one of the columns. They couldn't. The columns were covered with carvings of hieroglyphs.

At one point one of the men working as what Ed had called Guardians of the Temples beckoned Ed over, so he walked over to the man.

Heads, Hats and Tall Tales

"You want to see something very special not for all people?" the Guardian asked. "Small fee and I take you now. But your Queen stay here OK and wait." motioning at Ana.

Ed always was one to explore so, with me still sitting firmly on his head, he followed the man who walked behind a building and started to climb, scramble, up and around until they came out on the very top of what Ed thought to be one of the temples or chapels. It was a bit of a scramble upwards but Ed thought well worth while. From there he had a 360 degree panorama and could see the Sacred Lake and the countryside beyond; he could see the Nile and the West Bank. Ed took some photos, thinking he could maybe put them together as a collage one day. He wanted to sit and absorb the view, but the Guardian was saying they had to go back down. Ed thought it not entirely safe, that climb and descent, and probably illegal. He paid the Guardian who gave a big smile and shook hands and then immediately called over another tourist.

Ana had waited and Ed told her enthusiastically about his expedition. She said she was not keen on heights and glad she had not followed, as she had at first been inclined to do.

They walked on past side-chambers or chapels and statues and spotted the two big obelisks that were standing and then the fallen one; unless of course it had never been raised. Ed didn't know.

Then they reached the Sacred Lake.

The rectangular lake was quite large and the water was blue. Ed could see at the far side were rows of seats in tiers. They walked up the left side and found a place to sit. There was a hoopoe bird standing on a block. It was very tranquil away from all the Guardians and hawkers. They sat in silence for a while, and Ed read from the information page.

Tired now, the two humans decided to walk back to their taxi and go back to the Sheraton, which is what they did. Ed was pleased to have seen and read about the two big temples.

Karnak was the largest open temple site in the world. He had read that it covered one hundred hectares, larger than many ancient cities, and thousands of years old. In fact, it had been added to and added to for about a thousand years.

"Karnak was not built in a day," he mused.

Heads, Hats and Tall Tales

That evening Ed and Ana enjoyed a meal in one of the hotel restaurants. Ed ordered a bottle of local white wine. Once opened, he smelled the stuff and sent it back. He ordered a bottle of local red and sent that back too. The waiter did not even smell it; Ed thought maybe religion prohibited him from inhaling alcohol, or maybe he simply knew it smelled so bad that it was undrinkable. So Ed ordered local beer instead and, surprised as he was, he found it quite palatable. They had a good meal and an early night, knowing that no doubt the calls to prayer would wake them again at sunrise.

The following morning, Ed and Ana had a slow and prolonged breakfast at the hotel buffet. There was a huge selection of mostly serve-oneself dishes: muesli, porridge and cereal with milk or soya milk or yoghurt, fruits, fish dishes, various breads, cold meats such as lamb and turkey, cooked English-style breakfast including eggs, fried, boiled or scrambled, fried meats, hot tomatoes, onions, courgettes, egg plants, potatoes and the local dish called ful which is mashed cooked beans; there was a whole range of salads and a long line of different cakes as well as pancakes with different dressings. Also a selection of drinks available including local champagne, which they did not try.

Ed ate far too much.

So, after that slow breakfast, Ed and Ana decided to go for a walk along the Nile and head towards the *souk*, an alleyway marketplace.

They left the Sheraton and were immediately approached by a man selling papyrus approached them. They smiled and returned his "hello" and said no. He followed them but they kept saying no. Then a man selling small statues and some children offering postcards supposedly made from papyrus. Other men were inviting us to see their shops, buy spices, change money, go for a tourist trip or even ride a camel or donkey. Every *kalesh*, the horses and carriages, and every motorised taxi that passed tried to get Ed and Ana as customers. I could tell Ed was becoming impatient with what was becoming harassment although he well knew they were mostly trying to make an honest wage or commission.

They walked to a low wall between the pavement and the river and sat down. It was no more than minutes before a young man dressed in a blue tunic approached them. He asked where they were from and how long were we in Egypt and was it our first time and did we like it. He said that his name was Horus and that he was the captain of his own *felucca* boat and pointed to a wooden boat with its tall sails. If they wished, he had said, they could go with him and sail down to the crocodile island and eat a meal that he would cook on board, all very cheap. Three hours.

Ed knew that Ana loved sailing on boats and sure enough she wanted to go. Ed on the other hand, although he had been on boats, had never been sailing, did not swim and had heard about the risk of illness from the water in the Nile. He thought to try to delay what may have been the inevitable few hours sailing by saying that they were heading towards the souk, so maybe some other time. Horus did not seem upset and smiled and said "OK, maybe later. I will wait for you."

Then they chatted about families and Horus recommended they go to the West Bank to see the tombs and temples. Ed and Ana said goodbye and carried on down the road towards the turning to the *souk*. They dodged the street hawkers, boat captains, taxi and *kalesh* drivers, just smiling and saying "no thanks."

They walked as fast as was comfortable towards the *souk*, with Luxor Temple on their left, they spotted what looked like an army of *kalesh* carriages.

"God, look at that!" said Ed, "It's going to be like running the gauntlet and when we get in the market I can see it being a real hassle. You sure you want to go shopping?"

Heads, Hats and Tall Tales

Ana said that she wasn't bothered as there were lots of shops and they had tourist stuff in the hotel shops too. She told Ed that there was not actually anything she really wanted to go there to buy.

So they turned back, and instead went into the large hotel and café across the road from the Nile, for tea.

It was called the Winter Palace It had been built in the times when Egypt was a colony of Great Britain. It was a large building with a beautiful and clean-looking facade. They walked up steps and around to the grand entrance, inside and through to a grassy courtyard where they saw tables and chairs and then sat down and ordered tea. Ed thought that it was probably six times the price of anywhere else, but cool and pleasant to sit there, just the two of them.

Ana persuaded Ed, then, to walk back to Horus and take a journey in his *felucca*.

Sure enough, Horus was waiting for them, or seemed to be, and waved to them as they approached. It did not take long before they had an agreement on the price, although Ed knew, and he thought Horus knew, he would give *baksheesh* at the end of the trip.

They were soon in the boat, and Ed was surprised to be feeling quite comfortable about that. Horus explained that they would slowly sail up the river to Crocodile Island and they would stop somewhere and he would cook a lunch of fish and salad and rice and not to worry because everything was cooked and washed in bottled water.

Ed thoroughly enjoyed the journey there and back, just watching the riverbanks as they seemed to drift by. It was a calm afternoon. They had only a small problem at one stage when the boat became stuck close to the bank, but Horus' "boy" who was on board quickly jumped into the Nile and pushed the boat away from the bank; Ed thought that the locals must be immune to whatever the bacteria was that posed such a threat to tourists. Ana said she'd had a lovely day too, out away from the salesmen and taxi drivers.

They reached the hotel just as it was getting dark.

The following morning, Ed and Ana decided it was time to see some tombs on the West Bank. The tomb of Tutankhamun was a must, according to Ana, and the best way, they thought, would be by taxi. There were always taxies at the hotel so pretty soon, filled again by a hearty breakfast they set off in a taxi to the ferry. The driver said he would leave his taxi with his brother and they would cross the river by ferry, then get another taxi at the West Bank landing. He said his name was Mustafa, and that he would take them to the Valley of the Kings and then to see a Queen's tomb and some Tombs of Nobles.

THE VALLEY OF THE KINGS

It did not take long before they arrived at the car park where the taxi was waiting and soon Ed and Ana were walking up a dusty road towards the tombs in the Valley of the Kings.

They could see ahead of them the pyramid apex to the mountain, which was said to have been the reason that this valley was chosen, in recognition of pyramids being something special in Egypt.

Heads, Hats and Tall Tales

They reached the point in the road where signposted tracks led to the individual tombs. Ed and Ana had already decided to visit the tombs of *Tutankhamun*, *Seti* the First and one of the *Ramesses*.

First they went to *Seti* the First. By now Ed and probably Ana knew that Seti was a powerful warrior Pharaoh, the son of *Ramesses* the First who had founded a new dynasty.

At the entrance of course there was the usual Guardian, this time with a battery powered torch, and as they entered and showed their tickets, he simply followed them talking non-stop, shining his torch where he wished.

"This tomb very big," he said.

"It is one hundred twenty metres along. It was opened by Belsoni, he strong man from Italy, 1817. Everywhere we see beautiful paintings of Seti and the gods."

We walked along corridors and up and down ramps into side-chambers as the Guardian pointed out *Seti* and the gods and goddesses. "Here is *Seti* praying to sun, *Ra*, also *Amun-Re*. There is *Isis*. Here is *Hathor* and there, *Osiris*. Now we see *Hathor* and *Isis* again."

We saw a chamber with pillars where the Guardian pointed out scenes from the 'Book of Gates'. We arrived at the Burial Chamber where the roof had been decorated with stars.

The whole tomb complex was incredible. Ed wondered just how long and difficult it must have been, just to carve this all out, cover so much with detailed depictions and symbols, then probably fill it with treasure and a dead Pharaoh to then be sealed up, as they thought, for all time. He thought about how fortunate it was that the climate here had helped the beauty survive.

There was far too much to comprehend here. Ed vowed to read up on it later.

All too soon they were ushered out, back into what now seemed like incredible bright sunshine. Ed gave the traditional *baksheesh* to the Guardian and they headed back down to look for the sign to the tomb of *Ramesses*.

They spotted a sign that read '*Ramsis* I Number KV16' and followed the path.

This was a much smaller tomb and had apparently never been finished before the king died, according to their new Guardian who led them inside and down quite a long flight of stairs. The walls here were not decorated. The stairs led directly to the actual burial chamber.

Within the burial chamber they saw a red granite sarcophagus. The chamber was not very large at all; there would not have been so much room for treasure. Here the wall paintings were astoundingly colourful and beautiful. There were scenes of the Pharaoh being carried to his burial. They saw images of *Osiris* on one wall, and *Kephri* on the other.

On each side of the entrance, we saw paintings of the goddess *Ma'at* welcoming the deceased king. On the left wall, we saw the king depicted making an offering of two vases of wine to the god *Nefertum* who wears an open Lotus flower on his head. On the right wall we saw more scenes from the 'Book of the Dead' showing the gods in judgement of the dead Pharaoh's soul.

On the back wall there were more beautiful paintings of the gods with the Pharaoh *Ramesses*.

Heads, Hats and Tall Tales

After leaving that tomb, Ed and Ana, once again impressed, headed down towards the entrance to the most famous Pharaoh of all, *Tutankhamun*, one of the few Egyptians kings that Ed had even heard of before this holiday trip.

Well, Ed had read about the supposed curse that was put on all who enter the tomb. Apparently the Earl of Carnarvon had been bitten by a mosquito after leaving the tomb and later died. He had been a sponsor of Howard Carter who rediscovered the tomb in 1922, Ed knew, and he had not been the only person that entered that had later suddenly died. Of course, Ed considered the hundreds of thousands that had been inside since. But something was niggling him enough, and he was already tired and wanted tea. So he decided to sit on the wall outside whilst Ana went inside.

Ed knew that *Tutankhamun* had been a teenager when he had died, apparently suddenly, and that his tomb had been crammed full of treasures from his life, things that he would have wanted in his afterlife. Much of that treasure they had seen in Cairo in the museum. But, in fact, Ed knew, Tutankhamen had been quite a minor Pharaoh and that his tomb had been hidden away and probably never robbed, as so many others had been.

It was not long after she came back out that Ana had in fact been bitten by a mosquito. They laughed about it, but I felt Ed was a little concerned too. Ana did say that she was really impressed by what she had seen.

I can tell you now though, that Ana did not die from that bite.

Later, they paid a brief visit to the Mortuary Complex of Pharaoh Queen *Hatshepsut* which stood alongside the ruins of the temple of *Mentuhotep* and a few other ruins.

Ed had seen on the map that there was a tomb fairly close by, that had been built for this *Senemut*, so he suggested to Ana that they visit it and she agreed. They had to scramble a little up a hill to get to the tomb entrance which was like a large stone doorway. There was a guardian waiting there and he took them inside with his torch. There were no electric lights in there.

Inside the tomb the chamber had incredible ceiling and wall decorations, full of detail. This was their first tomb of non-royalty. *ahri. Senenmut's masterpiece building project was the Mortuary Temple complex of Hatshepsut at Deir el-Bahari. It was designed and implemented by Senemut on a site on the West Bank of the Nile close to the entrance to the Valley of the Kings.*

That was the last day trip for Ed and Ana. They felt dumbfounded by the amount of information they had tried to absorb. They had met some friendly people and there had been no hostility or problems at all. Most of the locals in Luxor smiled and waved at them, the children, often without shoes and wearing rags, all asked for "*baksheesh*", some few coins or sweets; the older children also asked for "*Ben*". Ana told Ed that they were being asked for pens, as all the children had only pencils and crayons in their poor schools. Sadly though, we did not have *bens* to give them.

This was Ed's first visit to Egypt. I know he was more confused about the almost 2500-year history (mystery) than before he arrived, and he took a year trying to make lists of Pharaohs, Temples, Pyramids and tombs, with dates.

1990: AYMAN

The following year, Ed returned on another tourist package holiday, for another week in Cairo and week in Luxor with Ana. Before they left Norwich,, Ana had given him a gift to open when he arrived. Ed had also purchased a hundred ball-point pens, which he remembered all the locals wanted and called "*ben*".

Ed and Ana were booked on a similar two-week holiday as previously, spending one week in Cairo and one week in Luxor. Ed knew he wanted to see some places again, and some ones additional too.

Ed had started to try to make sense of names and places and dates since his last trip.

When they arrived in Cairo, Ed opened the gift from Ana. It was another hundred "*bens*".

Ed had two hundred pens to give away to the people in Luxor when they were out on the West Bank.

Ed took Ana to see the pyramids and Sphinx at Giza again. This time there was no Moses to guide them and they strolled around on their own, which brought Ed pleasure in itself; well there were plenty of other tourists and some in groups with an expert guide telling them about what they were looking at, and Ed and Ana had a listen too.

The Great Pyramid of *Cheops* also called *Khufu*, was closed to tourists this time, but the second pyramid, supposedly built some five thousand years ago for a Pharaoh called *Khafre* also known as *Kephren*, was open. They also took a look around the outside of the relatively modest-sized Pyramid of *Menkaure* also known as *Mykerinus*, along with a number of smaller satellite edifices known as 'Queen's pyramids'.

A day later, they took a tourist trip to the oasis of Fayoum, also to see the ruins of a pyramid built for a twelfth dynasty

Heads, Hats and Tall Tales

Pharaoh called *Amenemhat* the First. Fayoum is about sixty miles from Cairo but it took over two hours, even though the bus was in good conditions and the roads not very crowded. It was a hot ride. The hostess explained a few things about the town.

The next day was their last day in Cairo so they decided to spend the morning back at the pyramids, the afternoon in the museum and in the evening they would go by tourist coach back to the Giza plateau for the Sound and Light show.

It was a tiring day and a cold night. The hotel had provided rough woollen blankets and they enjoyed the show. The show was a bit amateurish using what was probably out-of-date equipment. Lights were directed on the pyramids which where quite a distance away from the wooden tiers of seats where we sat. A commentary about the site was broadcast through tinny speakers.

Ed enjoyed it for what it was, as he said to Ana on the way back to the hotel by coach and she agreed.

Soon it was time to take the pre-booked flight to Luxor.

The next day, shortly after leaving the hotel, they were approached by a man who offered donkey-riding days to explore the West Bank. His price was so low that Ed and Ana agreed to meet him the next morning near the ferry crossing and spend a day with him. He said his name was A

The following day, they set off in the morning to meet their donkey-ride host, Ayman. Sure enough, he was waiting near the entrance to the ferry. He quickly led them passed all the other men offering boat rides, donkey rides or souvenirs, and bought the ferry tickets.

Ed thought it was a bit of a rickety old ferry boat with two levels, that shuddered its way across the Nile. It was quite crowded, mostly what seemed like local people with bundles. Most were dressed in *djellabas* although some young men wore jeans and T-shirts. There were what looked like a few other tourists too.

Upon arrival at the West Bank disembarking point, Ed realised that he was about to enter a quite different Luxor where things appeared to be more basic. The walked up the ramp and followed Ayman a short distance to where two donkeys were being held by a boy. Without many words he helped Ed and Ana to get onto the two donkeys.

Ayman told them "Always wait until I hold donkey before you get on, otherwise maybe problem.

Heads, Hats and Tall Tales

Ayman said "I take you now on full day trip with lunch. We see Colossi, Temple Hatshepsut, Deir el Bahri, Temple Seti, Medinet Habu, Deir el Medina workmen village and Ramasseum. We have lunch half way. Later we see village life and we see sugar cane and alabaster factory. OK?"

Well, all Ed knew now is that he had heard some of those names but he did not know what was what or where or how old or which Pharaoh had built what or was buried where. I sensed he was keen to learn, so just said "yes", as did Ana.

We set off as Ayman continued talking and chatting about who we were and where were we from and how many children and what do we do in the UK. He called Ana "Your Queen".

First they had to buy tickets at a small kiosk at the side of the road, that would entitle them to enter some of the tombs and most of the temples.

Ed felt surprisingly comfortable on his donkey as they rode past the Colossi of *Memnon*, which Ed read out to Ana were two massive statues that *Amenhotep* the Third had built showing images of himself, which had been just at the entrance to a huge mortuary temple where he would be worshipped after his body was hidden in his tomb in the Valley of the Kings, which they would maybe see one day.

Ayman explained that our first stop would be at the village of the workmen at Deir el Medina.

The village of the workmen itself was quite large with ruins of houses gathered quite close together.

Heads, Hats and Tall Tales

They rode on past the gigantic statues towards the ticket office. Ayman went across and bought the necessary tickets, which were cheap enough.

After leaving Deir el Medina we started ascending the mountain.

Ayman pointed to the right and looking back one could see the Valley of the Queens and further away the mortuary temple of *Ramesses* the Third at *Medinet Habu.*

Medinet Habu

At the top, Ayman pointed out the connection between the Valley of the Kings and Hatshepsut's Temple much more clearly. It seemed only a short distance between the two. The Valley lay beneath us and we could see what looked like small ants scurrying around going into tombs, the entrances of which we could see clearly. On the other side we could look straight down on the top terrace of *Hatshepsut's* temple and the ramps of the lower levels. We could see the remains of part of the even-more-ancient mortuary temple of *Mentutotep*.

Ed and Ana got down from the donkeys to take in the scenery and take some photographs. The view was simply amazing for them.

Soon it was time to climb back on to the backs of the donkeys. Whilst Ayman was holding the one donkey for Ana, Ed decided he could get on without help, so put his one foot in the stirrup and tried to hoist himself up. The donkey started to move forward. Ed was stuck with one foot in the stirrup with one foot on the ground. He had to hop. He was very close to the edge. I fell off his head and started being blown by the wind even closer to the edge. Ed felt he was about to fall over the edge and I felt I was about to be blown over. By some sort of miracle, Ed thought, or even his guardian angel, there was a wooden post which he grabbed. It was just seconds before Ayman grabbed the donkey's reins and he had somehow even managed to scoop me up on his way. He held the donkey still as Ed managed to get onto its saddle. "I told you," said Ayman, "always wait."

We descended on to a road and Ayman guided us back to see the Temple of *Hatshepsut* itself.

As we rode towards **THE TEMPLE OF HATSHEPSUT.** I knew that Ed was thinking this must be one of the most beautiful temples that he had ever seen. It had been renovated.

Heads, Hats and Tall Tales

Hathor

I wondered if this *Hatshepsut* and *Hathor* were anything to do with hats.

Ed and Ana walked towards the temple, passed a short statue of some sort of falcon representing *Horus*, and walked up the stone ramp.

Heads, Hats and Tall Tales

At the top there were rows of stone statues, some with heads and some without, some showing residual blue and red coloured areas, all with arms crossed. These were lined up on each side of the entrance. They were at least 15 feet tall.

Cartouche of Hatshepsut

They were soon approached by a temple Guardian looking for *baksheesh*, no doubt. He quickly said hello and without pause started explaining what was what but in such a way that it was quite meaningless to us. Yet he took control and Ed and Ana followed him. He pointed out that *Hatshepsut* was a woman who claimed divine birth and was often depicted with the head of a cow, like *Hathor*. *Hatshepsut*, he said, had sent an expedition to the Land of *Punt* to bring back precious stones and gold and spices.

The Guardian showed them to what he called the Hathor Chapel and pointed out carvings that showed depictions of Hatshepsut suckling on a cow's udder, dancing for *Hathor* and seated between *Hathor* and *Amun-Ra*.

Nearby he pointed out beautiful *Hathor*-headed columns which were once part of a Hypostyle Hall.

Then he led them to the Temple of *Anubis*, a jackal-headed god. He showed them where carvings that, he said, were of Hatshepsut, had been destroyed.

Anubis,
God of the Dead

To one side of the ramps, looking down, they saw a vast array of blocks of stones that looked as if they were waiting to be sorted and put back together. Ed said he thought that must be part of the ruined Mortuary Temple of *Mentuhotep*.

"We'll have to come back here again if we get a chance, there's so much to see but I want to read up about it," said Ana.

After leaving *Hatshepsut's* Temple, they rode their donkeys and stopped at a Temple called the *Ramasseum*, the Mortuary Temple of *Ramesses* the Second. It too was impressive, but by this time Ed for sure was tired and not absorbing much, so they did not stay long.

Ayman said he wanted to take them to an alabaster factory but Ed made it clear that at this time they were tired and hungry and did not want to go. So Ayman told us that we could go to a house in the village for mint tea and then to his house for dinner and to meet his family.

"Let's do that," said Ana. Ed thought he'd be happy if he could just sit on a chair.

AL QUNAH AND UNCLE MUSTAFA

The village was called *Al Qunah* and this was the village they had seen from afar. Ayman said that there were tombs under the village and the people were always digging looking to find new tombs and precious things to sell. He said that his brother in the big house would show them some items whilst they had some tea but that there was no need to buy anything. Ed said that he did not want to buy anything.

Inside the house, we met a large chap dressed in a blue *djellaba* and a coloured headscarf. He smiled broadly and motioned Ed and Ana to sit in two armchairs, whilst he sat on a third. Ayman sat on the floor near the door, Minutes later a teenage boy brought in a large brass tray with a brass teapot and brass goblets. Black tea with sugar was poured for all and the boy took a goblet to Ayman; Ed noticed that Ayman took about six lumps of sugar.

Our host said his name was "Uncle" Mustafa. I could tell that Ed immediately felt suspicious of this Mustafa. There was some sort of mischievous or dishonest glint in his eyes. Ed determined himself not to buy anything.

Mustafa showed them a partly-disintegrated wooden figurine representing the dog-headed god of the underworld, *Anubis*.

Mustafa said, in broken English, that it was three thousand years old and that it had come from underneath one of the houses here. He told them that people could not buy these in shops and that it was very precious but for them there would be a special price of one hundred UK pounds.

Ed said that he had heard there were a lot of copies and forgeries on sale and that wood could be made to look old by soaking it in tea.

He asked Mustafa: "How do I know it is from the time of the Pharaohs?"

Mustafa said: "My friends, you can trust me. I am an honest man and I offer this to you because you come with my brother Ayman and he says you are good people."

Ed said: "It is so beautiful that I would buy it if it was a replica but If you are saying this is three thousand years old it should be in a museum. It must be more precious than one hundred pounds!"

Mustafa kept the same grin on his face but Ed could see he was disappointed. He did not even show them anything else, but as they finished their tea he stood up and offered his hand, saying "Bye bye, my friend, you very wise."

After leaving the house and village, Ed and Ana handed out pens, which the locals called bens, to many children but also to adults and, at one point, to a policeman who said "and *ben* for my wife and *ben* for son, mister please."

They set off, again on their donkeys,

At one place along the track and heading for Ayman's family house, they were approached by a young maybe teenage girl who offered them a rag doll; it was simply stitched and stuffed, but colourful enough, probably made from rags but certainly by hand. It had a square head with a funny face. It was very crudely made but then again, thought Ed a rare gift for somebody back home. The first asking price was cheap enough, so he handed over some Egyptian coins and a few bens as backsheesh.

They rode alongside fields growing crops and suddenly turned off up an even smaller road where there were several houses with small walls around. There were ragged barefooted children playing in the dust and chickens running around pecking at what must have been donkey droppings. Several of the young children ran towards us, greeting Ayman, who proudly said "My children. Come, my friends, my wife will have some food for us ready now. Please come, relax, eat and drink. I will take you to ferry after, before night comes."

Ayman's family house was a small brick building with a small courtyard outside where the donkeys were tethered. Ayman proudly introduced his four boys, who were called Mohammed, Omar, Youssef and Amir; he also had two daughters, Sara and Sofia, the youngest child. The youngest boy, Amir, looked about four years old. There was no sign of Ayman's wife.

First, Ayman brought water to wash, and then plates full of food; chicken, rice, bread, chips, vegetable dips, yoghurt and salads. They all sat cross-legged on the floor and feasted. The drink was water. Afterwards Ayman supplied fresh figs and sweet cakes with black tea.

Ayman seemed keen to learn as much as possible about Ed and where he and Ana were from; he asked about their jobs and their interest in ancient Egypt.

Ayman offered to take them to the entrance to a secret tomb that had many inscriptions that they could see and copy. He said that the entrance had been used to break into other tombs to look for artefacts, by some of the local people for many years, but now there was little left but the inscriptions. It was possible, he said, for a small fee, to be allowed to go inside.

Their time in Luxor was coming to an end, so Ed said no but promised one day to return to Luxor and see the tomb.

Sure enough, Ed and Ana found themselves back in the cold weather in Norwich, all too soon for them.

Ed thought a lot about what sort of technology and construction methods could have been used to create the magnificent and buildings that we had visited. He could accept that many temples, tombs and obelisks could have been cut using a large labour force, but when he thought back to the time of the Great Pyramid, or at least to the time that they had been built, supposedly, he realised that manpower alone would not solve the problem of time taken.

Ed had read that the Great Pyramid of Cheops or *Khufu* contained an estimated two and a half million stones, most weighing over seven tons, some weighing over twenty tons each. Those stones had to be cut, transported and placed with great accuracy and some had to be raised hundreds of feet into the air.

Egyptologists had written that it was completed in just twenty years and had to be finished when the Pharaoh died. They also claimed that the king had been buried within although there no body was found within.

They had written that a hundred thousand men would have been employed, which of course, Ed reasoned, would have needed a large number of other people such as architects and engineers, foreman and more people to feed them all.

So Ed did a calculation. He worked out how many minutes were in twenty years, assuming that the workmen worked for eighteen hours a day, for every day of the year.

There are 10,512,000 minutes in twenty years.

So, he thought, to place 2,500,000 in 10,512,000 minutes would mean accurately placing a stone about every four and a half minutes.

That, Ed thought, must have been impossible; after all, they were not even supposed to have yet invented wheel or pulley.

Heads, Hats and Tall Tales

That made Ed think that there must have been either some form of stone-age technology that has been lost, or it took a lot longer than twenty years, was not built for the Khufu we talked about, and maybe even built a great length of time earlier than 2,500,BC.

There was, Ed mused, a lot more mystery than history, when it came to ancient Egypt. He was determined to collect what information as he could about those days, try to put it in some sort of order and sense.

2010 BACK TO THE THE NILE

It was two decades before Ed was able to visit Egypt again and, once again, I found myself happily upon his head.

Again he went with his lady-friend called Ana.

He had seen Ana during the last twenty years and they remained good friends through her two unsuccessful marriages.

Ana was fascinated by the tombs and the prehistory.

She was also very clever with languages, including, by now, Arabic and Berber, which she had studied since 1990. She had also studied the ancient Egyptian hieroglyphics and demotic scripts used in ancient times which had been discovered on the Rosetta stone along with Greek. It was the Rosetta stone that first led to a better understanding of hieroglyphs after the time of Napoleon, in 1799.

Ana was slender in build with long red hair which Ed loved; she was naturally friendly, almost flirty, by nature. Ed knew that Ana done a great amount of travelling herself, to India and Nepal, North Africa and many places in Europe, as well as her previous trips to Luxor and Cairo with Ed, Ed thought she was quite capable of looking after herself, but also, feeling that he would do his best to protect her in Egypt.

I felt a little upset that he would put Ana before me, maybe cared more about her. Yet, quite often, he had left me on a chair or table and I had been lucky that somebody reminded him, including Ana; so I also appreciated her myself.

Ed was keen to see how Luxor had changed in twenty years. During those two decades, there had been trouble, even riots, in Cairo and other cities and a terrible incident when a tourist bus was shot at near the Temple of *Hatshepsut* on the West Bank at Luxor and people had been killed. Ed took advice and carefully considered the situation and decided Luxor was still one of the safest places to go. So they booked a three-week stay in a hotel on the West Bank which was closer to the tombs and a more authentic experience; not the standard of the hotels back in 1989 and 1990, but there was everything they needed.

Ed wondered what had happened to Ayman, the man who had taken them on the donkey ride in 1990. Would he still be alive? His children would have grown up by now and maybe even doing their own donkey rides. Ed had brought with him a photo of Ayman and his family taken back in 1990. He asked the guys at the hotel reception if they knew the man but they did not. They agreed, however, to get the photo copied and pass it about; if Ayman was still alive, somebody would know him, or maybe recognise the children.

On their first day, Ed and Ana crossed the Nile and visited the Temples of Luxor and Karnak as well as the Museum of Luxor on the Cornice beside the river. The Museum contained some of the most spectacular and well-preserved statues and artefacts that he had ever seen.

Although Ed had seen both temples several times already, he enjoyed spending the time with Ana again, able to point her to some of the sections and cite some statistics. He showed her the entrance to the climb that he had made at the invitation of a temple guardian, in exchange of course for *backsheesh*, decades earlier when he had been there with Ana. The guardian and Ed had scrambled up to the roof of a huge section from where they had a fantastic panoramic view. Sadly, Ed thought, the entrance was now barricaded.

The Luxor Museum, which cost just a small sum to enter, included entry to a film show and access to the main galleries.

Therein, Ed and Ana saw items that had them standing in awe.

Heads, Hats and Tall Tales

Among the items on display were grave goods from the tomb of *Tutankhamun* and a collection of twenty-six statues from the New Kingdom that were found at Luxor Temple. The mummies of the Pharaohs *Ahmose* the First and *Ramesses* the First were also on display. There was a reconstruction of one of the walls of *Akhenaten's* temple at Karnak. Amongst the featured items in the collection was a calcite double statue of the crocodile god *Sobek* and the eighteenth Dynasty pharaoh *Amenhotep* the Third.

That evening they went to Karnak Temple for the Sound and Light show. Again, he had seen the show twice decades before; it had not changed much, Ed thought, but he enjoyed being there again with Ana.

Afterwards they took an excellent but quite pricey fish dinner at a restaurant just down the road, before heading back to cross the river and back to their hotel. It had been a tiring day. They planned to head to *Hatshepsut's* Temple the next morning before it became too hot, then spend the afternoon in the cool courtyard of the hotel.

Heads, Hats and Tall Tales

The following morning there was a message at reception to say that the hotel Manager had found Ayman, the donkey owner who had taken him on a ride with Ana twenty years or more earlier. The Manager had left a message to say he could arrange a meeting the next day.

To Ed's surprise and pleasure, the following morning the hotel manager told Ed that he had indeed arranged for Ayman to be brought to the hotel that evening, by taxi as he had problems walking. Also Ayman's son was the taxi driver. Ed thought how strange it would be to meet again.

Ed and Ana went to visit *Hatshepsut's* Temple again.

They were surprised to see that the site had been cleaned up to some extent and some restoration work had been done.

Heads, Hats and Tall Tales

Ed had always had a fascination with *Hatshepsut*, a female pharaoh that future rulers had tried to erase from history but had failed.

Her mortuary temple at Deir el Bahari was one of the most beautiful in all of Egypt. *Hatshepsut* had claimed divine birth and was often represented as the cow-headed goddess *Hathor*. She had dressed as a man, wearing a kilt, false beard and crown. She had had temples constructed and raised obelisks at Karnak Temple on the east bank, sent expeditions south to the mysterious "Land of Punt" and been very powerful in her time. Ed and Ana both had a certain admiration for her although they knew also that she had been a very cruel and powerful tyrant too.

That evening, they took a meal at their hotel and at about seven o'clock, in walked a young man and an elderly man with walking sticks. It was Ayman.

Ed and Ayman first shook hands and then hugged; Ayman introduced the younger man, his son called Youssef, the taxi driver.

Ed felt a great warmth towards Ayman, even though they had met just once twenty years previously; in those days Youssef was just a child. Ed felt that he could trust them both.

Ayman's wife, he said, had died five years earlier; his daughters, Sara and Sofia, were married and had young babies of their own, his other two sons, Mohammed and Omar, were both working as tourist guides. His youngest son, Amir, had sadly disappeared years earlier.

Ayman no longer lived in his little house and now shared a different house in the "new" village belonging to his brother, Mustafa, who was ten years younger.

Ayman, Ed and Ana spent about an hour together, drinking tea and asking and answering questions, and laughing about their lives and how everything had turned out.

Ayman invited Ed and Ana to have dinner at his house the following evening and said that Youssef would collect them from the hotel at six o'clock and bring them back afterwards. Ayman was proud that they had mobile (cell) phones so keeping in touch would be easy. They exchanged numbers. There were no such phones in Luxor when they had first met.

The following day, sure enough, Youssef took Ed and Ana by taxi to Ayman's house. Brother Mustafa was not there. Ayman said he that he had gone to Cairo for important business. He explained that Mustafa had been an English teacher in Cairo, then moved back to Luxor and set up a business in antiques, made a lot of money and bought the house. He did not spend much time there, he said.

Ayman explained that his son, Amir, had disappeared when he was just twelve-years-old; apparently he and his friend Kareem had last been seen playing near some old houses in the old village. Amir and Kareem had never returned to their homes despite extensive searches including in the tunnels and tombs that lay beneath and connected to the old village houses. Ayman said that those tunnels had been a secret well-kept by the locals who had used them to find ancient artefacts that they then sold on the illicit market to rich tourists. Ayman said he remembered taking Ed to the house of such a salesman twenty years earlier It was his brother Mustafa, who had offered Ed a wooden carving of the jackal-headed god Anubis and Ed had said that if it was a replica, he would buy it, but if genuine then it should stay be in a museum in Egypt. Ayman said that he had thought Ed wise. Ayman and the authorities believed that his son Amir and Kareem had either been kidnapped, or had gone into the tunnels, fallen into the river or wandered into the desert and gotten lost

Ayman also told Ed and Ana that he could arrange, for a small fee, for them to be shown the entrance to the tunnels and a rough map, but that they should dress in Djellabah's, take some torches and spare batteries; also, he said, they should take some chalk to mark their way and notebooks and pencils if they wanted to copy the inscriptions, which there were plenty of, but he did not think they would find much in the way of artefacts from the time of the Pharaohs.

"Maybe some old Pepsi Cola cans or cigarette packets!" laughed Ayman.

Dinner was served and they sat on the floor eating with their hands: a local feast of chicken, salads, dips, bread, French fries and rice, yoghurt and fresh figs.

Afterwards, Ayman told his "boy" to bring tea with milk (most tea in drunk Egypt was not with milk), with biscuits and sweet stuff that Ed had never seen before.

Ayman asked if Ed and Ana smoked Alfalfa.

Ed never knew that plant could be smoked and wondered what it would be like. However, when Ayman passed Ed a metal tin with a green plant material inside it, Ed soon realised that it was, in fact, cannabis buds.

So Ed and Ana spent the next couple of hours smoking the cannabis plant along with Ayman and Youssef. Ed did not think that the cannabis was very strong, probably a good

Heads, Hats and Tall Tales

thing as Ayman explained that almost everyone there grew and used the plant, sometimes to ease pains but also just to relax.

They chatted about how Luxor had changed since Ed had been there twenty years previously with Ana. Ana. Ana was able to speak with them in Arabic and help with translation and explained how the whole world had changed. Luxor had many new buildings and many more people, like so many other places and, being a major tourist attraction, the emphasis now, said Ayman, seemed to be on the big hotels who charged more for one night than the average worker earned in a month. Of course, business had boomed for kalesh and taxi drivers and also the *felucca* men. But, he said, the number of kalesh and taxies had already grown so, at many times, especially in the summer when there were less tourists because of the heat, there were many drivers just sitting in hope for a fare. In the summer, many hotel rooms were empty and they had to lay off staff, so there were many unemployed and poor people in the summertime.

After a brief chat, Ed and Ana decided to take up Ayman's offer and explore the tunnels. It was to be in two days time and they would be taken to the house where the entrance to the tunnel was hidden in the garden at the back, setting off just before dawn so they would not be spotted by police or official tourist authorities. They said their good nights. "Mighty Night" said Ayman.

Sure enough, two days later, as planned, at five o'clock in the morning, Youssef arrived at the hotel. Ed and Ana had donned d*jellabas* on top of T-shirts and jeans. Ed took a small bag with his ID, some money, a torch, a box of matches and some pieces of chalk; also a ball of string which he could use to mark their way in the tunnels if they were damp; a bottle of water and some biscuits to eat. He took his mobile phone too. I was very glad that Ed decided to wear me that day too; I never would have guessed just how glad I was to be.

Youssef explained that he would show them the concealed entrance to the tunnels but that, as far as he knew, nobody had been inside for a long time; they should not expect to find any "old pieces" but they would see inscriptions inside the tombs. There were several tunnels leading to several tombs. Of course, he said, they must be careful not to get hurt or cause anything to collapse, although the tunnels had been there for decades without incident since they were built.

When they came back outside the tunnels, they should cover the entrance again and they should try not to let anyone see them leave the house, but once outside the house it was OK, he told them.

"And," he said, "If policeman sees you then say you are tourists exploring but do not say about me or father, then do not worry, you will be OK."

The journey to start of the bottom of the hill which led to the house was only minutes; they could have walked.

They scrambled up the hill. The house was boarded up and looked quite ruined, as did the other houses. It was just starting to get light.

Following Youssef around the side of the house to the back, they entered what was probably once a garden. They had to squeeze through a rough wooden fence. They helped him move some old garden pots that were broken, and some rusty corrugated iron that was probably once part of an out-building that had collapsed. Behind that, he showed them a wooden door which was laying on the ground, and when they moved that, they saw the entrance.

The tunnel went down almost vertically for what looked like twenty feet, as Ed could see in his torchlight.

Youssef showed them a rope ladder and how to attach it to pegs in the ground by the tunnel entrance. He told them again to be careful. He said that when they got back out, they should put the rope ladder back and cover the entrance with the door. Then they should phone him and go back to the hotel. He would hide the entrance again later.

Ed climbed through the hole in the ground and started to climb down the ladder. It was only a few steps before he knocked me off his head and I went falling down into the darkness. Oh how I wished he'd get some sort of strap to keep me on his head at times like this.

Before I knew it, I was alone at the bottom of this horrible place. Ed and Ana may well have been in places like this before, on rope ladders, but I had never enjoyed it when I was there. I remembered the time Al, my previous head, had climbed up the side of a ship that was bobbing up and down in the Mediterranean, the day he had left Antalya in Turkey, on his way, at that time, to Beirut. That was back in 1972. I was on his head, the wind threatening to blow me off into the sea, as Al had climbed from a small fishing boat and ascended the ladder. Al could not swim and, as far as I know, neither can I. Yet he obviously made it to the top.

I also remembered Ed descending a ladder near the Great Pyramid twenty years earlier, down into the darkness, not so many steps, and turning back upwards, never to reach the bottom where the tomb was supposed to be. But at that time he had no good source of light, now he had a torch.

I had hope.

My hope paid off, for it wasn't long before I sensed Ed was still climbing down the ladder and ... standing on me! I was not happy about that, I can tell you. He should learn to be more careful!

As he picked me up, dusted me off and put me back on his head, I realised, once again, that Ed was more concerned about Ana than Myhat.

Now, with Ana besides him, they headed down the underground corridor.

The tunnels were not high enough to walk upright. They did not have the feel of real ancient tunnels, being roughly hewn with wooden roof supports and a lot of rubble with trash on the ground. They were not level either.

Of course they were completely dark without the torches.

Ed drew arrows on the wall, pointing back the way we had come, as we passed more rough-hewn stone corridors on either side. Ed thought they may have led to tomb chambers, but he and Ana agreed to see how far the main corridor would go, first, seeing the side chambers on the way back.

At one point they almost missed a tunnel which went off from a small chamber that they arrived in. There were inscriptions on the walls, some looking very ancient and some with names and modern dates. It was as they looked back behind them that they saw two tunnels going, seemingly, in the same direction. Ed was keen to mark the correct passageway to take on their return. He wondered where the other tunnel would lead but decided to "check that out later" as he said to Ana.

Heads, Hats and Tall Tales

They continued along the main corridor until they reached another chamber which was blocked off on all sides; the way they had come was the only way in and out of this chamber. It was blocked by what looked like a large bolder, put there almost deliberately, thought Ed, and on the bolder was an inscription.

As the duo shone their torches on the inscription, Ana said that she would try to read what it said.

"Something about danger of death from what has gone before... that the great must rise towards the skies but only the Just will prevail. This is Anubis, the jackal-headed god of the dead," she said.

"Look there is Ra, shining upon the king."

"There's not much else here," said Ed; "let's head back and check out the side-rooms and corridors. We haven't been here even an hour yet," I guess.

"OK," said Ana, "but first can we just turn off the torches and sit for a while, see what it feels like. I think that inscription could be thousands of years old, judging by the style."

So they turned off their torches and sat quietly in the dark for some minutes.

"It's not completely dark," said Ed suddenly, "I can still see your outline. Look there! There's some light seems to be coming from behind that boulder: maybe there's another tunnel! We may have somehow linked up with one of the tombs that is open to the public and has electric lighting in its corridors."

"Well, we've been in here for almost an hour, I reckon but I don't think we've moved far enough to be anywhere near the Valley of the Kings yet. I can't get a signal on my phone, even the clock isn't working, but we're under a big hill so I am not surprised. I wonder if we can climb up and look through?" said Ana

Ed climbed up the side of the boulder and was able to squeeze through a gap; sure enough there was daylight. In fact, it looked like the daylight was coming through a gap along the top of another large boulder. He called through to Ana who, very nimbly, thought Ed, quickly joined him.

They climbed up to the top of the next boulder and could see through and, sure enough, could see the world outside the tunnels. There were green fields of crops, tended by a few workers, and beyond they could see the Nile.

As they walked outside. Ed looked back, and used his chalk to mark the boulder, which, looking back, he realised was quite difficult to distinguish from the other boulders along this side of the hill. The exit through which they had climbed was invisible from just yards away.

"Don't want to get lost," said Ed, "although I guess we'll just have to walk round the hill to get back to the village."

"It looks very different from here," exclaimed Ana.

"Look, there's the fields going up to the river, but on the other side there's what looks like a town but it's not Luxor. But there's no sign of the Luxor Temple and further up the river I would have thought we could see Karnak from here. There's just one or two buildings there. And not a lot of boats and no *fallucas* at all? No buildings at all, no tourist boats or hotels on the other bank. Where the heck or we?"

"I'll ring Ayman and ask him what's going on, where we are. We can't be far away but this view just doesn't make sense." So Ana took out her mobile phone.

"The phone's not working, it won't even switch on," she said. "We'll have to walk down the hill to the field, maybe we'll get a better signal or something, down there. We should do, it worked in the village and on the East bank too. Let's go and chat to that guy in the field."

As they walked, Ed took out his own phone.

OO – ARE – SET

Ana pointed to a worker who was doing something amidst a field of green crop. He was wearing just a loin cloth. It was very hot, much hotter than Ed had expected for quite early in the day. Ed felt overdressed in the *djellaba* over his jeans and tee-shirt, with me still clinging onto his head.

When they reached the worker, Ana spoke to him in Arabic.

The man shrugged and said something back. He was staring straight at me; I knew that I fascinated him and he wanted me on his head – not that Ed knew, but I would not have minded for a while, just to see through the man's eyes.

"He's saying hello, I think," Ana said, turning to Ed.

"It's not Arabic though, it's more like Berber, the language they still speak in the desert in Morocco. I didn't know they spoke it here. I'll try and ask him where we are."

Ana tried a few words and pointed around the place where they stood."

The man pointed across the river and said "Oo – are – set."

Ana looked at him and pointed also across the river. She said "Luxor?"

The man shrugged and said "Happy".

Ana said said something that was not English and smiled. "Temple of *Hatshepsut*?" she asked.

Another shrug.

"Temple Karnak? *Ramasseum*?"

No response to that, just a big smile on his face and a small bow.

"Oo – are - set! Oo – are - set!" he said pointing and laughing.

"I don't know those words," said Ana, "maybe it's somebody's name, like his boss? Or just an oo - are"

"Oh well," said Ed, "From what I can guess, if we go round the hill we should find the road back to the village or at least see something familiar. It's kind of weird here. It doesn't look at all right. I just can't fathom where we are."

They bowed slightly to the smiling man and set out to walk around the end of the hill that covered the tombs and tunnels they had passed through. From there, Ed thought, they should be able to see Luxor and the Temple.

In fact they did see a town spread out on the other side of the Nile, quite a large place but it was certainly not Luxor.

Heads, Hats and Tall Tales

There were no big buildings or hotels, no Temple, just what looked like a palace. There were no tourist cruise boats moored there, no *feluccas*, just small craft, going back and forth across the river. There was no ferry.

Ed was quite stressed out by now, I could tell, and I too was getting concerned that they were lost. Yet this side was not exactly a huge area, just fields between the hills and the river.

It just looked like somewhere completely different, as if they had exited the tunnels many miles up or down stream, somewhere they had never been before. They found no road, saw no trace of human habitation except for the few men working in the fields.

"The phone's still not working," said Ana, "I think we better go back and find that boulder and get back to Ayman and find out what's going on. Maybe he knows where we are. Maybe he has been here himself."

They walked back round the hill and scrambled up to find the chalk marks.

As Ed was about to climb through the gap above the boulder with the chalk mark, Ana asked "Is this yours?"

She passed Ed a small lighter which had a picture of the pyramids on. Ed flicked it, but it didn't work. He put it in his pocket anyway. It was a very hot day and I knew that Ed was keen to get back into the cool tunnels.

They quickly climbed back into the tunnel and followed the chalk marks, much faster than it had taken them coming this way, not stopping so much. There were several other tunnels leading off at points, so I sensed Ed was glad he'd marked the way. He had not noticed them all on the way through.

Just about half an hour later, they exited through to the garden in the dilapidated house.

"I'll phone Ayman," said Ed.

As he looked at his own mobile phone, he said "Well I get a signal but my phone says it's only eight-thirty"

Ana checked her own phone. "Weird, mine too. But it must have been two o'clock at least when we turned back, the sun was really high and I'm sure we were away for longer than that. We've definitely been gone for more than a few hours. It took over an hour to get through to the other end and we were there for at least four hours."

Ed phoned Ayman and said that they were back but that they had a problem so would like to meet him again later.

Ed and Ana left the garden, covering once again the entrance to the tunnels behind them.

They walked back to the hotel; sure enough it was only late morning.

They had black tea with milk and a late breakfast of corn flakes with milk, eggs and bread and sweet cakes and orange juice. They were both very hungry.

Ed took out some maps of the area and began scrutinising them.

"I can't work this out at all," he said, "whichever way we went and wherever we came out on the hillside, we ought to have been able to see Luxor and the Temples and we should have found the road. And I don't know why there weren't any boats. There aren't any towns that size for miles"

Heads, Hats and Tall Tales

He decided to walk the short distance from the hotel towards the river. Ana said that she wanted to take a rest so he went alone.

Ed saw everything was as as it should be. There was the river, the ferry and, on the East Bank, he could see the cruise boats and Luxor town along with its Temple and tall lush hotels. Plenty of people about too, as usual, carrying on their daily business, taxies and trucks, donkeys pulling carts.

Puzzled still, he went back to the hotel.

Ana said that Ayman had phoned her to say that Youssef would pick them up at six o'clock.

"I've been thinking about what that guy said. You know when he pointed and said Oo – are - set?

"Well there's nowhere here called that and I asked the manager at reception if he knew anyone called that or any place and he said no. But he said that centuries ago the old place was called *Waset* even before it was called *Thebes*."

"I looked it up and he's right but that was four thousand years ago, in the time of Pharaohs *Senusret* the First and *Amenemhat* the Second."

Ah, another Hat, I thought, maybe an ancestor. Remember dear reader, that I had also heard of a woman Pharaoh called *Hatshepsut*, who also had a temple built here.

Ana continued: "The books say they were Twelfth dynasty, after *Mentuhotep* the Second, Eleventh dynasty. They'd had a war with the North which lasted for about fifty years and then many of the *Nomes* were united. The town was called *Waset*. *Waset* was a Goddess."

"Maybe what we saw was some sort of touristy replica or something, but it must be a huge site. We"ll ask Ayman about it this evening," said Ed.

"Pretty weird. I'm going to ask Ayman if we can go back; we'll cross the river and find out what's going on," said Ed.

That evening, Youssef arrived at the hotel a little after six o'clock and took the pair to Ayman's housed again. His brother, Mustafa, was still in Cairo on business, but would return maybe in a few days time, but, he said, Ed and Ana should indeed go back to the tombs and explore beyond, for he himself knew of nowhere or nobody with the name Oo - are – set or *Waset*. Youssef did not know the name either.

Once again, Ayman's boy brought in a small feast, this time fried fish with vegetables, chips, rice and bread, with a selection of fruit and, this time, Ayman proudly announced that he had "Ingleese teas with milk from cow".

Once again, after eating, they sat smoking the green buds and leaves from locally-grown cannabis, chatting away about what they had seen and about how Luxor had changed in twenty years.

Ayman said that Youssef would meet them and take them back to the entrance to the tunnels early in the morning in

Heads, Hats and Tall Tales

two days time.

That would give Ed a chance to check out all the old maps of the area to try to work out where they had been.

Ayman explained that there was certainly no tourist exhibition in the area. He said they should look again for the roads and agreed that they should take the ferry across the river, or another boat, and find out the name of the town.

He said that he was thinking and wondering if that was where his son Amir had gone to years ago and even had a "little hoping" that they would bring him back, even though now he would be a man of about twenty years of age.

Ed showed Ayman the lighter that Ana had spotted outside the exit boulder.

"It has a picture of the pyramids on it but no gas. I'll give it to you. I guess it doesn't mean much but it was the only thing we found.

"Funny thing to find right there, though, right outside the exit boulder. So it's a small memento but in the distant future it may mean more for your descendants, it will be antique!" Ed laughed.

"Mighty Night", said Ayman.

The following day they crossed the Nile by local ferry, always filled with locals and people touting tourists for trade for taxi or *felucca* trips.

They planned to go to the small house of a man whom Ayman had called "Professor Bertie" and who, Ayman had said, had several old maps of the area around Luxor and other places along the Nile.

"If there is place now called *Waset* or Wasat or anything like that, he would know.

"In Arabic, Luxor we call *al-Uqsur*. It sounds similar but not like *Waset*."

Ayman said the man's name was Albert but he was called by most people as Professor Bertie and he was "Ingleese".

SALEEM AND CINDERELLA

Ayman had told Ed and Ana that they would be met by a *kalesh* driver called Saleem who would recognise them and meet them at the ferry port on the East Bank. He would take them around the town and to the house of Professor Bertie, wait for them and then bring them back to the local ferry.

As they were getting off the ferry and starting to climb the steps leading up to the Cornice, the road that ran beside the Nile at that part of town, they spotted a man wearing a brown d*jellaba* who was smiling and waving at them.

He quickly descended the steps to greet them with a broad smile and handshake, saying that his name was Saleem. He led them back up the steps and kept away the other men touting for trade, almost as if we had become his property. He said he would show them around "real life Luxor, where people live" as well as the *souk*, the marketplace and take them to the Government shops. After that he would take them for lunch in a "cheap local-not-tourist restaurant" and, after lunch, take them to the house of Professor Bertie.

Ed said that they had been to the Government shops before and did not want to go but that they would go to the *souk*, then go to Luxor Museum, have lunch and then see Bertie.

They climbed aboard the *kalesh*, with Saleem sitting in front driving the horse. Ana commented that the horse looked healthy and well-fed. Saleem said: "She called Cinderella, my best horse; very good girl. I have another horse and she named Black Isis."

Before they even knew it, within minutes they had arrived at the *souk*. Saleem said that they should walk through the first street where shops were selling souvenirs, then at half-way point he would meet them with the *kalesh a*nd drive through the "local market".

So that is what they did. As they climbed down from the *kalesh*, Saleem said to Ed "I like your hat. You give to me as gift?"

Ed just said "No chance!" and pulled me down firmer on his head. I gripped tighter. I did not want to go with a *kalesh* driver. I wanted to go to Oo – are - set.

They walked fairly quickly through the *souk*, not wanting to buy much. Yet as they walked past one of the shops in a row of shops selling tourist souvenirs, Ed spotted and then bought, with very little bartering or haggling as was the custom here, a small statuette of the Pharaoh *Akhenaton*, black, made out of basalt; I know he had wanted one for twenty years at least. I wanted him to buy a statue of *Hatshepsut*, but he didn't. Ana bought some silk pyjamas and Ed looked forward to seeing her wearing them. She told him: "I'll wear them under the djellaba when we go back tomorrow, they'll be much cooler."

Heads, Hats and Tall Tales

They had seen pyjamas on one of the many stalls but none of the correct size, so the young man working on the stall offered to take them down the street to a shop where they had more variety. So they followed and inside the shop were offered a whole range of silk and cotton pyjamas. Ana did well to haggle down the price from two hundred and fifty Egyptian pounds for one set to one hundred for two sets. Ed was very pleased to see that.

Then the man who had taken us to the shop asked for *baksheesh*. Ed gave him ten Egyptian pounds.

Then he asked for *baksheesh* for the young man working in the shop, as he said did not earn much money and it was not his shop. So Ed handed over another Egyptian ten pound note. Ana laughed and said "Purchase tax!"

They walked along to the half-way point, not stopping to buy anything else. Saleem was waiting in his *kalesh*. They boarded and he drove them along the rest of the market which was less touristy. They drove past people offering spice, and stopped outside an open-fronted shop where Ana bought several packets of spice, including green peppercorns, saffron and some unknown spice that the salesman called "Egyptian Viagra".

Further up the street they drove past shops selling clothing, tools and foodstuff. Saleem gave a running commentary: "Chickens, meat, flowers, silk and cotton cloths, fishes, rice, beans, bread ...", most of which we on open display on stalls, in dishes or hanging. It was quite a smelly place and quite crowded and several times people had to move things out of the way so we could get along in this narrow track in our *kalesh*.

Then Saleem drove us back along a main road towards Luxor train station, turning off to drive us through narrow streets of old and simple-looking houses of several stories, streets filled with rubbish and smiling, waving, ragged children. Ed had read somewhere that parents had told the children not to beg or ask *baksheesh* as they had years earlier. So instead they shouted "hello" or "welcome".

It was quite smelly and very dusty.

Finally the *kalesh* pulled up outside a restaurant close to Luxor Temple. Saleem asked what they wanted to eat and Ed said fish or chicken. Saleem said that they should allow him to pay the bill and later they could pay him, as it would be cheaper.

Inside the restaurant, they went upstairs. Saleem ordered the food: it was to be chicken. The food arrived and Ed was not surprised to find the chicken accompanied by French fries, rice with little bits of fried onion, breads, hummus and other dips and a tomato and bean salad.

As soon as Saleem had eaten his fill, which was not much, he said he would pay the bill and wait outside and feed Cinderella.

As Ed and Ana were about to leave, some ten minutes or so later, the waiter came to them and said "Bill Sir is one hundred twenty pounds for all."

"Oh I thought the *kalesh* driver had paid." said Ed.

"Yes yes, he paid. I only want you to know how much!"

Ed thought the price reasonable although they left more food than they had eaten, yet he knew that it was probably cheaper for locals, just as is almost everything else in Luxor.

When they were outside, Ed asked Saleem how much but Saleem just said "No problem my friend, you pay me later."

He was feeding the horse on what looked like grass.

PROFESSOR BERTIE

Saleem took them through the back streets towards the outskirts of Luxor, and pulled up outside a new-looking two-storey building surrounded by a green and well-attended garden. "Professor here", he said.

Ed and Ana climbed down from the carriage and Saleem said he would wait. They walked through two large open decorative iron gates, along a short path between the lawns and flower beds, up a few stone steps and were about to knock on the door when it opened.

A middle-aged man with almost no hair and long black beard stood before them with out-stretched hand, which they shook as he said "Hi, I'm Bertie. From London. Welcome to Egypt and my house."

Bertie explained that he had moved to Luxor five years previously, bought this house which had been quite run-down and employed local workers to turn it into what it was today. He showed them around; on the ground floor there was a large reception room with table and chairs, a settee and cushions on the floor; it was dimly lit but had brightly-coloured throws hanging from the wall; it felt quite cool compared to outside. Bertie led them through another door into a large kitchen complete with what looked like a well-stocked bar. The Kitchen opened, at the other end on to a smaller room and off that, to one side, was the bathroom and on the other side a door led to a terrace with easy chairs and a hammock. He took them back inside through the kitchen and opened another door; beyond that, to Ed's surprise, was a home cinema with a dozen of so comfortable chairs.

He led them back to the main reception room, opened another door and led them up some wooden stairs. Up there was another bathroom, toilet and three bedrooms, each with a door opening onto a balcony. The main bedroom had another set of stairs leading to the terrace on the roof, filled with small bushes and flowering plants, along with adjustable sun beds and chairs.

The view was amazing. They could see a large part of Luxor, with Luxor Temple on one side and Karnak Temple on the other. They could see the hills on the West Bank, just able to make out what was probably the Valley of the Kings and the *Mentuhotep* and *Hatshepsut* mortuary temples.

"Wow this place is just incredible!", exclaimed Ana.

Bertie led them back downstairs and out to the back terrace. He turned to a young teenager boy and told him in English to bring black tea with milk, cakes and hasheesh.

The three of them sat down in the shade of the trees as Ed explained that they had come to Luxor for the third time, from Norwich where they lived, in England. Bertie said he knew Norwich well but had himself lived in London, where he had been running a secret club for rich pop stars and actors: he dropped many names of people who had been in his club.

He had moved to Luxor because, he said, he was fed up with London and he was happier here. The locals called him a

Professor but in fact he wasn't; just an educated and travelled man.

Ed and Ana excitedly explained to him their experience beyond the tunnels. They did their best to explain the appearance of the town which should have been Luxor itself, telling of the worker who had pointed and said Oo – are – set.

The tea arrived, Bertie filled a small pipe with some light-coloured hasheesh which he said had come from Sudan and, as they sat and smoked and sipped, explained that there was in fact nowhere close to Luxor of the size and appearance they had described.

"I know a lot of people here," he said, "but nobody called that. They call the city here *al-Uqsur*, which is the name in Arabic. Before that it was called *Thebes*. But before that it was called *Waset*"

Ed interrupted: "the only thing we came up with was *Waset*, which is what it was called here, but that was thousands of years ago. That doesn't make sense. It's not like we're time-travellers", he laughed.

They did not reach any conclusions, despite the hasheesh which inspired a lot of imagination and speculation, including the idea that the exit boulder was some sort of TARDIS, a time and space travelling ship used by the fictitious Doctor Who, a highly-successful TV series spanning decades. They laughed a lot about that and the prospects of going back and forth in time. Ed told Bertie about the lighter with the pictures of the pyramids on, that they had found outside the exit boulder and that he had since given to Ayman.

"That's it then," laughed Bertie, "Doctor Who is a smoker!"

A couple of hours later they left, with no solution to the mystery and with Bertie saying he would like to join them on a future trip, but not the following days as he was going to be quite busy.

Saleem was still outside waiting in his *kalesh* and quickly took them back to the boarding place for the ferry.

Once there, Ed asked Saleem how much the restaurant bill was.

He said "Two hundred pounds for the day and two hundred and forty pounds for the lunch."

Ed immediately knew that Saleem had doubled the price of the food, but handed over 500 Egyptian pounds saying "Plus little *baksheesh* for Cinderella."

Saleem smiled broadly and gave them a scrap of white card with his name and phone number written on it and said "My Fader, I am always here when you need to make another journey, only phone to me and I will come. You want go further, I will get taxi. Or you want to fly to Cairo for pyramid visit or Abu Simbel, I will do that all for you too."

Ed liked Saleem and could see that he looked after his horse well, so did not begrudge the money.

"One day you come my house meet my family and we will give you food, my wife will make fry chickens."

Ed and Ana, led by Saleem who cleared their way of young men touting for trade for taxies and boats. They were soon aboard the ferry, across the river and back in their hotel room.

Heads, Hats and Tall Tales

The remainder of the day was spent resting, chatting, eating and sleeping.

That evening Ed and Ana went to the rooftop gardens of the hotel, where several lounge chairs and low tables were laid out.

Instead they lay on the woollen mats and cushions on the ground. It was a full moon that night. I was on top of Ed's head, as usual, as they lay and smoked many pipes of the *hasheesh* that Bertie had given them.

They also drank a few bottles of the local beer.

Ed felt warm and cosy, glad to be there with Ana. He wanted to get closer and closer to her as they chatted about the possible interpretations of their experience beyond the tunnels and their talks with Ayman and Bertie.

They shared ideas on what would happen if they went back and asked each other how long should they stay and what should they take with them. Ana said she had wondered about the significance of the lighter she had found. She told Ed that she wondered who would have left that lighter there and thought it important.

All too soon it was the next morning and they found themselves walking with Youssef towards the house on the hill and then climbing down the ladder back into the tunnels.

Ana wore her new pyjamas, as she has said, under her *djellaba*.

Ed had decided to wear just his underpants beneath his. He carried a small leather bag containing his phone, torch, candles, matches and chalk, a small notebook and pencils and a bottle of mineral water.

He also had several hundred pounds in Egyptian money and some coins which was customary to hand out to tomb guardians and guides. I was on his head and he managed to climb down the rope ladder without knocking me off again as I clung on tighter than ever.

They walked through the tunnels faster this time, following the previous chalk marks and were soon, once again, standing beyond the exit boulder. It was still dark.

It seemed darker than when they had climbed down the ladder but it was now starting to get light here too. Ed thought that was just another mystery as they sat looking across the river to the town that appeared again as the morning mist was dissipated by the already warm sunshine.

Since it was light enough, they headed down the hillside and towards the river to look for a way to get across it.

It took almost an hour for them to reach the river; they walked slowly. It was getting hot fast and Ed was glad, I knew, to have me on his head shading his eyes, even though his spectacles, as usual, darkened in the bright light. Now, Ed realised, they were back in the different world, far from Luxor. Maybe, he mused, even a different age.

They arrived at the river bank where some small wooden boats were moored. As they approached, the man who sat in one waved to them to climb aboard. As soon as they were seated he started to row across the river using two long wooden oars. It did not take more than a few minutes.

As Ed looked back across the river towards the West Bank, he could see the place where he knew *Hatshepsut's* temple should be but instead of that, set in the cliffs was another temple. He wondered if it was representing the Temple of Mentuhotep.

Funny, he thought, when we were in Egypt in 1990 I really wondered what *Mentuhotep's* temple would have looked like before it had been destroyed and the newer temple of *Hatshepsut* was built alongside and partly in front of it, using some of the materials.

As Ed stood up ready to climb ashore, he handed the man a small Egyptian bank note, ten pounds. The man looked at it and smiled. He held it up to the light. He folded and unfolded it. He bowed and placed in beneath his short garment. He pointed ashore and said "Abam – ee – ra."

Ed asked Ana if she knew what that meant. She responded that she did not know for sure, but often in Arabic they put 'Ab" before somebody's name to indicate that it was somebody's father; so, she said, in this case it could mean the father of Am - ee – ra. Like the name Amir, but with the 'ra' added.

Ed mentioned that it was coincidence that Ayman's missing son had been called Amir and now the first person they were being sent to, if in fact it meant a person's name, was quite similar.

"So," said Ed, "my father would be Abed?"

"Guess so," she laughed.

Ed laughed. "And Ana means sexy one!"

"Maybe," she said, "but it also meant 'goddess'."

ABAMIRA

They climbed some stone steps to the top of the bank where they saw some sort of ceremonial-dressed guard wearing a purple tunic over a brown kilt, a dagger at each side and carrying a spear. He bowed to them. He seemed to have been expecting them.

Ed said "Abam-ee-ra" and the guard motioned for them to follow him.

They were led towards the centre of the town which seemed to be consist mostly of mud huts, in the direction, as Ed thought, of the palatial-looking building they had seen from the other bank of this river.

They were joined by six other men, dressed in brown kilts, carrying spears, clubs and knives. They each wore a purple sash across their chests. They said nothing.

There were many people around, some leading donkeys, others carrying things. Most of them were men, dressed in simple loincloths, some even naked, working on the roads, if they could be called roads. Naked children played or lounged around everywhere. There were no *kalesh*; in fact, no horses, no wheeled carts.

Most of the buildings seemed to be made of mud bricks and were single story. The ones closest to the track looked like both housing and business premises.

There were stalls selling fruit and vegetables or flat breads piled high, fish and the occasional animal carcass. There was a range of colourful spices. The frontage of the buildings was multi-coloured, like the village back on the west bank of Luxor.

Men were sorting fruits and vegetables, others piling up flat breads. Some dressed in white robes and had bald heads, that made them look much like the ancient priests Ed had seen in books about old Egypt.

We passed by one shop where men were having their heads and beards shaved by a small team of barbers, which reminded me of Greece.

It was dusty but otherwise quite clean, although it smelt strongly of sewage.

"And another thing", Ed said aloud, "there's no street lamps or telegraph poles. This is obviously some sort of representation of the way people lived centuries ago but how the fuck we got here and where the fuck we are, I don't know. They are all looking at us; some are even bowing. But nobody is making any noise. What happened to all the kids shouting welcome?"

They could see men constructing more buildings, whilst other buildings seemed occupied by a variety of men doing their tasks. Men and small boys herded goats; others carried fish hanging from sticks.

The few women that were visible were bare-breasted, which was most unusual in a Muslim country, even in simulations made for tourists.

Ed felt considerably over-dressed in his *djellaba* and me, Myhat, on his head. Hardly anybody wore anything on their heads.

Thinking of *djellabas*, Ed could not help himself thinking of Ana's body beneath hers. He became aware of his thoughts and decided to focus where they were being taken; or at least try to.

Soon they could see the palace just ahead. It was a two-storey building decorated with coloured flags, fronted by large wooden gates with a row of guards dressed in purple tunics and holding spears and shields.

Beyond that Ed could see a large open courtyard with what looked like a pool of water where ducks and geese were settled beneath the surrounding trees. Beyond that, the palace looked exotic and grand. The building looked like it was made out of stone, with stone statues of gods flanking the main entrance, and two more guards standing each side.

The guards with whom Ed and Ana were walking turned off this road, which was looking in better condition here, and walked a short distance towards a two-storey house made out of stone; another two guards stood outside. Our escort spoke to one of them and they allowed him to go inside. Ed and Ana stood near the doorway, surrounded by eight armed guards who said nothing.

It was not long before the first guard returned from within the house, accompanied by a young man who looked about twenty-two years of age, dressed in some sort of ceremonial gown of blue colour, a blue tunic over a short blue kilt, a blue sash across his chest and wearing a dagger at each side, with sandals on his feet; he had long dark hair, braided on one side; he wore a chain that looked like gold around his neck. His hair looked like a wig.

He beckoned Ed and Ana inside and spoke to them in a language that Ed did not recognise, although he knew it was neither Arabic or English. It was a sort of clicking and guttural-sounding language.

Ana turned to Ed and spoke "It's like Berber, but not the same; and it's not Arabic that I know either."

With that the man moved closer. He said in a quieter tone: "you speaking Ingleese?"

"Yes, English," said Ana, "We are visiting here. We come from Luxor. My name is Ana and this is Ed."

"Very good, I speaking little Ingleese from my father. He from place Luxor, which is our language we called *al-Uqsur*. Here now, father is Abamira, he is Master of House and Greeter of Foreigners for Great King; my name is Amira and I welcome to *Waset*. I take you now My Lord and Lady Ana, to meet father."

They stood in quite a large foyer with mats on the stone floor, large water jugs and pottery urns holding a variety of leafy plants. There were wooden stairs going to the upper storey and several wooden doors which were closed. They could see through some open sliding double doors into a courtyard beyond.

They could see a man sitting on what could have been a raised throne, being fanned by a large dark-skinned man dressed only in a loincloth. As they were led towards the courtyard by this Amira, Ed could see that there was running water passing through the courtyard and, in the water, what looked like water lilies and other plants, including rushes.

As they entered the courtyard the man, who looked to be about sixty years-of-age, older than Ed or Ana, stood up and stepped down from his raised chair, which we could now see was not a throne at all. He stepped towards us with his hands reaching out in greeting, saying "Hello I am greeting you good Master and Lady Ana. I offer the respect of Pharaoh and his house, oh wise man. We talk now and I give food and drink. Later we make all ready for his holiness."

"We are very pleased to be here," said Ed, "But surely this is not the house of a Pharaoh; is this some sort of touristy thing? Where are we?"

"This place is *Waset* and this is Palace of *Kheperkare Senwoset, Ka of Ra* is created, begat of *Nefertitamen Amenemhat*, Father of *Nubkaure Amenemhat*, Glory be upon his name and his family and those that be amongst his friends; Glory be upon you."

I thought that there are more hats here and wondered if I had any connection with them. Ed did not know this, he was oblivious to the possibility.

"I am Amira called Abamira, father of Amira, First Friend of the King, Greeter of Foreigners, Master of the Spoken Tongues."

This Abamira was a well-fed middle aged man dressed in a purple gown that went from his shoulders to his feet. He wore a bright blue and red sash across his chest and what looked like a heavy gold chain and some sort or medallion. His head and beard were shaved; his face carried heavy blue make-up, mostly around the eyes. He wore heavy-looking gold earrings. His smile was broad and friendly. He did not have many teeth. He wore no hat.

"Now please sit and eat arrival feast. Tomorrow we may meet *Ameny*."

"I wonder who Ameny is," whispered Ana as they sat on small cushions on the floor mats and as naked boys brought in plates laden with grapes, figs, breads, pots that they later saw that contained honey with jugs of what turned out to be a not-unpleasant beer. There were cakes that Ed thought were made from spicy lentils and tasted delicious. Young girls who looked about twelve years old, wearing nothing but tiny loincloths and shining beads, brought water which they poured over the diners' hands and then they all ate with their fingers.

Abamira said he would answer their questions later and was keen to hear their story and how they had travelled. He asked how long they planned to stay.

"Well, if we are welcome, we would stay three or four nights, I think, but we don't have anything to exchange," said Ed.

"Kind and wise Lord, your company and tales will be payment enough. And you will give your seed.

"Tomorrow, after you have been washed and shaved of body hair, you will be ready and fit to have audience with the blessed and Golden are the Souls of *Ra, Nubkaure Amenemhat* the son of the Great God, *Kheperkare, the Ka of Ra is created."*

Ed looked at Ana, upon hearing that. She simply looked ahead.

Ed asked himself if Abamira was actually telling him he had to fuck some maidens. I knew about the sex acts that some people engaged in and knew that Ed had experienced that himself, although I had never been close enough to feel what he felt or see what he thought about sex.

On those other occasions, I had been either hanging on a hook or inside a box.

I quietly hoped that I would experience more this time, as I knew that sex was not only the way humans reproduced, but often highly pleasurable and pre-occupied much of the subconscious drives of many people.

Ed knew, and he knew that Ana knew, that in the time of ancient Egypt, they had encouraged travellers to impregnate girls chosen for that purpose, to enhance the blood-line. He also knew though, that amongst royalty in those times, there had been much incest. Normally the crown had passed through the wife or sister of the Pharaoh, to another male, which was the reason why many Pharaohs married their mothers or their sisters.

It was not, though, the reason for incest, which was either under the mistaken belief that it would keep the royal bloodline pure, or else it was simply lust.

Not that we are in ancient Egypt, thought Ed but at the same time thinking it was beginning to look like a very realistic simulation or else somewhere completely different to Luxor, which in theory, was no further away than the other side of the hill on the west bank.

Ed excused himself so that he could think about what was happening and asked for the toilet. He was shocked to see what was actually pretty much a working flush toilet. It consisted of a stone seat above a hole in the floor. Above was what looked like a wooden tank of water with a cord attached and when he pulled the cord, the water flushed away the excrement, to wherever it went. Presumably there was some sort of pump mechanism to refill the wooden tank. Maybe something similar to the *Shaduf* mechanism that the ancients had used to divert the Nile and irrigate the fields at the side of the river.

After Ed had returned from the toilet, Abamira started to tell them his own story whilst more beer was poured and consumed.

"Now I will tell how I come here and how I speak Ingleese."

"I came to this place *Waset* from my city *al-Uqsur* or Luxor as they call it in Ingleese, many years ago; now I am 56. Then I was boy 12 years old. I came with my friend after school that day. His name was Kareem.

"That day we saw the brother of my father, who was named Mustafa. My father's name was Ayman."

Ed looked at Ana. She was boggle-eyed and puzzled. She just nodded.

"My uncle was going towards a house on the hill and we knew that nobody lived in that house, so we followed him, Kareem and me, and watched as he entered a hole in the ground.

"We followed him down a rope ladder and into a tunnel. We saw a torch near the entrance so took it with us, along with our school books, which were about the language Ingleese, which is how we were able to carry on with our lessons.

"But my uncle was too far ahead of us and we got lost, in those tunnels. We became frightened as we tried to find our way back. We became hungry and thirsty and tired, and then the battery in the torch started to fade.

"Kareem had one lighter from Cairo. I remember it had a picture of the pyramids on it. We used that until that too was no good for us. Then we sat in darkness, huddled together crying.

"But it was not dark! We could see light above a big stone and we climbed up onto it and then saw the way out. That is how we come to be here.

"But we did not know the way back. We had to stay.

"And you say that was over forty years ago when you were just twelve?" asked Ed.

"Yes." said Abamira, "Soon after I arrived with Kareem we saw my uncle again. He told us we would stay with his wife in a house just outside of *Waset* but that it was impossible for us to go back to Luxor. He told us we must learn the local language and to speak Ingleese and Arabic. Uncle Mustafa had been a teacher of Ingleese in Cairo and used to come and visit and bring us books written in Ingleese or Arabic. Later I started to teach the languages to some of his children and his friends. I taught the tongues to *Ameny* and I still do that today."

"Do you still see your Uncle Mustafa?" asked Ed.

"No My Lord, I have not seen him for about thirty years.

"When I was seventeen, Mustafa arranged that I marry to daughter of the Pharaoh, which I did, the Great Lady Titiatum whom I grieve for, she gave me three sons and two daughters.

"My youngest son is Amira who is now of thirty years and married with two sons and one daughter.

"My other sons I named after my father and brothers in Luxor. My first son I called Ay-Min-Ra; my middle son is Omar-Min-Ra who will marry *Nefru-Ptah*, sister to the boy god *Ameny*.

"After that, Kareem became a Royal Soldier and my uncle took Kareem to the North to marry a princess from another land and he became very rich. I have not seen Mustafa or Kareem for those thirty years since. I have had no word from my uncle.

"I received news that Kareem's wife, after giving him two daughters, was taken at her will as a mistress by another man from a far off land.

"I was told that the wife of Kareem and the stranger were both killed in a big fire and Kareem took another wife, the daughter of a local merchant and became very rich himself, a huge wealth and a private army. I have not seen him for many years and now he is old man like myself.

"My uncle Mustafa was as old as my own father, Ayman, or similar age and would now be about eighty years old and I believe he is dead. Yet I hear nothing.

"I am happy here.

"When I was twenty-five years of age, I was already here for more than twelve years in the reign of the great king, *Senwosret,*, The *Ka* of *Ra* is created, Master of All Kingdoms North and South, husband of Great Lady *Neferu*, that I was made Friend of the King and given this house.

"Later I was by God appointed as Greeter of Foreigners and Master of Tongues.

"I was there when Ameny, Lord and Prince of *Waset* and all the Lands, *Nubkare*, Golden are the Sons of *Ra*, was brought into this world. As the future Pharaoh grew, I talk to him the tongues of Ingleese and Arabic.

"Ameny has three sisters, and first is *Nefru-Ptah* who is pledged to marry my second son, Omar-Min-Ra.

"We have not had visitors from Luxor since many years and we welcome you. I think Ameny will be very happy to speak Ingleese with you."

"How many people live here?" asked Ana.

Abamira smiled: "Forty thousand are looked upon, by the grace of *Atum* and the Goddess *Waset*," he said.

Abamira clapped his hands and a boy brought a long pipe into the room: it looked to Ed like an Opium pipe.

Sure enough it was, and as the boy placed a small black sticky lump at one end, ready to apply a flame from a small burning twig, Abamira motioned Ed to smoke.

Ed smoked one pipe, inhaling deeply. It was just enough to make him relax.

As darkness fell outside, Ed could see through the un-shuttered windows and lamps were being lit. Abamira told the two travellers that he would get a boy to show them to their quarters. He said that they should stay within the building and should ask the boy servant for anything they wanted. He said that they would be brought beer and food and clean clothing. The next morning they would eat well and then go to be prepared for meeting The Young Lord.

"Mighty Night," said Abamira.

The room that they were shown to was quite small, There was both a large raised bed and two smaller ones. They saw mattresses stuffed with straw and cushions that felt like feathers. Each bed was covered with a large sheet.

Around the rooms were statues of birds and animals. The boy lit three lamps. He indicated to outside the door and said "I am here, you want, you call."

The room was very cosy and warm. There was a wash basin off to one side, next to a door that opened on a commode, which Ed went to use almost immediately.

After that I knew nothing of what happened or did not happen, except that when Ed put me back on his head in the morning after he had eaten breakfast, he felt good.

The morning passed slowly with the couple chatting in whispers, trying to understand what was happening to them.

They agreed that what they were experiencing was real, not a dream but how could people go back and forth in time. That was for fiction.

SEX AMONGST THE ANCIENTS

It was early afternoon before Abamira came to them.

"Please you like to smoke of the milk of poppy? Then to bathe and we go to welcome celebration feat and meet the First Prince, *Ameny*."

Ed did not relish the thought of smoking a lot of opium here. Yet he knew that it would not put him to sleep so, sure enough, he accepted the pipe again, putting it between his fingers so that his lips touched only his hands, and took in a deep draw of opium smoke.

Back in 1972, as Ed and I both knew, Al, my previous head, had caught infectious hepatitis and was very ill for many months, probably from sharing an opium pipe, or cannabis joints, in Kabul in Afghanistan, a friendly and fascinating country that lacked hygiene and was the host to thousands of drug-taking travellers who had been blamed for bringing the illness to that country.

Ed did not want to risk illness. I had been with Al at that time. I knew how opium smoke felt: not unpleasant but dream-like.

So I was glad that Ed now smoked through his hands.

As he blew out the smoke, I felt him relax. The opium took effect quickly. The boy filled another pipe and Ed sucked upon it again.

The pipe was not offered to Ana.

Instead it was passed to Abamira who put his lips directly on to the wooden mouthpiece and sucked. He smoked three pipes and it was passed back to Ed who smoked a third.

Ed's world became pleasantly hazy as he and Ana were led each by hand by two middle-aged ladies wearing flimsy gowns and what were obviously wigs, their faces covered with black and purple make-up.

Ed and Ana were taken through large double doors made of dark brown wood, into a large chamber.

The chamber was filled with wooden chairs and benches, many plants and idols of Gods and Goddesses in alcoves around the walls. Ed recognised some; certainly there was Isis, Ptah, Hathor, Thoth and some he did not know. Several were with a sceptre and feather headdress that he thought was the local goddess *Waset*.

Then he spotted *Min*, the god with the erection, god of fertility.

His mind suddenly became filled with images of Ana.

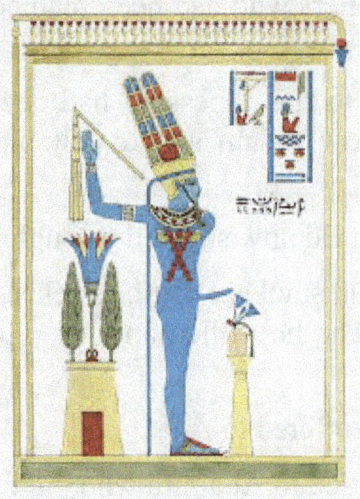

MIN, God of Fertility

In the centre of what he now realised was another large courtyard, open to the roof, was a wide and almost circular stone bath into which naked women were pouring steaming water from clay pots. It was late morning and very warm. The sun lit up the courtyard. There was a strong and pleasant smell of flowers, probably incense.

They were greeted by four women who looked like they were in their late teenage years, dressed in flimsy gowns that left nothing to the imagination and wearing what were clearly braided black wigs that made them look even more beautiful, Ed thought, than they would have looked if bald.

The women smiled as they first removed their own clothing, then stepped forward and started to remove the *djellabas*. Ed did not resist. As he watched Ana as she stood there in her pyjamas, the women laughed as they pulled down his boxer shorts. Through his haze he now saw that Ana, as well as all the other women and girls in the room, was totally naked.

The four women encouraged Ed and Ana to step into the warm water, which was deep enough to just cover their knees as they stood. Ed took me off his head and placed me on a table close to the bath; From there I could easily sense what was happening in the bath.

Two women started to wash Ed with soft cloths covered with pleasant perfumes, first washing then pouring.

l thought he was in some sort of dream as he saw that Ana was being washed too; she was not resisting.

As he watched her, inevitably I thought, he felt a stirring and a rising and very soon, as the one woman washed his belly, his penis was hard again. He was too high to feel embarrassed while all the women, as well as Ana, laughed.

"I thought this was going to happen, Ed. Remember back in ancient Egypt they regarded sexual activity as holy and necessary. I think they're going to want you to fuck at least one of them."

"I'd rather be with you. Come over here and come over here!", Ed laughed.

"Later my darling. I love you; I don't own you."

He was going to find this hard to resist, I felt. I certainly hoped that he would do his duty. I wanted to know if it was the same with all women, for Ed.

The woman was now washing his erection, sliding the slippery soapy wet cloth up and down the stiff shaft and around and under his scrotum. He looked at Ana and almost came then and there.

Suddenly he saw that they held long razor-like stone knives.

He panicked slightly, wondering whether he was about to be killed. Maybe he'd been caught out with the boss' wife or sister?

But he relaxed when he saw them gently sitting Ana on a wooden chair in the bathwater, one of them holding her back and the other sat crouched in front of Ana, gently opening her legs to reveal that delicious cherry-blossom pubic hair.

"Oh my God," he thought, "they're going to shave her pubes."

Just then he felt a razor on his own back, and then another on his chest. They were shaving him too. It felt delicious. They shaved his armpits.

Ed did not have a very hairy back, so it was not long before that razor had reached his more hairy buttocks. The front razor-holder had finished with his chest, seemingly spending a considerable time around his nipples, brushing them until they were hard and erect. Then the ladies shaved his legs. She shaved the top of his belly, then she too got him to sit on a low chair in the water. It was not low enough to cover his groin and she helped him lay back into the arms of the other woman as she parted his legs and brushed against his hardened penis. His head was spinning and dreamy in a delightful way. He felt he had no resistance. Here we go again, I thought.

Of course I was no longer on his head. I had been placed on a wooden bench close to the bath. I was close enough though.

As he allowed himself to relax backwards his penis was now standing fully erect and felt huge again. It was pointing to the Gods. He knew that Ana and all the other women, and who knows who else, were watching.

He felt the razor being softly and delightfully moved from the end of his manhood down the shaft slowly towards his scrotum, which she was gently caressing with her other hand which was also holding his hard-on at its base.

She then held Ed's penis by its head, gently massaging around it and tickling him, drumming her fingers on its very end, which sent him into ecstasy. As she started to shave his scrotum, whilst playing so skilfully with his erection, squeezing gently at its base, he thought he would orgasm, then that it was passing, then felt his come ready to spurt out.

Yet he didn't. He just leaned back and relaxed and enjoyed the sensation, until suddenly it changed.

He opened his eyes to see that one of the bath-ladies was now sitting on his erection, with it inside her, lifting herself up and down until he spurted his hot semen inside her. He could not help himself. It was like a rocket taking off, feeling full of power.

He immediately felt guilty and looked at Ana. She had been watching and was now laughing. He thought he would have to apologise and make it up to her later.

For now, his first thought was that he may have made the lady pregnant and that was probably her purpose.

They made no attempt to shave their heads or Ed's beard.

They stepped out of the water, now completely shaven apart from heads, as several ladies brought them each a clean set of clothes to put on.

One carried Ed's leather shoulder bag, which he had forgotten all about.

It contained his and Ana's passports, some Egyptian money, his torch, phone, notebook and several pencils, chalk and the bottle of water.

Ed wondered if anyone had looked inside it or taken anything. He wondered if the items could change this society in any way, if indeed it was not modern on his terms. How dangerous would it be to take things from the future to the past.

He suddenly remembered reading stories of how travellers had unknowingly infected Pygmy tribes with the common cold virus and wiped out thousands of people. He hoped the same would not happen here.

As he looked into the bag he saw that everything seemed to be there except the water bottle.

"Oh my God, the water bottle's not here; somebody has taken it!" he exclaimed to Ana.

They dressed Ana in nothing more than a very fine purple gown that left little to the imagination, placing a garland of flowers round her neck and more flowers as a headdress. Her shaven fanny was not hidden at all by the gown.

He could see her silhouette, every shape of her lovely body, every time she stepped in front of one of the many oil lamps or flaming torches.

Ed was given a blue tunic with a purple sash above a purple kilt that reached half way to his knees, with nothing underneath. It felt good and comfortable and probably looked very grand, but he could not sit down without revealing his privates.

When he told Ana, she laughed. "Serve you right," she chuckled. "They are not shy here are they? If you get another hard-on, they'll all see it", she toyed.

One of the women handed me to Ed and he put me back on to his head. I was well pleased. He may have forgotten the risks of sex with strangers but there he was again now, his head back inside me where it belonged. It was the closest I would get to sex!

AMENY

Abamira approached through a doorway followed by two naked young boys, each carrying clay pots.

"Greetings My Lord and Lady, I bring more beer and now rest a while and we will attend the Royal Greeting celebrations and you will meet the Divine Son."

Abamira led them through the door to a smaller chamber that was filled with coloured cushions on top of reed mats on the floor. They lay down side-by-side.

Ed gently pulled Ana towards him and kissed her on the lips.

They lay there chatting and supping beer for an hour or so, questioning where they were. Ed said he was wondering if any of this was real at all; maybe they had been drugged back in Luxor and this was all some sort of dream?

Ana, though, said that it would have to be a strangely shared dream, asking that if it was, was their love making part of it and were they now dreaming that they were discussing a dream, "Inside the dream, sort of," she said.

She said that she favoured the idea that it was all in fact real, not a simulation and that they had come out of the tunnels into history and, based upon the names that Abamira had given them, they were about four thousand years before the time they had left.

She said that she thought that it was certainly possible that Abamira was the son of Ayman, although Ayman had said that Amir was just twelve years old when he disappeared, which was only eleven years ago, which should make him about twenty-three now, yet he looked about fifty-five and had adult children himself. Also there was the story of his uncle, Mustafa, the same name as Ayman's brother, whom they had yet to meet.

"And," she continued, "they speak English! That's pretty weird. I'm half expecting to see the time-travelling Doctor Who appear in his TARDIS. Surely time travel's not possible Ed? What if we changed the past? What if we introduced something that they copied, like your hat? Or if one of those prostitutes got pregnant by you, which I think was the idea. Certainly in ancient Egypt they used to do that. Or if we make them ill, or cause a death, or slip up and tell them the future? I know a little about this time, it was part of my course, *Mentuhotep* and *Amenemhat* the first and second, and *Senusret*. *Senusret* the first was supposed to be the son of *Amenemhat* the first and *Senusret's* son would become *Amenemhat* the second. I think they co-ruled for some time."

"Yes,", said Ed, "and that was after *Mentuhotep*, twelfth dynasty I think. He was the Pharaoh that fought a war that lasted fifty years and eventually he united the red and white crowns and brought together the local *nomes* to make *Waset* the capital. *Amenemhat* the first moved the capital to a place called *Itjtawy*, in the North, what we call the *Fayoum.*"

Ana responded enthusiastically: "If that's all true and that is where and when we are now, then there should be the finished Mortuary Temple of *Mentuhotep* on the West bank at *Deir el Bahari*, but no Temple of *Hatshepsut*. I know she was supposed to have built hers alongside and in front of *Mentuhotep's* which was in ruins by her time."

"I did see what looked like a temple," said Ed, "from the boat, when I looked back towards where *Hatshepsut's* Temple should be, but it wasn't as we know it."

Anna continued: "Yes. Maybe we'll get a chance to take a look tomorrow. I think we should stay tonight and tomorrow night and maybe head back to the tunnels the next day so we can get inside when it's dark and we won't be seen. We don't want anyone from here following us. And we should try to find out more about that Mustafa chap and

Heads, Hats and Tall Tales

Abamira's old school friend, I wonder where he is now?"

Ed agreed.

So we would ask some questions and find out what was going on, being careful not to reveal the future or change anything. It was a mystery.

Actually, I thought, it was a mystery I could easily solve, if only *Abamira* or somebody would put me on his head. Another problem for me was how I could communicate with Ed. He was hardly receptive to my messages; always thinking that they are just his own thoughts in his own head. Well, I ask you the reader, who is the clever one? Who is the one that remembers most?

The hour of whispering and hugging and kissing passed quickly and *Abamira* reappeared beckoning them to follow him.

"You must address the God as 'My Lord' or 'Divine Son' You must bow on one knee before him, with lowered head. You must not look directly at him unless he speaks directly to you, in which case you must smile always and answer all his questions. You must not tell untruths or insult him in any way, or his Divine Father the Pharaoh or his family, on risk of death, you must not approach, you must stay on the lower level unless he calls you forward. You are fortunate that now *Ameny* my Lord speaks your tongue, Ingleese."

"Can I ask how old he is?" said Ana.

"He is now nine years of age," answered *Abamira*.

"I hope those women in the bathing pool were not his relatives!" said Ed.

"They are his sisters." said Abamira, "by lesser wives to the Great God *Kheperkare Senwosret.* They did their duty.*"*

Abamira led them out through another large wooden door now held open by a guard. Beyond the door stood four more guards, dressed in kilts with sashes across their naked chests, carrying swords, daggers and spears. Two took up the lead and two followed behind, as they walked down corridors decorated with wall paintings of Gods and Goddesses on one side and paintings of scenes of workers with crops, fishermen, animals being led by boys, servant-girls with plates of food, soldiers and priests and what looked like bakers and brewers with flat loaves and barrels before them. Towards the very end were paintings of builders who looked like they were raising large pylons and obelisks. It was very colourful and seemed to show many aspects of local life. There was even a painting of a woman helping another give birth, or so it seemed to Ed. Then at the end, scenes of men carrying what looked like mummy-wrapped bodies on stretchers.

They exited into a very large grassy courtyard, rectangular in shape, with a tall circular structure ahead of them. Ed noticed many guards armed with spears high on the walls. Ahead he could see that the circular area had wooden structures at angles similar to the pyramids covered with fabrics bringing cover from harsh sun or maybe rain and probably keeping the whole inside warmer at night. Where they were standing, there was no roof, and Ed and Ana looked up to see a blue cloudless sky.

"I'd like to try to draw some constellations later when it gets dark," he said softly so only Ana could hear (and myself of course, but Ed did not know that!), "because if we are back in time, they will look different over four thousand years ... and another thing ... those supports for the roof look to be at just about the right angle for a pyramid and that made we think that even four thousand years ago the Great Pyramid would have been hundreds of years old and known about. I will ask about them later. Now I'm thinking I'd like it if we stayed longer, or if we get back to Luxor, come back again. Maybe we could get a trip down the Nile to Giza?"

"Yes and a few other things I bet, like sex and drugs and beer and food!" she laughed. "But I reckon we should go back to Luxor first and get some more information and see what Ayman says about his brother and what we've found out. Funny that *Abamira* is about the same age as Ayman though, and *Abamira*'s sons about the same age as Ayman's.

"Happy?" she said.

"Very happy but knackered."

"No I mean *Hapi*, the God of the Nile. Remember how that chap in the field pointed to the river and said '*Hapi*'?"

"Wow, I forgot about that!" said Ed.

Ed, Ana and Myhat, Happy with *Hapi* on the Nile, I chuckled to myself. I knew how English people often played with words.

Ed and Ana looked around. There were bright oil lamps everywhere. There were two tiers of seats, on both sides with stone statues of the Gods and Goddesses. He did not recognise them all, but could see *Ptah*, *Osiris*, *Isis*, *Horus*, *Hathor* the cow-headed Goddess, *Min* as usual with an erect phallus, *Thoth* the scribe, *Sobek* the crocodile, *Sekhmet* the lioness and the war-god Montu; he spotted several statues of what he now knew was the local Goddess *Waset* with her sceptre and feathered headdress.

The width of this courtyard was almost a hundred yards, he guessed, and about fifty yards in front the area where the covered roof started.

Abamira led them towards it, quietly reminding them not to move towards the God unless he beckoned them, not to look at him unless he spoke to them and not to speak unless spoken too. He told them that they would be served with food and drink, beer or wine as they preferred, and when the God arrived he would take his seat and the celebration would begin. Abamira said that he would call them forward and present them to the God. He said that thought *Ameny* would like them.

Ed could see now that on each side within the area covered by the pyramid roof, there were two tiers of seats, almost all filled by people in a variety of dress and undress. Most of the women were bare-breasted and wore black wigs; the men's heads were all shaven; men and women wore dark make-up around their eyes and some had very bright red lipstick.

There were several palm trees and flowering bushes in this area too. It smelt very heavily of incense, lots of it.

Directly ahead were two tiers filled with what may well have been courtiers or minor royalty.

There must have been seats for three to four hundred people.

Abamira pointed to two women sitting off to one side and said "Young God's half-sisters who washed you." Ed would never have recognised them, from this angle.

Above that was an empty tier apart from the guards who stood each side, as they did on each tier, and above that a large golden throne piled high with cushions. That was also well-guarded. Each side of the throne was a large and beautiful wall hanging. There were large vases of flowers around the throne.

To either side of the throne, on the same level, stood two very large Negroes; one looked as if he was holding a large fan and the other stood by a row of earthenware pots and dishes on a low table.

Abamira led them to two sets of beautiful cushions on the lower level off to the right, pointing out where he himself was to be sitting, on the third tier. He told them they could sit or stand, but should be on one knee and bow as the Divine Son of God entered.

Abamira introduced them to some of the courtiers as they entered, both men and women. This included men whom he said were *viziers*, masters of constructions, astrologers, heads of army and of sailors, keepers of records of stock, of weapons, of history and a whole group of the royal household. Most were dressed in robes and names included the Vizier *Khnumhotep*, and Vizier *Antef,* Master of Divine Construction *Interfikuer*, Lady *Nefertitanen*, Master of Ships *Aker*, master of Cattle *Hanaf,* the Ladies *Fent Ankhet*, *Input* and *Zara,* There was a savage looking priest called *Ptah-em-hebi*. What a good memory I have!

There was an air of expectation and the crowds murmured as Ed and Ana were shown to their places and sat down.

A group of musicians came forward with drums and flutes and harps and other instruments that Ed did not recognise.

They started playing a very soft and relaxing tune.

It wasn't long before this supposed boy god walked from behind the beautiful hangings and took his place on his throne. Everybody stood up and then bowed down. Ed kept his eyes on Abamira, waiting for some sort of signal that he had forgotten to arrange. Abamira soon made movements with his hand, and everyone except the already-standing guards stood up.

Well, sensible or stupid, whilst people settled down again and the music continued to play, rising in tempo, Ed could not resist a tiny peek. What he saw was simply astounding.

There sat this young boy, wearing a large hat showing the colours of red and white Egypt, dressed in gold and blue, complete with a large gold medallion that looked almost too big for him to carry. He wore an obviously false golden beard.

Behind the boy there was a large mirror that reflected so much light that the boy looked as if he was surrounded by a silver aura. He had a broad smile on his face. He seemed to looking directly at Ed and Ana, and Ed quickly looked away and downwards again.

As the music stopped, the boy, *Ameny*, Son of God as they said, spoke down to Abamira. Abamira promptly stood up and motioned Ed and Ana to stand up.

"Step forward six paces!" he said to them.

They did so.

Abamira turned towards the boy and bowed; he spoke loudly first in what was presumably the local tongue (Ed recognised his own name) and then in English.

"Oh great and wondrous Son of God, *Nubakre*, Golden are the Souls of *Ra*, Protector of the Red and White lands and the peoples of *Waset* and all the territories of the Great King and all that is Holy and Good, oh innocent and wise teacher of all, for your great pleasure I bring to you tonight, two travellers from afar, speakers of Ingleese, washed and prepared, humbled by your magnificence, the Wise One and his Lady consort, the Goddess Ana."

Abamira bowed again and stood awaiting response.

"Welcome to *Waset,* welcome to God's house. I am pleased to meet you." said the boy in excellent English.

Ed took this as his chance to get a good look at this rich and powerful boy and his regalia. He understood now that he was worshipped as a god.

Ed looked at the boy, then bowed to one knee again and looked up.

"My Lord, I and my Lady Ana are very pleased to be here in your divine presence," he said, "and we hope to serve you well during this brief time of what we hope will be the first of many visits."

"Step forward and approach."

Ed and Ana stepped up to the level beneath *Ameny* and stood below and before the boy that was said to be a god. Ed suddenly realised that what was hanging from a chain around the boy's neck looked very much like a clock.

The boy leaned forward and spoke softly:

"I have much to talk about and, as you are from the distant land of Luxor and the world beyond, I have many questions;

I wish to speak of the big birds that fly and carry hundreds and thousands of men and women through the sky to far away places, of the power of *Amon-Ra* that runs beneath the good earth and so men are able to use the will of gods to grind their wheat and carry their crops, light their streets and houses and send messages through the air. I want to know about the boxes of pictures that move with spoken word and music and are in the homes of every man. I want to know about the creatures that are called, in that place, horses and pull carriages through the streets. And the big boats said to be bigger than the Most Royal Barges of the King and carry people along the Great River *Hapi*.

"First though, we have fun and drink. Tomorrow we will speak together."

Music was playing again and dancing girls, wearing different coloured and loose fitting almost translucent gowns with their black wigs covered with flowers, began to move their bodies to the sounds, gathering speed so that their gowns whirled in the air around them. Jugglers entered the arena, throwing daggers and spears high into the air and catching them as they did their acrobatics: some juggled with flaming torches.

Ed became concerned in case a sharp spear or even a fire-stick was ill-thrown and hit one of the dancers.

Ed was drinking beer fast and his cup was being filled often.

He found the dance stimulating and imagined Ana as a dancer too; one dancer did in fact look much like her. She had a nice body, he could see. Ana was happily sitting next to him, quite close and warm so that he could smell her own perfume above even the smell of the incense. She was swaying to the music and also drinking beer. He hoped he would not get an erection right now. In this kilt everyone would see. It was difficult enough keeping his manhood out of sight. Not that anyone seemed bothered. There were plenty of bare chests on display and genitals too and, as he looked around, he saw that several spectators seemed to be proudly displaying their erections.

As the dance continued, another group joined in from the sides.

These all had painted faces or wore masks. They had much shorter dresses; in fact above the knee. They seemed much more clumsy than the other girls. The girls moved aside so that the new dancers had more space. *Ameny* was laughing loudly and clapping his hands.

As the new girls swirled around, their short dresses were swirling in the air around them. Ed looked closer. He was sure some of the 'girls; had penises.

The dancing seemed to get worse and they started to bump into each other; one or two fell over, naked arses pointing at the roof. A couple started to push each other and wave their arms in the air. *Ameny* and the whole crowd were now roaring with laughter. Some of the dancers started to pull at each others garments, tearing them as they fell to the ground, revealing the nudity that was underneath.

Yes, for sure, Ed could see now, some were men and some were women. Closest to them he could now see a dwarf with a huge erection; it must have been a foot long. Several naked women started dancing around him, rubbing their bodies against his. Suddenly one girl jumped on to him; he clasped her as she seemed to slide onto his erection and he started to perform a very strangely funny gyrating movement, much exaggerating the sexual act. She threw her head back into the air and jumped off, the erection was still bouncing along.

Ameny was laughing so hard that he was spilling his beer. Ed thought that at nine years of age, maybe he should not drink much beer.

Ed looked at the audience. They were obviously getting quite drunk, jumping about, clapping their hands, laughing and shouting. It looked like a chaotic orgy.

Men and women were in various states of undress, touching each other in sexual ways.

Several men were masturbating quite openly. He spotted some men openly having blow jobs given by the women next to them or in the tier below. Others were having sex in various positions.

Quite clearly, public sex and nudity were not illegal here: in fact they seemed to be encouraged. Briefly Ed thought he should ask Ana but in fact he felt no stirring in his own manhood at all. It was out of the question. In any case, he thought, I couldn't ask her now in a public arena. That he had wanted Ana in the bath when he was high on booze and opium was one thing; but he loved her too much to ask for a blow job in clear view of a nine-year-old boy, even if the boy thought it all so funny.

This scene continued for a couple of hours: music, dancers, jugglers, acrobats, weight-lifters with trials of strength that looked like Sumo wrestling; at one point several lions were brought in to perform tricks, jumping over people, standing up and rolling on the ground; there were public sexual acts with various combinations of men and women; at one time there was a circle of men with erections seemingly penetrating the behinds of the man in front as the circle moved.

I knew that Ed found that quite distasteful, but again everyone was laughing or else busy with their own or somebody else's genitals. Men in the audience were clearly engaging in mutual masturbation too. Not Abamira though, or the other Royal Guests close to the boy and not the boy himself.

Abamira was smoking opium. For some reason Ed thought of the value of *Pi*, the ratio of the circumference of a circle to its diameter. Then he wondered why he thought that.

Suddenly, without word or gesture, *Ameny* stood up and walked to the side, exiting behind the long curtain.

The music stopped. The dancing stopped. The sex stopped. Everyone starting moaning or crying loudly, some shouting. Obviously what they are meant to do when the Son of God walks away, thought Ed.

The arena started to empty rapidly, people leaving through a variety of doors.

It was not long before Abamira approached them, telling them once again, to follow. He told them it was time to sleep and he would show them to their beds. That meant going back down the corridors through which they has passed, into what Ed thought must be Abamira's private house.

He led them to a large room filled with flowers, decorated clay pots, small statues of various gods and goddesses, and several raised beds covered with soft cushions. He said "Mighty night" and left.

Ed headed for one of the beds and Ana joined him.

"Ha!" laughed Ed, "He said Mighty Night! Let's hope it is!"

Ayman used to say Mighty Night too," said Ana. "Do you think that suggests recent contact?

LOVELY ANA

Ed wondered now whether Ana would let him make love to her.

He had known her a long time and they cared for each other, shared a lot and loved each other's company. Yet there had never been any sexual contact between them.

As Ana spoke softly next to him about the plans for the next day, all Ed could think about was her body: he knew that she was quite slender and included firm breasts and buttocks. With that, he felt a stirring in his loins as his penis started to rise and stiffen. He adjusted his position.

I was enjoying this sensation too: if I was right, it may lead to sex. How would he communicate this to Ana? He wanted to smell her. Would he just ask her? Would he pull out his penis and show her?

I was fascinated. Best of all, I was still on his head!

As he drifted in and out of this sexually-arousing daydream, Ana suddenly turned towards him, moving closer.

"Ed," she said, "Kiss me, I want you to kiss me; we've never had more than a peck for decades!"

He reacted immediately, turning towards her, pulling her gently towards him so they were pressing bodies together, he held her head gently and kissed her full on the lips.

That felt good, to me too: I never knew about kissing like this. It was as if they were exploring each other's mouths with their tongues, brushing lips against lips.

Ed felt his stiff manhood, and could not stop himself pushing it against her belly.

Ana moved suddenly away and he did the same. She looked him straight in his eyes: he was about to say sorry but before he could, she said: "Make love to me now."

"Are you sure? It's not just the drink? I really want to if you do too."

"Yes, yes, make love to me, kiss me all over. I've wanted to know you like this for years. Don't worry, Ed, I won't be getting pregnant."

So Ed moved closer again. They kissed and started to undress each other gently. He kissed her neck and then her breasts as her nipples now stood erect. He didn't even care if anyone saw them.

Whilst Ana kissed him on his lips, she had slid down and took hold of his manhood.

I was just laying there close to the mat on the floor, but close enough to see what Ed saw, those wonderful breasts glistening in the moonlight. That beautiful shaven place. Those wonderful eyes reflecting the light. I could smell and taste as he did; best of all I could hear his thoughts, feel as he felt.

Ed thought he had never been so hard.

Ana was making sexy little murmurs as Ed's breathed slower and then faster. He felt he was in heaven.

They had sex. It was certainly very enjoyable for Ed.

"Wow, that was incredible." said Ana. "I am so happy."

Ed felt happy too. He pulled Ana closer again, now they were both naked, pulling a sheet over them, concerned in case anyone was watching.

It was over, as Ed was soon asleep in Ana's arms. She laughed as he snored for a while, then went silent.

I can tell you that Ed felt very happy and pleased with himself when he put me back on his head. Ana seemed to be glowing.

I had been on Ed's head the whole time whilst we were in that arena and it was as new an experience to me as it was, I knew, to him. I wondered what else could happen in this place so different from anything I had ever witnessed before, so very far in time and space from that barber's shop in Thessaloniki in Greece, where I had first met Al almost forty years earlier. I must say now that I was having a wonderful education on our travels. And, I felt, I was becoming more and more fond of Ana.

"Mighty Night, Ed."

The following morning Ed awoke and his first thought was that he had been dreaming the whole previous day, that he was in fact still in Luxor or even Norwich, that he had not had sex with Ana at all, let alone the two in the bath. He turned to see Ana laying naked, still asleep and close to him.

Then he wondered if it was, in fact, real.

He sat on a wooden stool and started to munch on some bread and eggs: the eggs looked as from not just chickens but also ducks. He smelt the beer. He wanted a cup of tea with milk and vowed that if they ever returned he would bring some tea bags, plenty of them.

There was nothing else to drink, so he supped on beer. He did not want to get drunk at this time of day. Ana was already difficult for him to resist and as he thought about her, he could not help it, his penis started to rise again in it's morning glory.

"Did I really fuck her?" he thought and soon decided that in fact he had. It must have been real, he thought, as he felt his shaven crotch. Then he remembered the women in the bath.

Ana got out of bed and stretched her wondrous body in front of the large window.

After they had eaten a small breakfast and taken some small amount of beer, the almost naked children returned and removed the trays, replacing them with plates of sweet cakes. They brought more beer.

After a while Abamira entered through the doorway. Ed and Ana were both dressed again, wearing the fresh costumes that Abamira had give them, with Ed in a pant-less kilt. A boy accompanied him, bringing their *djellabas*, Ana's pyjamas and Ed's boxer shorts. He put them on.

Almost sadly, he watched as Ana took off her transparent gown, put on her pyjamas, then put the gown on top. Ed was a little disappointed when he realised he may not see her body for the rest of the day.

Abamira told them to follow him and explained that the Boy God was taking them to fish on the river and wanted to speak with them. Their every need would be met and their total honesty required. Abamira said that he himself would not be with them but his son Amira would be. He said that both Amira and *Ameny* spoke quite good Ingleese, so they would not have a problem.

They were led back out of the house, by Amira, back down the road and once again accompanied by guards, to see and board a large and colourfully decorated wooden boat, with both sails and oars. They climbed on board.

Quite soon *Ameny* joined them with quite a few, a dozen or so, guards and about the same number of well-dressed men and women, most of whom boarded smaller boats also moored nearby.

Small crowds of local people cheered and clapped as he boarded the boat, also being followed by several young girls that were probably about his own age, all flimsily dressed, one or two with small breasts, maybe a few years older than him. They all giggled and hid their faces whenever he looked at them or spoke to them. It was strange that they hid their faces and not their bodies. Ed wondered if the future bride was there.

The boat had sails as well as oarsmen, about six on each side.

Ed knew that if *Ameny* was going to ask about planes and electricity and TV sets, it was going to be very hard to explain it. Yet, as *Ameny* already knew about those things, presumably from Abamira, he could not deny their existence. He wondered if he could just say it was magic.

He decided to say that those stories were true but he did not understand how it worked.

They not tell the Royal Boy that they had been on planes many times, or that their lives were almost controlled, in cities at least, by the power known as electricity, which men and women had to pay for.

He said that TV's were boxes powered by electricity and which told stories or news and showed pictures but he did not know how they worked.

Ameny asked if Ed and Ana could bring him a TV next time they came to visit. Ed simply said that it would be very difficult but that a TV would not work here without electricity.

Ameny said that he would ask his *Vizier* to make a box that a man could stand in and a window through which he could announce news or tell stories and show paintings. First, he said, it would be only for the palace but one day maybe all the people could watch them in the streets and markets in the town.

Ed thought of Egyptian 'Punch and Judy' shows and laughed to himself.

It was then that Ed saw that the gold medallion that he had seen hanging from a gold chain around *Ameny's* neck, was, in fact, another timepiece, as he had thought. A functioning watch in this age? He asked *Ameny* politely where he had gotten it from. The boy god replied that it was a gift from his father the Great God and that was able to count the time and show where the sun would be even if it was indoors.

They spent the pleasant morning chatting and laughing together until the heat of the sun became too hot and then they headed ashore. They had hardly moved on the river at all.

Nobody had actually done any fishing, not that Ed saw anyway. Ana had spent most of the time laying in the sun. She kept her clothes on though.

They were escorted back to the house of Abamira where they feasted on fish which he said *Ameny* had "caught that very morning", bread and fruit along with more beer.

There were piles of onions and garlic and green herbs, vegetables that looked a bit like carrots, olives and a bean stew. It was all delicious.

As he started to feel the effects of the beer he wondered if today was to be a repeat of yesterday. In some ways he hoped so, but in others he hoped not: mostly he wanted to be with Ana. Besides the possibility of more sex, they had so much to talk about, so many mysteries to solve.

Also, they had to decide when to leave and whether to take anything back with them? Maybe a small statuette of a god, certainly an oil lamp. He planned to ask Ana to do some sketches. He did not feel happy about taking pictures with his phone and it was not working anyway. He had to keep his phone well-hidden. He did not want to even try to explain what it was.

Ed remembered the water bottle, a sobering thought that replaced the constantly reoccurring images of the naked Ana in his arms, in his mind.

So this was their third night. In the evening there had been more entertainment in the arena, which they attended with Abamira and Amira, but the boy God was not there. It didn't seem to have the same sort of energy.

Ed and Ana had agreed that they would try to get back to Luxor the following day as they thought that by now people may be asking questions there. They wanted to talk with Ayman again.

So they told Abamira and he said that he would arrange an escort back across the river if they wished, or a boat along the river as far as they needed.

Then they made their farewells and went back to their room.

I know they had sex again that night. It made Ed feel good; that was good enough for me.

The following morning they donned their washed undergarments and djellabas, dressed as they were when they had arrived. They had another good breakfast with fish.

About mid-morning, Abamira entered their chamber. He told them that *Ameny* had asked him to thank them for meeting him and that he hoped that they would return soon and he would take them on his boat along the Nile to visit the ancient pyramids in the North and visit the camp of the Pharaoh.

Amira arrived and asked if they were ready and prepared to cross the river. They would be provided with a Royal Guard to escort them to the edge of the cultured land where they would make their own way.

That is exactly what happened, with no ceremony and no goodbyes. It was another hot day, but now the guards carried some pots and gourds containing beer. Ed had never found the missing plastic water bottle.

Quite soon, late afternoon now, they had climbed the hill towards the hidden boulder which Ed had marked with chalk.

On Ana's suggestion, they did not go straight to the boulder in case they were being watched, but instead decided to sit and wait until the sun went down. Once they knew exactly which boulder to climb, they could enter without being seen. They still had their candles and had also brought a small oil lamp. That and the gourd were the only physical proof of where they thought they may have been, which was four thousand years in the past.

As they sat there chatting about what had happened, they both said that it was all becoming less and less real, yet they had the oil lamp. Ana checked her phone. It still was not working at all.

Once it was dark enough, they quickly found the boulder and climbed through. Ed switched on his torch.

They climbed the other boulder and without delay, followed the chalk marks back through the tunnels. At some points there were other tunnels leading off and Ed said he would one day like to see where they led.

"If we actually went four thousand years into the past, those corridors could lead anywhere," he said.

As they climbed back up the rope ladder at the entrance, Ed saw that it was still dark, as expected. If they had climbed back into the tunnels at about eleven pm and took about forty-five minutes, it was now just before midnight.

"I'll phone Ayman, he may still be awake. Or else we'll have to phone him in the morning. That's if the phones are working."

He took out his phone and switched it on.

"It's working," he said, "but the clock's wrong. It says it's ten past four in the morning. Hang on, the date is wrong as well. According to this it's just the day after we left; in fact less than twenty-four hours.

"I can't phone him now, til we check the time. Let's just walk back to the hotel. It's not far and I don't feel sleepy at all."

As they left the house, Ana mentioned that it was starting to get light. She looked at her own phone and said that said now twenty past four in the morning. People were in fact starting to wake up. They rapidly walked back to the hotel which was already open, said good morning and collected their keys.

"I'll phone Ayman at nine," said Ed.

That is what they did, first lazing around chatting and planning, then pushing together the two beds, helping each other out of their clothing with plenty of kissing and touching, then, when Ed was standing erect once again, they had sex. I was on the bedside table and was able to share the joy of Ed's orgasm. I wondered if I could ever be on Ana's head and feel what she felt at a time like this.

At just after half past eight, Ed went to the hotel reception and ordered breakfast, orange juice, tea with milk, eggs, toast and butter and jam. At just after nine o'clock, he phoned Ayman, told him that they had important news and Ayman said he would get his son to bring him to the hotel that afternoon and that he would invite Professor Bertie as well.

Ed and Ana had at least a few hours to do nothing, so they decided to do something. They had sex again, Ana suddenly pulling down Ed's boxer shorts which was all he had on, quickly taking hold of Ed's cock and starting to lick the end of it. It did not take long for Ed to react, and before he knew it she was trying to get his whole erection into her mouth.

She's so good at this, he thought, think of England! He came in her mouth. He returned the favour, so to speak, pulling off her pyjamas and panties that she'd dressed in again, putting his head between her opening legs, as she moved herself slowly up and down.

She didn't take long to come either, but that did not stop him. Already his cock was getting hard again. He lay on his back and she moved on top of him and guided him inside her again. She moved herself up and down and round and round on his erection, making pleasant little sounds, until he came again. It seemed this time they both orgasmed at the same time.

Far too soon for Ed, she had removed herself and was looking at her phone.

"It's one o'clock already," she said. "Ayman could be here soon. I'm going to have to shower first. Join me and I'll wash you."

Leaving me on the table, they went into their tiny bathroom

and, well, you and I will have to guess the rest.

In fact, it was over another hour until they were dressed again, with Ed having put his jeans on beneath the *djellabah*, when there was a knock on the door. It was the manager telling them that Ayman and Bertie were downstairs and waiting in the guest living room which was equipped, as Ed knew, with comfortable arm chairs.

Sure enough, Bertie and Ayman were seated in the soft chairs. Ed was uncertain where to start with his tale of what Ana and he had seen.

Somehow he had to tell them that it seemed as if they had gone back four thousand years in time, which was not only going to be hard for them or anyone else to believe, but Ed was already doubting it himself, feeling that some sort of trick had been played on them, some sort of hallucination or dream. Yet he had the gourd and lamp and well as shaven genitals to confirm that something strange had indeed occurred.

How was he going to tell Ayman that he had met and talked with his missing son, Amir? How could he possibly explain that Amir had been about the same age as Ayman himself, with sons of his own named after his father and brothers, that he was called Abamira and was a man of considerable power? He was going to have to explain that Abamira had told him that it was forty-four years since he had followed and been left there by his uncle, Mustafa. He would like to meet this Mustafa chap and confront him. It seemed that they had spent four nights back with Abamira but, when they had returned to Luxor, only one night had passed, that eleven years here was forty-four years there, as if time was passing at a faster rate, although it had not seemed like it. He could see that Ana was almost bursting with excitement.

First Ed asked if Ayman had heard from Mustafa.

"No, my friend, my brother is still in Cairo," Ayman said.

At first Ayman smiled when Ed told him that he had found a man who seemed to be the missing Amir. As he continued to explain the age, the sons, the tale of how Mustafa had apparently left Amir and his schoolboy friend somewhere that seemed many years in the past, in the time of the Pharaoh *Senusret* and the future Pharaoh *Amenemhat* the Third, Ayman and Bertie started shaking their heads and laughing.

"What sort of joke is this to give Ayman such hope and then destroy it with nonsense?" asked Bertie. "How can you say you went back in time? What proof do you have?"

Ed showed them the gourd and the oil lamp they had brought back through the tunnels. He did not tell them about the episode in the bath and the shaving of his body hair, and Ana's pubic hair, and he certainly did not want to be undressing to prove that. Actually of course, it proved nothing except somewhere somebody had shaved them. Neither did he tell them about the celebration mass orgy.

Bertie inspected the oil lamp.

"It's certainly nothing like I've ever seen before. I'll take it and get in inspected; and that gourd. If it is genuine Pharaonic from the eleventh dynasty, the experts will know, and I will come through the tunnels with you when you go back, if you go back, or go alone.

"Yet it is a good story you tell, worthy of a book or film, so carry on, please."

Ana suddenly started telling them how they had been taken across the river and had armed guards, that some of the people including Amira and Abamira and the future Pharaoh spoke good English.

She told them all about the bathing, the shaving, the orgy and the fishing trip, leaving out only the details of their sex sessions.

During that time they had been drinking tea with sweet cakes.

"I did miss a cup of English tea with milk," said Ed; "all they had to drink was beer and wine."

Mid-afternoon, Ayman phoned Youssef who collected him and Bertie in his taxi and they left with the oil lamp and gourd. "It may take a couple of weeks to study these," he said.

Ed and Ana chatted and agreed that they would wait two weeks and in the meantime they would go by train to Cairo, visit the pyramids and museum and study the periods before the twelfth dynasty to see what was known. They would also ask about Mustafa, maybe even speak with him.

The following day they ordered a taxi and took a train, in such a rush that, unbelievably, Ed left me on the bedside table in the hotel room. I was placed on a hook in the reception area, where I had no choice other than to stay.

I wished and prayed, although I was not sure to whom, that Ed would in fact come back and that I would be on his head again, wherever he went. One again I thought he cared more about Ana than he did about me, yet that was not the first time that he had left me on a hook or put me in a dark box.

Heads, Hats and Tall Tales

I expect that you, the reader, can guess that they did come back, about six days later. They had learned something of the age they had travelled too, although little new information was available. They had found no trace of Mustafa although there were probably many thousands of Mustafas in Cairo.

They visited Ayman several times and together talked about the four of them going back through the tunnels, about what to take and what not to take. Ayman was unsure that he could himself make the journey, due the problems with his legs, and said he might send one of his sons.

At the end of the second week, Bertie called at the hotel and said that the lamp was authentic, "although," he said, "there was no genie when he had rubbed it."

Bertie told them that he had also been to Cairo and contacted several rich business friends, asking about Mustafa. He had discovered that Mustafa was well known in certain circles, often offering expensive artefacts that had origins in the eleventh and twelfth dynasties and owned a very large property in Cairo and several in other countries including the US, Japan and the UK. Mustafa had been selling such items for over a decade and was now a very rich and secretive merchant of antiques.

Bertie said that they should leave no more time as this discovery was to be investigated with urgency, although he had told the story to nobody else. He wanted to leave with just the two of them that very evening, as soon as it was dark.

So that is what we did. First though, they booked out of their little hotel, giving their bags to Youssef to look after, as they intended to be away for some time and did not want people to think they had simply disappeared, gotten lost or killed.

THE RETURNING

We entered, passed through, and exited the tunnels quickly. Bertie was not interested in anything but getting through. As Ed had suggested, all three wore *djellabas*. I gripped firmly on top of Ed's head. Ed made sure the chalk marks were all still visible.

When we came out over the exit boulder, it was daylight.

"Weird! We've only been inside for thirty or forty minutes, surely, now it's light already," said Bertie. In fact the sun was quite high.

"Check your clock on your phone!" said Ana.

Bertie took his phone from beneath his clothing.

"It's not working," he said.

"See, told you so," she laughed.

Ed suggested that they leave everything from what was now the future, except their clothing, hidden inside the tunnel, explaining how the plastic water bottle had been lost and the lighter found. He said that he did not want to contaminate history.

So that is what they did.

Heads, Hats and Tall Tales

They headed straight down to the river where, sure enough, as if he was waiting specially for them, a boatman waved them on board and rowed them across the Nile to where, once again, Amira and several armed guards were waiting to escort them through this part of the town *Waset* to the house of Abamira. He stood at the doorway waiting for them.

"I am very pleased, as will be the God, that you have returned. We thought that you may not return, it has been more than two moons since you left."

Ed introduced Bertie and Abamira.

They feasted and chatted and out came the opium pipe which Abamira, Bertie and Ed took turns smoking.

Abamira said that *Ameny* was about to go by Royal Boat up the Nile towards the camp where his father, the Divine Pharaoh was waiting. That was planned for two days time. Abamira told them that once again they would be bathed and shaved.

Ed was not so keen on that thought even though it started to turn him on, the images of Ana being washed and shaved in front of Bertie. He did not want Bertie fucking her; there would be other women there, he could do what he wanted to them as far as Ed was concerned, but not Ana.

The washing and shaving was actually filled with laughter. It was not long before both Ed and Bertie had erections; in fact it was not long before Bertie was engaged is rapid sex with one of the women, and soon Ed and Ana were also having sex in the pool.

This was certainly an enjoyable traditional reception.

Abamira suddenly appeared. He had been watching all the time. He walked over and picked me up and put me on his head. I was shocked; Abamira was actually a very fearful man, scared of the boy god and his father, the priests and other couriers. Also, then I knew, he had seen his uncle Mustafa far more often and recently than he had said. He told Bertie that his seed was welcome in many ladies of the temple and hoped that they would be fruitful by him.

After they were all washed and shaven again, Abamira led them through the courtyard and corridor to the guest suite, where all three would be sleeping, saying that in a short while they would be taken again to see *Ameny*, this time before the welcome party.

Bertie was grinning from ear to ear. "So it's true then! I didn't expect that. You never told me I could end up being a father here! Who were those women?"

"Relatives of the Pharaoh's son by lesser wives, half-sisters I guess," Ed explained. "I never got the sex, maybe because I was with Ana? I missed out there!"

She pinched him.

Ameny greeted Ed and Ana like old friends, welcoming Bertie too, saying that they would all sail together the very next day, to meet his father, in the North.

At the end of the evening, Abamira took them to their quarters. "Mighty Night," said Abamira.

It was the following morning when they set off early, Abamira having woken the three English people up. It was a much larger boat than they had "been fishing" on and had many oarsmen as well as large sails. This boat was going to move! We were accompanied by about ten other boats, many filled with armed guards. There were also many guards at intervals along the river banks, on both sides. Some were

Heads, Hats and Tall Tales

running to keep up with the boats, until others took over.

Abamira was on board another boat along with his son, Amira, and some other members of the Royal Court.

Nefru-Ptah, sister of *Ameny* who was pledged to marry the second son of Amira, Omar-Min-Ra, was on board the royal barge as well as Omar-Min-Ra himself. They were supposed to be betrothed. Yet Bertie became quite besotted with *Nefru-Ptah* and she with him, and they had sex together several times in front of others, unabashed.

Ed thought that may lead to trouble although it was not spoken about to his knowledge. Women here had equal rights as men and it seemed that people could take sexual partners without complications or social gossip.

All the boats were highly decorated with red, white and purple banners and flags. Their boat had food and wine everywhere, so they could just laze around and eat and chat. *Ameny* played many games, such as throwing hoops on to wooden poles held by the guards, and throwing fruit at other fruits balanced on the heads of soldiers, trying to knock off the fruit, supposedly, but laughing loudly when he hit one in the face. The soldiers stood, motionless.

There was also a game that involved throwing sticks and, depending on how the sticks landed, moving wooden pieces like two armies clashing with each other. It was a simple enough game. The boy god won most of the time, until he challenged Ana, saying if she lost she would have to spend the day naked. Ana won that game.

Each evening there were dancers and jugglers and clowns and a lot of sex as young girls and courtiers came on board from the other boats. Bertie, for sure, was having the time of his life. He spent a great deal of the time naked, with a girl or two at his side or sitting on his lap. He certainly was not shy.

Ed and Ana agreed to restrict their sexual activities to the covered sleeping section allocated to them. But they did not restrict the amount of sex that they had. On those occasions, Ed carefully hung me from the wooden struts.

One morning, *Ameny* invited the three English people to see his collection of drawings. There were sketches of pyramids and of gods and goddesses, many of the boy himself, some with his father the Pharaoh, one that the boy said was of his mother. Plenty of animals and plants.

To Ed's surprise, he found himself looking at drawings of planes, helicopters and what looked like astronauts with spaceships, even cars with wheels. He had seen no vehicles with wheels at all, during his visits to this time.

He spoke to Ana and Bertie later about those drawings and they agreed that certainly this could be seen as a corruption of the time-line. Somebody from the future had been here and left those drawings.

Ed wondered if it may have been Abamira's uncle Mustafa, who was not to be seen here and whom, in the future, was supposed to be in Cairo.

A few days later, I had the biggest surprise of life time since I first met Ed.

Suddenly, after playing hoops, *Ameny* asked Ed if he could try me on and if it would be agreeable with Ed to make a similar hat for himself, in the colours white and red, signifying Upper and Lower Egypt.

Ed knew that the white crown of Upper Egypt was officially known as the *Hedjet,* whilst the Red Crown of Lower Egypt was called the *Deshret*. After Egypt had been unified, the double crown, red and white, was called the *Pschent*. That was several hundred years before *Ameny* and the double crown would be worn by him when he became Pharaoh, as it was by his father *Senwosret*.

THROUGH THE EYES OF A GOD

Ed was not in the habit of letting others wear me, although I had been on Ana's head and a few others over the years. He could hardly say no to a boy god who was his host, so he took me off, bowed and presented me to *Ameny*.

What a revelation!

The boy totally believed that he was of divine birth, that he was a god and that he was all powerful. Only his own father was above him in rank.

I realised that that *Ameny* regarded everyone else as inferior, including Ed and Ana, other members of his own family and court, including the many Priests that he regarded with suspicion and as struggling to gain position in his eyes.

He had little genuine respect or care for anyone, not even his own family and, as *Ameny* knew his successors had done, was quite prepared to destroy people's lives and use people for his own purposes.

Ameny knew that one day he may have to dispose of his father. He felt that when he openly worshipped the gods, he was worshipping only what he was.

Ana's name meant Goddess. *Ameny* knew that Ed and Ana came to him from a very far away and mysterious place, a place where huge birds carried people through the skies and people communicated through the air even showing pictures through their mysterious boxes powered by an unseen energy called electricity which was, he had concluded, a great gift from the gods.

Ameny saw himself as indestructible: he could do whatever he wanted to or with whoever he wanted, except he could not fly.

The head of Ameny was nothing like the head of Ed, or Ana, or any other head that I been upon. The world view was so different that I became almost lost in it.

For the first time in my existence, I understood that it was I that was the superior being. I had a better memory and better understanding of many things than Ed. If I was to remain on the head of *Ameny*, I could rule the world. Ed could never do that. I also knew all about this land that Ed knew of as ancient Egypt. I knew the history and the geography of Egypt, several languages, the magic performed by his *viziers*, the secret ceremonies of the religions, the names of all the gods and goddesses. *Ameny* was descended from conquerors. Life and death were mere illusions for him; he was part of a greater plan.

Maybe I was more limited to where I could travel and what I could do than these human beings but I could experience and remember much more. Although they may not fully realise the truth of it themselves, I could even get my memories written down by whoever wore Myhat; well, that is how it had happened with Al.

Maybe with practice I could learn to use that connection to communicate ideas, even take control of people's decisions without them even knowing.

If I could do that, with *Ameny* when he ruled the kingdoms, I could surely be a goddess.

It was also whilst upon *Ameny's* head, that Ed mentioned that he and Ana wanted to visit the Pyramids. He asked *Ameny* if that was possible and he said that it was. The boy god knew that the pyramids were many thousands of years old, much older than the Egyptology experts and their books had speculated, which would have been a few hundred years before the time we were now in. *Ameny* believed that the pyramids which we knew as Khufu or Cheops, Khafre or Chephren and Menkaure or Mykerenus, as well as the Great Sphinx, had been built by the Gods that once walked these lands, using magic thousands of years earlier.

I understood that several of the previous Pharaohs had attempted to build their own copies, such as *Djoser* and *Unas*, but none were so godly, so big, so complex or so accurate in their dimensions.

The strange thing was that *Ameny* had never been inside the pyramids, whereas Ed and Ana had entered two, some four thousand years in the future, as tourists.

I must admit, I was almost disappointed when passed back to Ed.

Ameny spent some time telling Ed, Ana and Bertie about the history of his predecessors.

"Our great land was united about one thousand years before now, by a great military leader called *Narmer* who came across the desert. Before him the greatest king was called *Scorpion*. There have been uprisings since then, as well as foreigners coming to try to win Egypt, but they were all defeated.

"Hundreds of years later, some great gods, such as Kings *Djoser* and *Unas*, tried to build copies of the Big Pyramids in the North, which you may see. Those pyramids were built in steps, one on another, but were not as big or complex as the ancient ones.

"Several centuries ago, the Great God-Kings *Khufu*, *Khafre* and *Menkaure*, blessed be their names, had found it impossible to reproduce the Great Pyramids that bear their names, so took the names of the Great Gods that had built them many thousands of years earlier, before the flooding of the land, and claimed the Pyramids as their own.

"It is said that a few hundred years ago *Khufu* opened the greatest of all and sent in workers to explore the inside, telling them to leave their marks to make claim to all the God's that the pyramid was his. He had temples built in his own name, so that the people would worship him as the greatest god of all. Even today the priests run the temples there, allowing only certain people access, claiming them as theirs.

"There was a great drought throughout the whole land when the Great God Hapi abandoned the people and the river dried up, with many people dying.

"The land became filled with strife and wars, between the *nomes* that each wanted power for themselves.

"It was the great warrior *Intef,* son of *Mentuhotep* the first of that name, who overcame rebellion and brought together the nomes. There were three kings with the name *Intef*. But it was the Great God *Mentuhotep*, the second of that name, the son of *Intef* the Third and *Iah*, that brought true unification in the lands, and *Waset* became a great city.

"It was the time when *Waset* was first taken as the Capital City of the Lands of Egypt Upper and Lower.

"War continued until put away with by Divine Pharaoh *Nebhetepre Mentuhotep*, the second of that name who sent our armies North and South, bringing back great knowledge and gifts from Phoenecia, bringing also much wood of the cedar tree from Leban for the building of boats.

"Son of *Nebhetepre* and Big Lady Queen Tem and the third king of the name *Mentuhotep* sent armies to Punt and brought back many treasures.

"His son by Queen *Uni*, the fourth of the name *Mentuhotep*, *Nebtawyre* ruled for only seven years and was succeeded by his Vizier, the Great God Amenemhat *Sehetepibre* and his Great Lady Queen Nefertitamen, my own grandparents, who also built a great pyramid.

"My own father, the greatest king of all history, *Khepekare Senusret*, the first of his name and Lord of all the lands, ended the years of wars and rebellions. He is building his pyramid already, in the North, at I*ty-Tawy*, where he will make his capital city; close to the waters in the desert. That is where I will travel to meet him. That is where one day, I will build my divine pyramid.

"My father is building also a great white temple near *Waset*, in the Holy Place of *Ra-Atum*.

"Having ruled besides my grandfather and taken as his own wife, my Divine Mother, *Neferu*, my father became the

Great God himself upon the taking of the Divine Journey to his afterlife, by my grandfather.

"So you see Mister Bertie, Master Ed and Goddess Ana I am descended from the Gods themselves and one day I will sit alongside my Divine Father and then take my own position upon the Divine Throne, become ruler myself of the two lands and beyond. Then I will build my own pyramid, when my father is taken on his journey to become *Ra*.

"Great and Holy am I, though of short years until now, and powerful I will become, putting down the enemies of Egypt and of God and one day men will remember and speak of me, with reverence and prayer, I, *Nubkaure*, the second of the name *Amenemhat*.

"But at this time, you, my friends, may call me *Ameny*."

The boy clapped his hands and food and beer were brought to us.

I was, once again, amazed, that such a god could bear my name as part of his own name, *Amenemhat*.

It was then that, having seen through the eyes of the young god, that I realised that I too was Divinity itself, that my spirit had passed through all time, to be worn on the heads of people great and lesser sorts, and that my destiny was to be upon the head of Ed, known here as the Wise One; how thankful I was. If only Ed knew!

The whole journey from *Waset,* later known as Luxor, to what was to become known as Cairo, was one of over three hundred miles, over five hundred kilometres. It took over two weeks, by Ed's reckoning, but he was unsure.

Heads, Hats and Tall Tales

Finally it was announced that they were approaching the camp of the "Army of God". I wondered if I would ever be on the head of the living God, the Pharaoh that ruled the world.

The boats were moored on both banks of the Nile. Messengers came abroad to announce that The Great God Senwosret was not in the camp. He had gone to the area of *Iunu* the Place of Pillars, known later by the Greek name of *Heliopolis*, the City of the Sun, to inspect the restoration of the Temple of *Ra Amun*, which was some miles North, to inspect the works and the erection of a great obelisk.

Ed knew that little remained of *Heliopolis* in his own time, much of it having been destroyed over the centuries and now laying beneath parts of northern Cairo.

So it was announced that the Royal Party would wait, some staying on the boats and others on land along with the majority of the army guards to await the call from the Pharaoh.

Ed and Ana were keen on visiting the site of the Great Pyramid and Abamira told them that he would arrange a royal guard escort and that they would travel by camel.

Bertie decided to visit some of the nearby settlements and was also offered an escort. He told Ed that he wanted to ask about Mustafa and Kareem, Abamira's uncle and his schoolboy friend.

Ameny's sister, The Princess *Nefru-Ptah* announced that she would accompany Bertie, along with some of her ladies and an armed escort. They would ride donkeys.

Omar-Min-Ra was not to accompany them; he was to stay on board with the boy god and Abamira.

That evening, Ed was taking a short sleep when he was awoken by the sound of Ana shouting loudly. He looked outside and saw Ana towards the middle of the ship, seemingly arguing with Bertie. As he approached he realised that they were both speaking in Arabic, a language that few spoke here, but Ed recognised. He knew that Abamira and *Ameny* both understood Arabic, but most people here did not.

As Ed approached, they lowered their voices.

Ana turned to Ed.

"Tell him Ed, please, how stupid he's being. All the women available here, all the times he's fucked and god knows how many babies could come of it, now the idiot has told me he's in love with *Nefru-Ptah* and wants to marry her. He says he'll stay here with her or take her back to Luxor!

"Not only that, but now he just walks up to me with a hard on asking if I want a fuck!

"Damned stupid messing around with a princess already promised to Abamira's son.

"I know it doesn't seem important here who has sex with who and not frowned upon but talking of marriage and taking her back to Luxor is just fucking crazy!

"What if she gets pregnant?"

Ed was shocked. He did tend to agree, although he didn't think it was any of his business what Bertie did, so long as it did not involve danger for himself or Ana.

Heads, Hats and Tall Tales

So he told Bertie that he was just going to say once that he thought it was a stupid thing to let people know about, that it was probably understandable if Bertie had fallen for an Egyptian Princess, but she hardly spoke English or Arabic at all. As for taking her to Luxor, that was beyond reason. He told Bertie to stop putting them all at risk and enjoy himself while he could, but forget about any future with a Pharaoh's daughter who was already promised to another man, a man of some power here.

Bertie just said "Fuck you, both of you, I'll do what I want and you do what you want. If she gets pregnant then the next Pharaoh or the one after Ameny could be my son and he'll be Senwosret the Second, I didn't come here to be told how to behave by you!" and he walked off.

Ed could see that Abamira was within earshot and had probably heard the whole argument.

Bertie tried to avoid any conversation with Ed and Ana the following day, seemingly spending most of his time naked aboard another boat along with the Princess.

PYRAMIDS

A couple of days later, Ed and Ana found themselves riding camels, accompanied by about fifty soldiers on foot, and the Master of Divine Construction *Interfikuer*, who was to serve as their guide, riding his own camel.

Interfikuer spoke in broken English to them, telling them not to stray from the camps or the guards and to avoid contact with the priests at the site of the pyramids or near the surrounding chapels and temples, as, he said, they did not like foreigners or people that did not share their religious beliefs and could be very dangerous men. They struggled for power, often trying to undermine the wishes of the Pharaoh who was the true God, whilst they mumbled their prayers and curses. They studied not only preparing the dead for the Afterlife, but also often employed the "Servants of Seth", such as deadly spiders, snakes and poisons, to kill those that stood in their way.

"Crazy men," he said.

It was a journey of some miles and they were to spend three days or so, there and back, camping overnight in tents supplied by and for the army, although most of the soldiers slept on the ground when not surrounding the camp on guard. They had plenty of food and beer, including fish and goats meat, which Ed and Ana did not eat, being vegetarians of sorts; there were plenty of different fruits and vegetables and flat breads, figs and dates in abundance.

Ed and Ana decided to wear the gowns, tunics and kilts provided by Abamira, "By the Grace of the God", with their underwear beneath. It was a very hot ride.

The nights spent under the stars were actually quiet, uneventful but beautiful. Although the soldiers drank plenty of beer, there was little noise or partying. Ed and Ana spent a great deal of the darkest hours looking at the stars, looking for familiar constellations and counting shooting stars.

The following day, they set out on their camels at dawn. It was late morning and before the main heat of the day, that Ed and Ana saw for the first time the great pyramids as they were then, gleaming white in the sun, shining golden capstones, no pyramid overshadowing another.

Heads, Hats and Tall Tales

They were mindbogglingly massive, as they could see as they rode towards them, and nearby stood the Sphinx with its human head but without a beard but the head seemed as out of proportion as he remembered it from 1989.

The Sphinx also looked well-weathered, much the same as in 1989.

Ed considered it just as mysterious in its origins as the pyramids at Giza.

In 1989, Ed and Ana had walked around and even been inside the pyramids. That and this were things that I knew Ed would never forget.

As we got even closer, Ed could see white-robed priests and semi-naked construction workers, in the walk-ways and around the temples.

Ed could see that the head of the Sphinx was different from that of 1989; a different face and one with a beard. He realised that it had since been re-carved.

Interfikuer explained to Ed that the structures contained great mathematical secrets such as the divine ratio of the radius and circumference of the circle, which Ed knew as *Pi*, 3.14 and so on, and that they were laid out upon the plain in the formation of the belt of *Osiris* (what we now call Orion's Belt) as seen in the night sky.

As they rode right up to the pyramids on their camels, flying their Royal banners with an armed escort, the bald-headed priests seemed to stay out of the way.

Ed was fascinated and, as he could see, Ana, was too, by these huge monuments that were far older than the Egyptologists of his own time had claimed. Older by many thousands of years: "Before the flood", he had been told.

Plus he had been informed that they had not in fact been built by the Fourth dynasty Pharaohs Khufu and Khafre who had, as he had been told, taken the names of the gods that had the pyramids built after the previous dynasties had failed to reproduce them, claiming the constructions as their own.

"If only we could prove what we are seeing when we get home," Ed shouted to Ana.

They rode around the pyramid and were amazed that it was preserved quite well, if it was indeed so old.

After riding around for a while, they took shelter from the hottest part of the day under large coverings that had been erected over long wooden poles, and ate lunch and drank beer.

Their rest and refreshment completed, they set of for the journey to the camp, where they arrived just after dusk. They stayed that one night and set off back to the royal barge early the next morning, stopping again in the hottest part of the day and arriving before nightfall. Ed felt welcomed by the many lanterns and torches that lit up the boats and the banks on each side. He felt almost as if he was returning to his friends, although he was well aware that they were all tyrants and powerful tyrants at that. He knew that they had power over the living and believed themselves to have power over the dead, as gods.

They feasted that evening and were told that they would be taken to the east bank and given quarters along with Bertie.

It was a small mud-brick house that had been "donated" by a local merchant. It consisted of just one living room with an open fire in the middle, smoke going up and out through a hole in the roof, which was made of wood.

There were comfortable rugs and cushions scattered on the stone floor. All three of them were to sleep there. The only other spaces under the roof being used for storage, or for a basic run-away latrine.

Bertie was already there when they arrived, giving them no time to settle in before he made an announcement.

KAREEM AND MUSTAFA

"I have found Kareem, you remember the boyhood friend of Abamira when he was called Amir in Luxor?

"Well they took me round by donkey to a few settlements and I just asked around: not so many people called Kareem round here.

"I was directed to quite a large house where he lives with his wife and youngest daughter. They had four children, two have died and one has moved south. Kareem remembers Luxor and his own family. He's mid-fifties now, like Abamira.

"Thing is, he told me Mustafa is a bad man, that he forced him to leave his friend in *Waset* and always prevented them from meeting again. And Kareem said he had never been in the army. He said that Mustafa had told him that Amir, his school friend we now know as Abamira, had joined the army and that he, Mustafa, had seen him regularly until about five years ago when he was killed in battle. Somebody is telling lies!

"Mustafa would not take him home or show him how to find the tunnels. So he stayed here and met his wife and worked

Heads, Hats and Tall Tales

for Mustafa who brought him gifts of things from Luxor and paid him enough money to support his family well. But our old mate Mustafa, Kareem said, was very very rich. He owned boats that crossed the great seas and owned palaces in other countries, like Lebanon and Greece, as we know it. He has a private army. But he keeps himself away from people and authorities.

"He said Mustafa collects things from these times, like statues and manuscripts, jewellery and even every-day items and things stolen from tombs of the dead. Then he buries them in places that he knows he can get too, back in Luxor in four thousand years time. Then he digs them up and sells them for fortunes.

"He brings things back here through the tunnels. He has some people doing that, and when it's here, he sells them to the rich and powerful. Stuff like foods and oils, perfumes and paintings, clocks and watches and jewellery. Kareem had a watch that works.

"It sounds like Mustafa's super-rich and enjoying life both here and there, best of both worlds. If I got that right. Kareem did not speak much English, just hello mister sort of thing. I had to speak in Arabic with him. Anyway, it sounds like Mustafa is a nasty piece of work.

"I haven't told Abamira or anyone else yet, though I bet they know I spoke with Kareem. I wanted to tell you two first. We'll tell him tomorrow."

This was big development in this adventure for Ed and he started to wonder again how safe they were. If Mustafa was so rich and so devious, virtually kidnapping and stranding the two boys, one being his own nephew, whilst leaving his own brother in ignorance in Luxor, what would he do to strangers to protect his secrets and his wealth?

Ed was also wondering how Bertie had managed to find Kareem so easily. Was it a mere coincidence that the boats had stopped here and, in the two days we had been away, Bertie had found the man? Or did he have some prior knowledge? Ed was wondering if Bertie knew far more than he was telling.

Ed told Ana and Bertie about his concerns. Ana looked really worried but Bertie said they were safe with so many Royal Guards and friends. They agreed to talk to Abamira the next day, but when they arrived back on board his ship they learned that he had in fact left with the boy god Ameny early in the morning, to see the God Pharaoh at a nearby site where, one day, another pyramid would be built.

So they lounged around most of that day, shading from the sun, eating and drinking, enjoying the river. Bertie chose his favourite woman of the day and spent most of the time laying naked with her, having sex.

That evening they returned to their house.

A local man brought tributes of food from the villagers. As the man left, he laughed and said "Mighty Night!"

There was a variety of chicken dishes and a spicy-smelling dish of goat which smelled delicious but neither Ed nor Ana ate mammals so it was eaten only by Bertie. There were baskets of fresh fruits and vegetables and cooked stews of peas, beans and onions, with delicious spice flavouring. There were flat breads and sweet cakes made from figs and dates and honey. It was all washed down with a good tasty red wine.

It was a feast indeed, yet without dancers or entertainment other than the stars outside, so after good drink, they started to move to where they would sleep. Ana told Bertie that he was to sleep at one end of the room, whilst she and Ed would sleep at the other. She kept all her clothes on and cuddled up tight to Ed.

It was the middle of the night when Ed was awakened by the sound of somebody retching outside their little house. He got up, picked up a lit lamp and went outside. It was Bertie. He was being sick onto the ground. As Ed approached it looked like Bertie was puking up blood. Bertie was groaning and panting, clutching at his abdomen.

What could Ed do? He called Ana. She called a guard and told him to bring a vizier. As they watched, Bertie stopped puking, stopped moaning and stopped moving. Then he fell forwards.

Ed rushed to him, hoping that he would not choke on his own vomit. He turned him over on to his side. Ana moved closer to Bertie too.

She said that they must not allow Bertie to choke. Then she put her hand on Bertie's chest.

"Fuck, he's not breathing!" she said.

She put her finger on Bertie's wrist to find the pulse, then on his neck.

"I can't feel a pulse, nothing."

She picked up a lamp and shone it in Bertie's eyes.

"Fuck it!" she said, "Eyes aren't moving. He's dead!"

It seemed over half an hour before what Ed supposed was some sort of doctor or medicine man dressed in a brown robe and carrying a large leather bag, arrived.

He casually walked over to the body on the ground. Bending down, he looked into Bertie's still open eyes, he took out a metal sheet like a mirror and held it at Bertie's mouth, he listed at his chest and then he grabbed and gave a tug on Bertie's exposed penis.

He looked at Ed and Ana, pointing at Bertie and then the sky, shaking his head.

Then he walked off as casually as he had arrived, saying nothing.

PANIC: DEATH ON THE NILE

"Shit, shit, shit, he's bloody dead. What we going to do?" said Ed.

"I thought they were going to arrest us when they came to take the body away. I wonder what they'll do with it?

"Nothing we can do now til Abamira gets back. I don't even know who is still here that we can speak to. Or if they'll think we killed him. He seemed OK earlier on, ate all that food and drank the wine. Same as we did.

"I hope he's not been poisoned. What the fuck, do you think we'll be OK, we ate the same food and drank the same wine as he did. Maybe he had an allergy to nuts or something?"

Ana looked at Ed. "The only thing I know is that he ate the goat and we didn't. Do you think he was poisoned? Do you think it was meant for all of us?"

"Well I can't see why anyone would want us dead," said Ed.

"I'm freaking out about that Mustafa. I thought it strange that Bertie found Kareem so quickly and wonder if he knew more than he told us. Mustafa may know what Kareem said. Or there's Omar-Min-Ra. He must be upset about Bertie and the princess. It could be anyone with money enough to get poison and get somebody to put it in the food. One thing, if it was only Bertie they were after and knew we did not eat goat, then it's somebody that knows that. Or maybe we're just lucky, you know what I mean?

"It could even be Abamira or a vizier with their own motives. Or the priests, they kill people, maybe they were afraid he'd get the princess or somebody pregnant and upset the dynasty. After all, Bertie did shout about how his son could be a future Pharaoh!."

My own thought was just how useless humans could be at a time like this. For I knew that if I could be on the head of each suspect, I would know the answer; but could I communicate it? Would anyone really bother to try to find out here.

"He's going to have to be buried here," said Ana. "We can't take the body back through to Luxor even if we can get it back to *Waset*. What we going to do when we get back to Luxor?

"We'll have to tell Ayman but how can we tell anyone we've been through a time-tunnel back four thousand years and Bertie got killed? We don't even know if Bertie had a family.

"Well I guess we've got to wait til daylight anyway. Nothing we can do now."

They went back inside the house and lay together whispering. This time I wasn't even close enough to hear what they said.

Daylight came and two soldiers came and led Ed and Ana back towards the boats. They hoped that they were not being arrested.

It turned out to be two more days before Abamira returned to the boat and met with them. *Ameny* was still awaiting the return of the Lord Pharaoh.

It was clear that Abamira knew that Bertie had died. He said that although no poison was found in the food served to the three of them that dreadful evening, it was thought that Bertie had eaten poisoned food. There were no wounds or marks on his body.

Abamira had sent soldiers to the nearby villages to seek out the man that had brought the food and found his body with the throat cut, in his own house.

Ed told Abamira much of what Bertie said he had discovered about Kareem and Uncle Mustafa: that his uncle was in fact a very rich man with several palaces in other lands.

"How is that possible?" asked Abamira. "When I first came here I was twelve years old. My Uncle was about forty years old. That was forty-four years ago. Now I and Kareem, we are both fifty-six years of age. My Uncle Mustafa will be about eighty-six years now. It must be another man called Mustafa."

Ed leaned forwards and said: "I must tell you some information that will open your eyes to a great secret, known only by Ana and I, Bertie and your own father, Ayman, in Luxor, and a few others in the whole world, know this secret about time.

"It seems like it is possible to move through time. That is how we all came to be here, in this land, in this time.

"And in different times, time itself moves in different ways and in time here, when four days pass, in another time, only one day."

"When you and Kareem followed your uncle through the corridor tunnels connecting tombs beneath your village, you came here, to a new place called *Waset*, you did not come to the same time as you left Luxor, in our year 1999, as we were told by your father Ayman in Luxor in the year 2010.

"Abamira, I swear to you now on all that is Holy for you and for myself, upon my life, it is my belief that we are now living in the twelfth dynasty of Egypt, under Pharaoh Senwosret the First, in our own dating that is four thousand year ago. We have moved four thousand years back in time to be here now.

Abamira laughed: "Why are you telling me this, you crazy? Your companion is poisoned and you say you are as a god from the future? You saying you can tell me what will come to be? Who will be dead and how? Who will be King? You telling me you can go back to Luxor and I can go with you, and my family, or my father can come here? That is a good story for another time, my Lord Ed."

Ed looked shocked: "I have no reason to tell you anything false now. I wanted to tell you before but you see how hard it would have been, even dangerous."

"It could be why Bertie was killed, to protect all that wealth.

 When he found Kareem and he told him all that stuff about Mustafa. Kereem told Bertie that Kereem had a timepiece. Did he bring it when you both left Luxor, forty-four years ago or did he get it from Mustafa. If Mustafa is bringing things from the future it could effect how the future turns out!

"I think Kareem and Mustafa would both have motives for killing Bertie.

"That may be so, my Lord, but there are others that could have reason," said Abamira.

"For there is suspicion cast also upon my own son, Omar-Min-Ra as he was not happy when Mr Bertie spoke about *Nefru-Ptah* bearing a child that would one day be Pharaoh; and Vizier *Interfikuer* himself has reason to protect the line of Senwosret as do the Priests. There may be jealousy amongst many Nobles that watched as Mr Bertie took more than a share of the women that he could, caring nothing for their feelings.

"The Lady Goddess Ana, although she is blessed, was heard arguing loudly with Mr Bertie only two days ago.

"Lord Ed, with respect, there are many suspects in these crimes. From your own mouth you have made me think of others unknown, from this or that age, who may have motive to protect their wealth.

"Indeed I have considered whether yourself and Lady Ana were also intended victims of a poisoner.

"It is not advisable to tell others your tales, my Lord and Lady.

"We must wait. I am sending out many to find this Kareem, and whether he was my friend or not, he will tell us and lead us to this Mustafa and we will know the truth.

"My lord and Lady, with respect, you must stay with us now on this royal boat until we see reports from our investigations into this death and the body of Bertie is made ready for his next voyage."

Ed decided to accept this as it was maybe the safest place in this world at this time, for them at least.

Later they spoke together and agreed that they would try to head back up the Nile to *Waset* and through the tunnels back to Luxor as soon as possible.

"It's right what Abamira said," explained Ed, "there's a lot of possible culprits and people with various motives, whether it's greed or protecting people or jealousy and even protecting the royal blood line, you know how the Pharaohs often married their sisters or mothers to keep it in the family and for sure Omar-Min-Ra would not have been happy. They even suspect us!"

Ana nodded. "Well I agree, let's get home. We don't know what will happened if they get hold of Kareem and Mustafa. There's the weird age differences too. Kareem and Abamira being the same age as Ayman and then how come Mustafa is not so old as Abamira thinks – he must have been going back and for in time for years, smuggling stuff. There could be lots of watches and stuff.

"Bertie was acting a bit crazy like he wanted to screw every woman he saw. He was shouting about fathering a future Pharaoh which must be blasphemy here.

"We'll have to tell Ayman and he may want to come here. We don't know where Mustafa is. Ayman said he was in Cairo.

"If I have my way I'll see those tunnels sealed up this end."

So they waited, six days it took before news came from Abamira that neither Kareem nor Mustafa or the families had been found, although there had been people that knew them. It was believed that they had left Egypt.

If only I, Myhat, could get through to Ed to let me sit on a few heads, I would know the truth. Then all I had to do was communicate it. I didn't think that would happen. Shame that guy had had his throat cut; he could have told us who'd paid him.

RUN AWAY

Ed and Ana told Abamira that they wanted to go back to *Waset* by boat. Ed was surprised that Abamira agreed so quickly. Then he added Abamira to the list of possible suspects, in his (which is my) head.

He told them a boat would leave in two more days and take them and his son Omar-Min-Ra back to *Waset*. It was to be a smaller boat and would travel with two boats of guards, but it would be less comfortable and faster, taking eight to ten days.

Ed and Ana had little to do but laze in the sun and eat and drink until then.

Their moods had changed so much that although they did a lot of huddling together and whispering, there was no sex. Ed was frightened more than I had ever know him to be. It was the first time that I knew fear.

There was no more news, other than that the body of Bertie would be taken back to Waset when it was prepared and it would be placed in a tomb for foreigners.

Sure enough they headed back to Waset by boat two days later, passing many small settlements, farms and waving people.

One day when Ed had left me on the deck, Omar-Min-Ra picked me up and very briefly put me on his head. I sensed hatred. He hated Ameny, he hated the priests, he hated his father and, most of all, he had hated Bertie.

Apart from the journey was uneventful: they reached the city of *Waset and* spent one night in the house of Omar-Min-Ra, which was far less grand than that of Abamira or the palace.

The next morning, before dawn, they arranged to be escorted by guards back across the Nile and towards the entrance to the tunnels in the late evening, so that it would be dark when they reached the entrance to the tunnels. So that is what they did.

They sat a short distance from the boulder and watched the guards walk away before finding the correct boulder and scrambling through the entrance. Ed certainly did not want to be seen doing that. Inside, they looked for the items that they had left there. It was obvious that they had been disturbed, but nothing seemed to be missing as far as Ed could see, although he was not certain about Bertie's stuff. Ed and Ana collected together their own belongings, deciding to leave Bertie's stuff near the bolder.

It did not take them very long to get through the tunnels and to the rope ladder. As Ed climbed up and out through the entrance, once again, I fell off his head, back down the shaft towards Ana.

This time she caught me and placed me upon her own hatless head and climbed up.

That was when I saw through Ana's mind the memories of what had occurred, from her point of view so to speak.

I can tell you I was pleased, surprised and shocked at how she had seen events turn out, what she thought and felt about Ed, about Ayman, Abamira, Omar-Min-Ra, Bertie and Ameny and the whole lifestyle she had witnessed. I can tell you that Ana has her own tales.

Let sleeping dogs lie, I have heard it said.

They agreed to contact Ayman and ask if he could help them seal up the exit to Abamira's time.

"Ed, do you think we'll ever know what really happened, who killed Bertie?" asked Ana.

Ed looked up: "Well I somehow doubt it. I'm not at all keen on going back and I wouldn't advise anyone else to. I'm not sure that their society had any real sense of justice, only tyranny and I think we were just a curiosity for *Ameny* and his crowd. There'll be nothing in the history either. Really we were not important and I bet Bertie's murder was just one of hundreds, let alone natural deaths, accidents and war.

"Abamira seemed to think there's loads of suspects. They don't exactly have forensics there. I bet they torture suspects and sooner of later one of them will confess, guilty or not. We can't exactly tell the police.

"Now we're back here, it doesn't make much difference who did it, unless it was Mustafa and he'll have to get back here too.

"I'm also worried about him, if he was taking things like watches and who-knows-what back through time.

"I'm going to start looking at the old tomb paintings, see if any of the gods or kings have anything like a watch on their wrist. I bet they do.

"And I bet if they've ever dug one up, they'd keep it secret.

"First thing I want to ask Ayman is if he's seen Mustafa since we left.

"We were gone a good few weeks there. If it was say thirty-six days, I've lost count, it would be just nine days here if its' really four-to-one. Let's get back to the hotel and see if they have a room, then phone Ayman."

So that is what they did.

They managed to rent the same hotel room as before.

They lay together speaking about what to tell Ayman. The whole truth or just part of it? Then they made love again. Then they phoned Ayman and he said he would be at the hotel as soon as possible. He had news for them too.

It turned out that his brother Mustafa had been arrested in Cairo for possession of ancient artefacts.

He had been fined a lot of money and apparently had then gone to Greece.

So, thought Ed, Mustafa may well have been back in time when he was supposed to be in Greece.

They told the tale of what had happened and how Professor Bertie had died.

They told the whole tale, from the moment they had first met Amira and Abamira, through the feasting and bathing and royal audiences with *Ameny*.

They told him about the orgies and how Bertie had behaved with the Princess and all the other ladies on the boat journey along the Nile.

They told Ayman that they were convinced that time had somehow moved faster there, in the eleven years here since Amir had disappeared with Kareem, forty-four years had passed there, so that back then Amir was fifty-six years of age. He had taken the name Abamira and had a son called Amira, Omar-Min-Ra and Ay -Min-Ra, some of whom already had their own children. They were living the lavish lifestyle of a Friend of the Pharaoh.

They told Ayman how Bertie had gone searching for Kareem and Mustafa and had found Kareem who Bertie had said, told him about Mustafa and his work of sending things through time, and that Ameny had a watch.

"But", they said, "the life of a foreigner was maybe only of diplomatic importance and no efficient proper investigation was possible. There were no fingerprints of forensics four thousand years ago."

They named the suspects: Omar-Min-Ra, the vizier, a jealous admirer, Abamira himself, even the boy god.

They did not mention that they too could have been suspects.

They told Ayman that they had left Bertie's few personal possessions near the exit boulder, hidden.

They said that Bertie's family would have to be told, and the police and British Embassy, but as there was no body and no evidence, what could they say?

They could hardly say they'd been through time or take the police back with them.

Ayman said that he would seek help and something could be done. It was not the first time somebody here had simply disappeared, wandering into the desert, falling into the Nile or getting lost underground.

Ayman seemed to take it calmly although he was looking more and more confused and more and more worried.

"I do not think it would be good for a man to meet his father when they are the same ages but must be so different. I will not go there and I do not want my son to come here.

"And, my friends, I must find out if my brother Mustafa is involved in some way and where he is now.

"What if," he said, "those people all start coming here through the tunnels?

"They'd be like savages to the people here. They could start robbing and killing and taking so much modern stuff back with them."

Ed looked at Ayman straight in the eyes and said: "That's why I think we should seal up the tunnels at the exit boulders. It won't be easy. We tried to hide the way in from that side but we've got to stop people going back and forth willy-nilly if more people from here or their find their way through. I'll go through one more time and wash off the chalk marks that we left.

"Do you think we could safely blow it up? Can you get dynamite? Do you know who can safely use it?"

To Ed's surprise, Ayman agreed. "I lost my son to those fucking tunnels and Kareem, and maybe my brother, all for riches and greed. I think it must be stopped. We can seal up the entrance from this side too, but not with dynamite as it would cause trouble and attract people. I will start making preparations already. There are plenty of explosives in the Valleys. I can get some and I know Youssef has a friend who uses it.

"I will send somebody to clean off chalk marks and bring back Professor Bertie's things. I do not ask you to go again"

So that is what they did.

Later, when they were alone, Ed said to Ana:

"I just thought, what if there are other tunnels through time? They could be anywhere, not just here. There could be one in Cairo or Greece or even London!"

"Even Norwich," laughed Ana. "There's plenty of old tunnels there and almost everywhere. Just think how many cities have had secret tunnels. I know the Vatican did. And the tubes and metros go pretty deep. I remember somebody telling me there was a long tunnel running the length of Britain. Gibraltar is filled with them. There may even be tunnels to the future."

They agreed to leave the 'who-dun-nit' mystery to four thousand years ago, seal up the tunnels and try to find Mustafa.

As their return plane had already flown, Ed and Ana bought tickets for another flight back to London a few days later. They spent those days in Luxor, staying in a hotel on the East Bank, lazing in the sun, making love and discussing what had happened and what to do next.

Two days later they took the long flight back to London and caught the train from London Liverpool Street to Norwich.

After a few days back in Norwich, I sensed more and more uncertainty in Ed about what had happened, He told Ana that he felt he had to tell somebody what had happened.

They decided to seek out Al and to tell him all about their adventure and catastrophe.

Ed also decided he would give me, Myhat, back to Al.

"It's his hat," he told Ana, "it might have brought me mixed blessings. Love and death both," he said.

Ayman had phoned them from Luxor and had said that the tunnels would be closed "for all time." He had not yet found his brother, Mustafa.

And so that is what they assumed.

AL AND MYHAT

Al seemed pleased to see Ed and Ana again, after quite a few years.

As they shook hands, Ed took me off his own head and leaned forwards, putting me on Al's head.

"Your hat, I believe, old chap," said Ed.

"Myhat indeed," he replied, laughing.

I knew he was quite pleased to get me back and I was actually quite pleased to know Al again.

The three sat and smoked some pipes of good hashish and Ed and Ana jostled to tell their versions of their exploits in

Egypt to Al.

Al listened as they outlined first their trips as tourists in 1989 and 1990, and of their next trip twenty years later.

But as they continued to tell how they had been through time tunnels to a time four thousand years in the past, meeting those people and even a future Pharaoh, Al laughed more and more.

"It's a very good story, a bit like Doctor Who, but he beat you to it; he went back to ancient Egypt too."

"Maybe I'll write it one day," said Al.

I was amazed, shocked, disappointed.

We had been through all that and Professor Bertie had been killed, even though I knew that Ed did not expect to ever find out who did it, yet now the problem was who would believe their stories?

Here was I, Myhat, full of memories and tales of what had actually happened, even those sexual experiences, drugs, travels through space and even time, and yet I feared I would never be able to tell anyone, not even another hat.

That was when I first focussed so hard of getting the idea of writing first the story of my visit to India back in 1972, through Al.

Now I gave him the idea of claiming that his hat, Myhat, wrote the book about 1972. Of course, you know that it was, but Al does not in fact believe it.

Of course it was I, Myhat, that told the story.

It was several years later, again, that Al wrote this book, about my time in modern and ancient Egypt with Ed and Ana.

It was I who told the tale, much better than Ed could have told it himself. I have the memory of a god.

I can tell you my reader, that when he started the tale, Al did not fully know everything that had happened: there were many gaps in what Ed and Ana had said several years ago.

Without me, Al would have never started and would never have finished the tale.

Al did not know all the details of what had happened.

So this book's author is Myhat. Only I know the truth, for it is I that is that I am the God Myhat-Ra

And there was still the mystery of who was behind the murder.

There is only one person that knows the answer, in this time and that. I have been on that head too.

Mighty Night for now.

AL AND THE UNDEAD

Ed's tales had awakened Al's interest and he and Ed went back to Luxor, especially after he read in the press of the discovery on rock carvings dated from thousands of years ago: they were depictions, it was reported, of a helicopter and a plane!

Al had read: *"The 3,000-year-old hieroglyphs found in Seti The First's temple in Abydos, Egypt, are said to depict nothing less than a helicopter, plane and futuristic aircraft among the usual insects, symbols and snakes."*

So, I take up my tale with the arrival on Ed and Al in Luxor and their meeting with Ayman, the man that ran donkey rides in the Valley of the Kings and who had shown the entrance to the secret tomb that had led them back to Waset.

Ayman told them that the tunnels had been sealed up.

He also told them that Bertie had "come back from dead." Bertie's body had been found near the boulder in the tomb corridor. Ayman was still living in the house of his brother, Mustafa.

Al listened as Ayman told us that much suspicion was laid on Mustafa who had not been seen, apparently since Ed's last time in Luxor and before Ed went back to England with Ana. This time, Ana had stayed in the UK after she had had her first child by Ed. Ed explained that he had agreed only to travel as far as Luxor with Al to introduce him to Ayman.

Ayman portrayed a very different picture of what had supposedly happened to Ed, Ana and Professor Bertie in those ancient days in Egypt; quite different and more complete than the impression Ed had given Al.

Ed had told Al, as Ayman had told Ed, that the entrance and exit from the tunnels had been sealed up.

Bertie had returned to Luxor several weeks after Ed and Ana had left but Bertie had asked Ayman to keep it as a secret for at that time. Bertie had sorted out some of his local affairs through officials. Officially he was still alive, but had gone into hiding, fearful of his life, until the whereabouts of

Mustafa had been ascertained.

Ayman made a phone call and it was not long before Bertie turned up at his house where he greeted Ed as if they were long-lost brothers. Ed had introduced Al to Bertie.

Bertie told Ed and Al that he had been employed, for over ten years, by an international organisation known as AFAR, the Agency for Artefact Recovery. They had been investigating the activities of Ayman's brother, Mustafa, as he was suspected of illegally selling stolen ancient relics from Egypt, many from over four thousand years ago and had become very rich in the process.

That was why Bertie was so keen to accompany Ed and Ana back through the time tunnels after they had reported finding Ayman's missing son, Amir, known there as Abamira, a successful and rich man living in *Waset*, a town that eventually became Luzor. Abamira, and subsequently his old school friend Kareem, had in turn told Bertie that Mustafa was bad man who had abandoned them there, telling them it was not possible for them to go back to Luxor and had been burying artefacts to be dug up thousands of years later in his own time. Mustafa had also been taking items such as time pieces back from this, our present era, to give and sell in the past, where he had also become rich and powerful.

Bertie also admitted that he had not behaved sensibly in particular regarding his sexual antics with the Princess *Nefru-Ptah* and tried to excuse his behaviour as a result of his consumption of alcohol, opium and cannabis.

That, he admitted, had made him very unpopular and was the possible cause of the attempt on his life by poisoning. Yet, he explained, the attempt on his life was not a solved crime. He suspected Omar-Min-Ra, a son of Abamira, who was promised to wed *Nefru-Ptah* and it was probable that the poisoning was a result of simple jealousy.

However, explained Bertie, he had also uncovered a conspiracy between Mustafa, Abamira and Omar-Min-Ra, at least. They were all profiteering from Mustafa's time-smuggling exploits.

Bertie told them that he remembered being sick and had realised that he had been poisoned. He remembered nothing after that until be woke up back inside the tunnels, in complete darkness, the exit to the old world having been sealed up from the outside. He had been left there along with a small plastic bottle of water and a modern-day torch, so had soon found his way out by following the chalk marks previously left there by Ed and Ana.

Since returning to the present day, AFAR agents had discovered that Mustafa was living in Greece or possibly Romania. They suspected that Mustafa had links to other times in other countries. No attempt, however, had been made to go back the 4000 years to *Waset*. By this time, in those days, several people such as Abamira may have died and Ameny, the "Boy-God" could well be co-ruling with his father, Senusret *Kheperkare*, also known as Senwosret the First. History showed that "Ameny" was to become the great Pharaoh Amenemhat The Second, *Nebkhaure*.

It was a very long afternoon spent smoking cannabis with Bertie, Ayman and Ed. Al was exhausted and stoned: his imagination was going wild: he had ideas of joining Bertie in his quest to halt the time-smuggling activities, to find Mustafa and to discover the truth about the ancient rock carvings of planes and helicopters.

Ed, on the other had, was quite insistent that the only place he was going to would be to Norwich to join Ana. He was not prepared to risk his life; he was a father now, Ed said. Ed was not going back to *Waset*.

Heads, Hats and Tall Tales

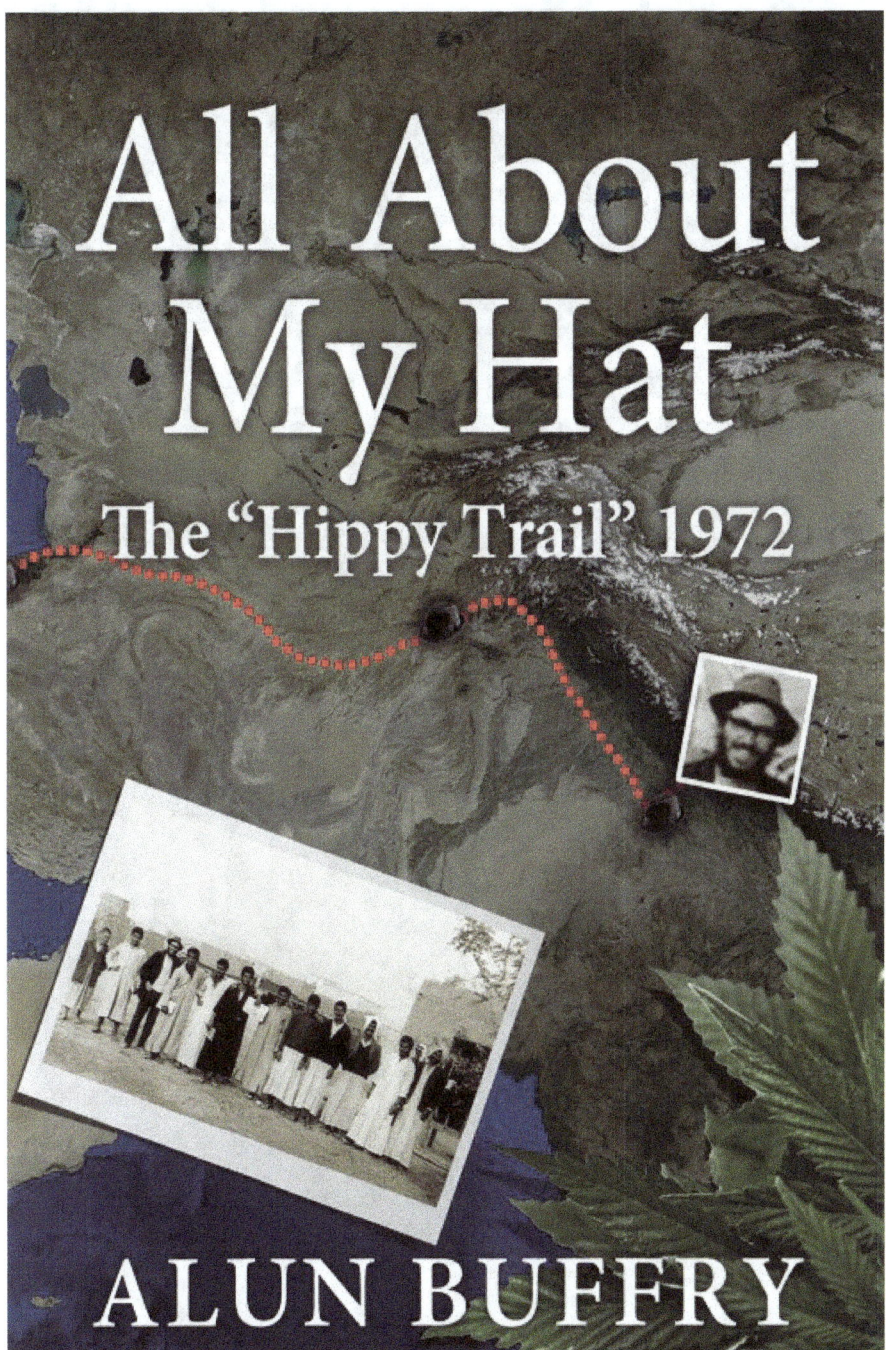

All About My Hat
The "Hippy Trail" 1972

ALUN BUFFRY

The Autobiography of a Head

Alun Buffry

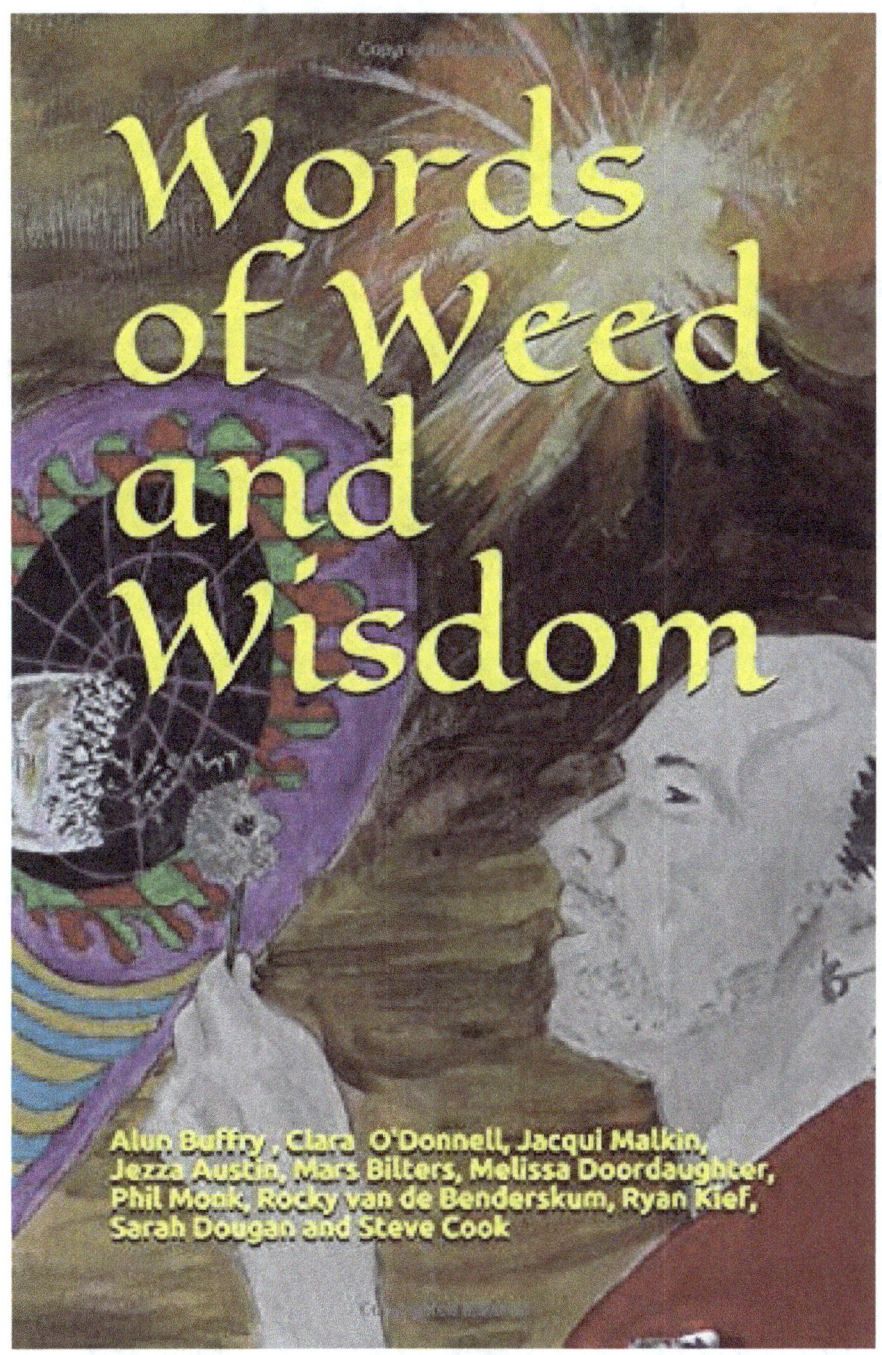

Heads, Hats and Tall Tales

Heads, Hats and Tall Tales

Heads, Hats and Tall Tales

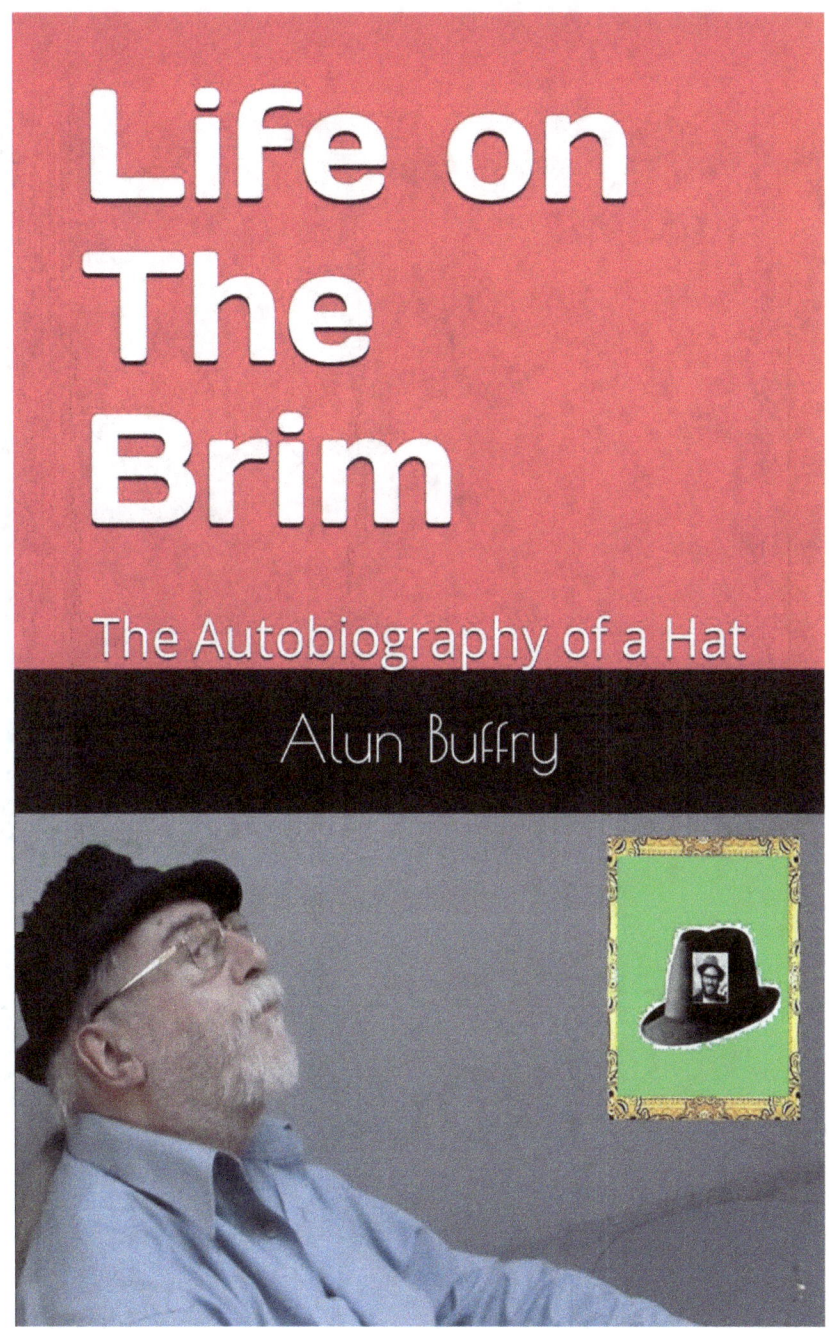

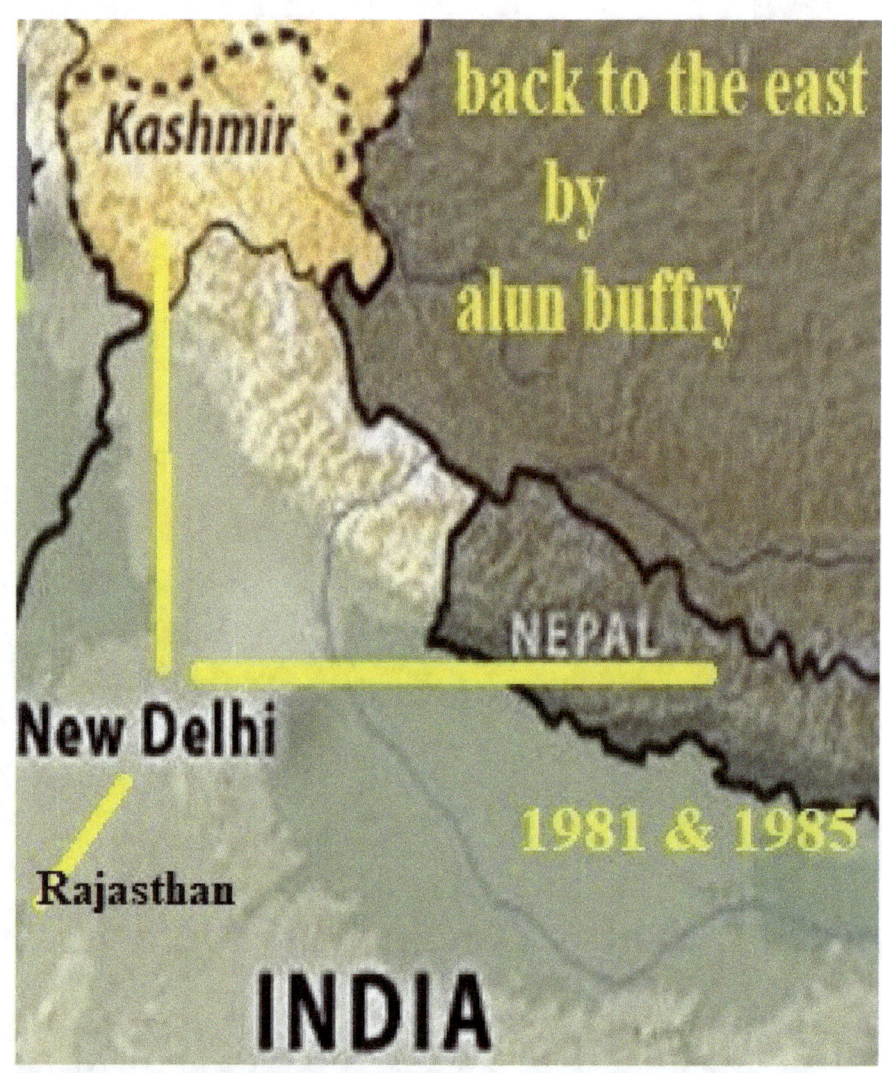

ALUN BUFFRY, WILLIAM D HUTCHINSON

Damage and Humanity in Custody

A Comparison of UK Prison Regimes by Inmates